# THE BROMLEY BOYS

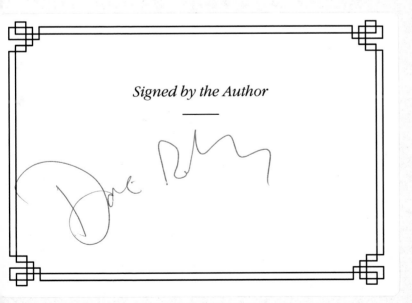

*Signed by the Author*

# THE
# BROMLEY
# BOYS

**Dave Roberts**

Happy Birthday Luca!
From Alan

January 2011

**PORTICO**

Dedicated to
John Maxwell Williams

First published in the United Kingdom in 2008 by
Portico Books
10 Southcombe Street
London
W14 0RA

An imprint of Anova Books Company Ltd

ISBN 9781906032241

A CIP catalogue record for this book is available from the British Library.

10 9 8 7 6 5 4 3 2 1

Printed and bound by CPI Mackays, Chatham, Kent ME5 8TD.

Newspaper clippings reproduced with kind permission of *Kentish Times* Newspapers.

Memorabilia courtesy of Derek Dobson.

This book can be ordered direct from the publisher.
Contact the marketing department, but try your bookshop first.

www.anovabooks.com

Expectation is the root of all heartache.
William Shakespeare

# Author's Note

As events in this book took place nearly forty years ago, I've had to take liberties with dialogue and the exact sequence of off-field events. Everything that could be checked has been checked and no names have been changed. The sheer ineptitude of the Bromley team that season is very real. No-one could possibly make something like that up.

If you'd like to get in contact with the author please email dave@stripeyjumper.com

# Prologue

The 31st of July 1969 had finally arrived. It was the day I'd been building up to since I was 11 years old. That was when I'd seen my first game against Wycombe Wanderers. That was when I started covering my schoolbooks in the names of heroes that no-one else had ever heard of. And that was when I started a lifelong love affair with a team that seemed to attract more than its fair share of eccentrics and misfits.

Bromley Football Club.

Back then, games like the one I would be attending today existed only in my imagination and on the Subbuteo pitch.

And now it was really happening. I had been too excited to sleep and the morning had seemed to go on for ever.

My Marmite sandwiches and newly cleaned football boots were already packed away in my duffel bag by 8am. It was the start of a new season and I was counting down the minutes until kick off. I left the house just after midday for the short walk to the Hayes Lane ground, where arguably the biggest game in Bromley's history would take place at 7.30 that evening. It was a friendly against West Ham. West Ham! One of the First Division's glamour clubs with 3 World Cup winners were coming to take on my local team of Isthmian League part-timers.

The Isthmian League was a long way down from the First Division. To get there, you had to pass through three divisions of the Football League, the Northern Premier League and finally two divisions of the Southern League. Even then, it was by no means certain that you'd find the Isthmian League. Depending on who you asked, the Athenian League was either of a higher standard, a lower standard or around the same standard.

Why did I take the boots? Even though I was only 14 and not a terribly good footballer, I had a fantasy that a couple of Bromley players would get involved in a non-fatal car crash on their way to the match and, for some bizarre reason, a call would go out on the PA asking if anyone could take their place.

And the reason for leaving so early? I wanted to make sure of getting a seat, so I could one day tell my grandchildren that I was there.

I had already decided who I was going to approach for autographs first. Obviously the World Cup winning trio of Bobby Moore, Geoff Hurst and Martin Peters would be a priority. Next up would be Billy Bonds and Harry Redknapp, both of whom I was sure would play for England one day. I was taking my A&BC Football Cards of Moore, Hurst and Peters as well as those of Robert Ferguson and Alan Stephenson in the hopes of getting them personally signed.

When I arrived, the picture that greeted me was slightly different from the one I'd imagined. The place was deserted. I stood by the turnstiles, first in line and waited. Three hours later, I was sitting eating my sandwiches not feeling quite so pleased with myself, but still with the same levels of excitement. I shut my eyes and played out various scenarios in my mind, all of which involved an upset that stunned the world of football.

At 6.20pm, I saw someone walking towards the ground. It was the groundsman who passed me with a quizzical glance.

Twenty minutes later, the Bromley players started to arrive. I greeted them with a 'Good luck today', while simulta-neously ticking their names off my mental checklist of possible non-fatal car crash victims. Obviously, I had mixed feelings about this. On one hand, they were my heroes. On the other hand, their presence meant I wouldn't be called upon to replace them.

Roy Pettet, the tall, elegant midfielder bustled past, looking all business. He was followed by Pat Brown – postman during the week, tough, reliable centre-half when Saturday came. And then David Jensen sauntered by. My goalkeeping idol. I always dreamed of emulating him and becoming Bromley's (and England's) goalkeeper. When asked my influences by *Shoot!* Magazine, I would simply reply 'David Jensen'.

Then came the moment I had been waiting for. Alan Stonebridge, last season's top scorer and probably the greatest player ever to wear the Bromley shirt, strode confidently past me, chewing gum nonchalantly. My one fear about today's game was that Ron Greenwood, the West Ham manager, would see how good he was and sign him. Stonebridge was the one player we couldn't afford to lose.

I had nicknames for all the Bromley players. Pat Brown was Postman Pat, Stonebridge was Stoney and Phil Amato was Tomato Face. Eddie Green was Eat Your Greens, Eric Nottage was Cottage and Jeff Bridge was Tower Bridge. Some of the new signings, like Roy Pettet, hadn't been allocated nicknames yet. Pettet's was proving a tough challenge. Petit Pois was the current frontrunner, but I wasn't sure that it really worked.

My thoughts were interrupted by the West Ham coach pulling up. Grabbing the cards and autograph book from my duffel bag, I watched the players climb down the steps and walk into the ground. Excitement was replaced by confusion. I only recognised a couple of them.

It had never occurred to me that they wouldn't be sending their strongest team and I ended up with a book full of unidentifiable autographs. The ones I could make out were players I had never heard of.

As I was in the process of trying to decipher some of the other scrawls, a turnstile operator arrived and I was in.

I felt a sudden burst of happiness to see the Bromley ground again after a summer without football. It felt like coming home after a lengthy absence, even though it had only been a few months.

The main stand (I never could work out why it was called that, since it was the only stand) had had a facelift and the large windows on either side had been cleaned, meaning goalmouth action would now be much easier to see than it had been at the end of the previous season. The picket fence surrounding the pitch had been repainted white. Even the floodlights, each of which had eight bulbs, looked in better condition than I remembered.

By the time the West Ham team strolled out, a small crowd was scattered around the ground. Many of them were wearing long, knitted black and white scarves and were either in the main stand, or on the open terraces opposite leaning against the white barriers. A small band of optimists were sitting on the covered benches behind the West Ham goal and a bigger band of realists stood behind the Bromley goal. Altogether, there wouldn't have been more than two hundred people there. I had apparently misread the fixture's appeal.

It seemed that some of the players had taken a similar attitude because two of them, Phil Amato and Graham Gaston, simply hadn't turned up, while Postman Pat Brown had withdrawn at the last minute due to a tummy ache.

But that didn't matter. My heart soared as I once again saw my heroes running out, David to West Ham's Goliath. I loved everything about Bromley and constantly fantasised about one day pulling on the famous white shirt with blue trim around the neck and wrists, stepping into the white shorts and putting on the white socks topped with blue.

Once Bromley had kicked off, I checked my watch every few minutes. Every minute without a West Ham goal was a minute nearer an incredible shock result.

By the time the first half was drawing to a close, I was

feeling the first stirrings of a possible upset. It was still 0–0 and if they could just hold out for another 45 minutes and get a draw against one of the best sides in the country, then winning the Isthmian League had to be a real possibility.

After an hour, something happened which would still be talked about today, if it had been against West Ham, as opposed to a team of West Ham reserve and youth team players.

Bromley took the lead.

A long, curling cross from Johnny Mears was poked home by the great Alan Stonebridge.

1–0 to Bromley.

I sat in stunned silence, unable to formulate any coherent thoughts. Was this really happening? Were Bromley really beating West Ham 1–0? A warm glow slowly came over me as I saw the referee run back to the halfway line and realised he wasn't going to find a reason to disallow the goal. My local amateur team were a goal up against a team which had won the European Cup Winners' Cup. I felt incredibly proud, as I left my seat and nervously paced around the ground. This was something I always did when Bromley took the lead in a big game. It usually helped to calm my nerves, but it didn't work on this occasion. Not with Bromley a goal up against West Ham.

It might have stayed that way, too, were it not for the somewhat unfair introduction of the Hammers' free-scoring Bermudan World Cup striker, Clyde Best. He made all the difference, making the home team look like a bunch of hapless amateurs and by the time the final whistle went, West Ham were comfortable 3–1 winners.

Still, coming that close to glory meant I approached the new season with even more optimism than usual.

If only I'd known what was about to follow . . .

# CHAPTER ONE

When England were winning the World Cup in 1966, I had been stuck on a ferry in the middle of the North Sea, bound for Sweden on holiday with my parents.

People were being sick everywhere as the waves crashed against the hull, tossing the boat from side to side. There was panicked screaming and shouting in a variety of languages. But I wasn't even thinking about what was going on. I was hunched by a huge radio catching intermittent bursts of commentary from Wembley, as the signal frustratingly faded in and out.

I knew about Wolfgang Weber's late equaliser. I knew about Geoff Hurst's shot that went in off the underside of the crossbar to put England back in the lead. But I didn't know about Hurst's famous match-sealing solo effort until we reached dry land.

When I found out, I was delirious. I had always loved football. Now my passion knew no bounds.

Once home, I went down to the local park every Saturday afternoon and Sunday morning to watch the matches involving teams with names like The Gas Board (South Eastern Region), interrogating the few people on the sidelines about what the teams were called, what the goal-scorers names were and what league they were playing in. After the games, the players seemed surprised yet flattered to be asked for their autographs. But soon I wanted more than park football.

Since I was only 11, my initial idea of going to watch West Ham (provider of three World Cup winners) on my own was turned down by my mum and dad. As was my compromise solution of me getting the bus and train to Crystal Palace instead, which was much nearer.

Eventually, I was allowed to go to Hayes Lane to watch the local team, Bromley.

My first time was a thrilling 3–2 win over Wycombe Wanderers. I loved the smell of liniment drifting up from the dressing rooms beneath the stand, blending with the harsh-smelling cigarette smoke. I marvelled at the sound of the crowd rising expectantly every time Bromley mounted an attack. The game seemed incredibly fast and exciting compared with the games at the park. There were plenty of goals and plenty of action.

I left wanting more and knowing this was the team for me. I had fallen in love with everything about them, from the colours of white and royal blue to the spacious stadium. It was great being able to sit in the stands and get an uninterrupted view of the action taking place just a few yards away. And it felt good to be watching a winning team.

Perhaps the win gave me false expectations – it was the only time they managed it in the first nine games that season. But it was too late. I was hooked.

●●●

Bromley were unique. Things happened to them that didn't happen to other teams – for example:

- Their record crowd was for a game in which the opposition played in bare feet.
- Their stand was hit by a hurricane. A few years later, it was burnt down.
- They would have lost 2–1 to Kingstonian a few seasons ago, but a rabbit intervened and the game ended 1–1.
- They somehow contrived to win the Kent Senior Cup

several weeks before the final was played. Even today, I struggle to work out how they managed it.

- The official club colours were black and white, yet they played in white and blue.

They also had the world's most embarrassing nickname. While other teams had intimidating sounding aliases like the Red Devils, the Gunners and the Eagles, Bromley were known as the Lillywhites.

Yet as the 1969–70 season loomed, I was feeling confident about Bromley's prospects. The previous season had been a pretty good one. Despite finishing a lowly 17th out of 20, there had been several highlights – a draw at the home of the perennial champions, Enfield, a win against high-flying Barking and an exciting, though goalless, draw with eventual runners-up, Hitchin Town.

Bromley would be playing all three of these teams in the first month of the new season and similar results would set us up for a possible top-five finish. Something I was quietly confident of happening.

Those with a more pessimistic view would have instead drawn attention to some of the previous season's lowlights – the 9–0 defeat at the hands of Sutton United, the 7–0 FA Cup humiliation at Hillingdon Borough, the loss at Leytonstone by the same score and the 6–1 thrashing by Wealdstone. I dismissed these as freak occurrences.

The weaker teams this season would probably be the ones who had finished below us last season: Corinthian Casuals, Dulwich Hamlet and Ilford. At two points for a win and playing each team home and away, that was an almost guaranteed twelve points.

It was going to be a huge season. And I was determined to watch every single game, home and away – starting with the away fixture against Wycombe Wanderers.

•••

I was now 14, a slightly tubby child with unflattering collar-length hair and a voice that hadn't yet broken. Outside of the house, I favoured a green anorak, which was covered with badges of all the places I'd been, most of them from the Lake District. There was also one from Aberystwyth, which I hadn't actually visited, but had acquired through mail order. I thought it would make me look more worldly and well-travelled.

I lived largely in my imagination, daydreaming of football glory, sometimes for me, sometimes for Bromley, but usually for both. I played out lengthy games of Subbuteo on my own, where I led Bromley to incredible last-minute victories over Real Madrid, Barcelona and Young Boys of Berne.

I didn't really fit in with others my age, preferring a solitary existence. My favourite times were spent sitting on the bank of the river at the bottom of the local park, staring at tadpoles and daydreaming of sporting glory.

The only friends I had were the ones I played football with at the same park. They overlooked my lack of social and sporting skills as I was always willing to fetch the ball when it went behind the goal and into the stream. They also put up with my habit of doing commentary while I was playing and remained unpeturbed when I was bearing in on goal screaming, in my best Kenneth Wolstenholme voice, things like 'There's just a minute left on the clock and the crowd roar with excitement as Alan Stonebridge gets the ball outside the area, he beats the defender and hits a glorious shot beating the Leeds United goalkeeper all ends up. What an amazing goal! Sprake had no chance with that one and Bromley have won the cup against all odds!'

Following one session, where I played way above my usual

standard and re-ignited my dreams of a professional football career, I ran home and wrote down a pretend interview with *Shoot!* Magazine, in which I answered a series of questions they had put to Terry Hennessey of Nottingham Forest in a recent edition.

This was the imaginary interview in full:

**Name:** David Alexander Roberts.
**Date of Birth:** 1 March 1955.
**Best friend:** Don't really have one.
**Car:** We have a white Austin 1100.
**Favourite player:** I have two – George Best and Alan Stonebridge.
**Most difficult opponent:** Barry Mace (played right-back for my primary-school team).
**Best goal ever scored:** In the playground, I kicked the ball on the volley from about ten yards out and it beat the goalie. It was a tennis ball.
**Miscellaneous likes:** My dog and Una Stubbs, the actress who plays Rita Rawlins in *Till Death Do Us Part.*

The next question was the easiest one to answer. My favourite food was Crispy Cod Fries and Chips. That was what I had for tea every night, sometimes for lunch as well. Crispy Cod Fries were chunks of succulent cod coated in crispy batter, according to the advert, and were the best things I had ever tasted. A rumour had swept school that they had to change the name to Crispy Cod Fries after printing millions of packs with the original name, Crispy Cod Pieces, which was apparently quite rude. Unlike most playground tales, this one turned out to be true.

Terry Hennessy's favourite food was steak, creamed potatoes, mushrooms and braised celery, all of which sounded disgusting. After wondering how he could possibly enjoy eating celery, I got back to my form filling:

**Miscellaneous dislikes:** Rugby, going to school, homework.
**Favourite music:** The Seekers, The Archies, The Beatles, Jane Birkin & Serge Gainsbourg.
**Nickname:** The Black Cat. (This was a nickname I'd given myself and no-one had yet used. It was taken from the Russian goalie, Lev Yashin.)
**Club supported as a boy:** Bromley.
**Biggest influence on career:** David Jensen.
**What would you be if you weren't a footballer:** I'd just go to school.
**What advice would you give a youngster:** Work hard and get qualifications.
**Favourite TV show:** *Dr Who, Tomorrow's World, Junior Points of View, Crackerjack, Match of the Day.*

For the final question, I couldn't think of anything so just copied what Terry Hennessey had said, which was:

**Biggest drags in soccer:** Players who feign injury.

There was one question I had deliberately left unanswered. The most embarrasing moment. It had dredged up unpleasant memories of the incident I had spent the past four years trying to forget about.

Inevitably, football was responsible.

I always sat in the back of the class and one of the advantages of this was that I could get changed for football just before the preceding lesson – in this case Maths – had finished.

I was in the process of slipping my shorts on when the teacher, Mr Barrett, noticed what I was doing. He immediately told me to come up to the front of the class to write the answer to a Maths problem on the blackboard.

I tried to pull my shorts up, but he insisted I get there immediately.

I trudged up to the front, shorts around my ankles, white Y-fronts pulled up around my waist, my face as red as a Liverpool shirt.

From that moment on, I was marked out as an oddity.

Girls found me odd, too. I'd joined the local youth club, specifically for the purpose of meeting them, but since I lacked the courage to speak to them, I never got very far.

I didn't fit in at school, either. Most of the other boys seemed assured of a successful future and knew exactly what they wanted from life, even at the tender age of 14. Some of them went on to become household names, including an Oscar winner, an England opening batsman and an obscure member of the royal family.

The one thing that made this particular school unbearable was the fact that they played rugby. I hated rugby and still do. For two years, I lobbied for the school to put out a football team. Eventually, they agreed and I immediately appointed myself captain and sole selector.

But the only time I felt I truly belonged somewhere was when I was watching Bromley. My love for them was so all-consuming that I had recently started a campaign to move to Downham, which was about two miles away and a far less salubrious area. In truth, it was a pretty rubbish place to live, but it had one thing Bromley couldn't offer.

A postman called Pat Brown.

I could imagine no better start to the day than having one of my idols deliver the mail and maybe hang around for a kickabout afterwards.

My dad weighed this up against having a perfectly nice house in a good area, close to the shops, park, library and schools, then decided we'd be staying put.

I stoically hid my disappointment and turned my attention to Saturday's start of the new season.

•••

Wycombe had beyond-cool shirts, made up of dark and light blue quarters, while their pitch sloped dramatically. So much so, that you had to tilt your head at a slight angle to watch the game properly.

The coach journey typified the unusual stresses of being a Bromley supporter, by getting hopelessly lost before we'd even left town. The driver had managed to confuse High Wycombe with West Wickham and wasted a valuable half-hour before he got his A–Z out and found the right route. As we drove past Bromley South Station for the second time, I saw a couple of park friends making their way to Selhurst Park, for the Crystal Palace vs Manchester United game, which marked Palace's return to the top flight. While they would be watching the likes of George Best, Bobby Charlton and Denis Law, I was travelling much further, just so I could watch a bunch of teachers, postmen and printers.

As usual, I sat at the back with Derek, Roy and Peter. They were all older than me, but we somehow gravitated towards each other. Derek was short, about 5'5". He was the one we all looked up to, due to him having his own home – a three-bedroomed townhouse just around the corner from me – and a tax-consultancy business. He was in his early 20s and very serious with a habit of pausing emphatically during speech, so you could absorb what he was saying. Roy was a wild-haired dustman with the thickest glasses I had ever seen and firm opinions on everything, which were generally misguided. Peter was an enigma. He hardly ever spoke and no-one knew what he did for a living. The only available information was that he lived with his mother in a small bungalow. Maybe that was all we needed to know about him.

Together, we made up a core group of supporters who followed the team everywhere, no matter how far we had to travel or how bad the weather. We were drawn together by an undying love for a club that rarely deserved such devotion.

We got to the ground and I quickly took up my place behind the Wycombe goal, so I'd have a perfect view of all the action. It didn't matter that the cold, driving rain was blowing in our direction. The atmosphere was one of anticipation mixed with relief. The three months or so between football seasons seemed to drag on for years.

•••

As the home team warmed up, their supporters gave them a rousing welcome, with several shouts of 'Come on you Chairboys' coming from the large group of Wycombe supporters. Or at least that was what I though they were saying. 'Did he say chairboys?' I asked Derek, who agreed that that was what it had sounded like. I felt strangely smug in the knowledge that someone had an even worse nickname than ours.

While the announcer was running through the teams I was shocked to hear so many changes. It was typical Bromley that so many players were out for so many bizarre reasons. Eric Nottage was best man at a friend's wedding. Postman Pat Brown had to work. Gaston, Green, Proud and Rhodes were still on holiday and Phil Amato simply hadn't turned up.

Amato always looked the perfect footballer. He was tall, dark and athletic. Only one thing prevented him from becoming a star: the fact that he was completely useless. He spent more time posing than defending, and was prone to temperamental outbursts which I'd put down to his fiery Italian nature and Mediterranean upbringing, until I learnt he was from Hayes.

His absence as well as the others', meant that a handful of hastily signed replacements like Graham Farmer and Dave Mills were drafted in alongside half a dozen regulars. The team played as though it was the first time they'd played together, which it was, and it was no surprise when they conceded their first goal of the season after half an hour and their second only three minutes later.

At half-time, the consensus amongst the Bromley fans was that we were lucky to be just two goals down. That luck didn't last as our makeshift defence was torn apart in the second half, with Wycombe winning 5–0 – despite missing at least four more chances that even I would have scored.

I had fallen into a state of shock by the time I took my seat on to the coach for the long journey home. I had set out that morning convinced that Bromley would be starting the season with a win and naively hadn't even considered the possibility of a more predictable result. I stared out of the window at the Buckinghamshire countryside feeling angry, hurt and betrayed, my ticket to the game torn up and deposited in the ash tray.

I had spent the afternoon getting soaking wet, peering off into the distance, as all the action took place at the other end. Bromley hadn't threatened the Wycombe goal and had played even less impressively than they had towards the end of the last season, when they had been terrible.

Little did I know that things were about to get even worse.

•••

A couple of days later I lost my part-time job and watched Bromley crash to another heavy defeat. Neither of these should have surprised me.

The Saturday morning job at the chemist was going well until the football season started and then I began making all sorts of unreasonable demands, including finishing an hour early when Bromley were playing away and a large pay rise to cover the coach fares.

I'd been there since I was twelve and had become proficient at washing and drying old medicine bottles so that they could be reused. I'd also perfected the art of peeling off the old labels, which had taken me years to get right. I thought the job was mine for life, so wasn't expecting them to decide it would be more prudent to replace me than to give in to my demands.

I tried desperately to backtrack, but it was too late. They even said I could leave straight away when I asked how much notice I'd get.

Perhaps even more predictable than this was the loss to Kingstonian. The last time the K's (another rubbish nickname) had been to Hayes Lane, a rabbit had robbed the team of a well-deserved win, but there would be no such help for Bromley on this occasion. Back then, a perfectly good goal had been disallowed because the ball had crossed the line and gone through the net, that had been gnawed by a rabbit that had wandered onto the ground from the nearby common. The referee, who obviously hadn't considered this scenario, decided that the ball had passed outside the post and awarded a goal kick instead.

This led to a brief burst of national infamy for Bromley (and the rabbit), which I was convinced would be used as motivation by today's visitors. I felt a pathetic gratitude to the rabbit and even considered lobbying my parents to get one I could keep as a pet. I had decided I would call it Nora, regardless of its gender, as a reference to it's gnawing of the net.

•••

As it was the first proper home game of the season, there was almost a festive air at Hayes Lane. The crowd was big considering what had happened at Wycombe the previous Saturday, and it was a beautiful late Summer evening.

The team, on paper at least, looked better. Postman Pat Brown, legendary striker Eric Nottage and the brilliant winger Eddie Green were all back. No-one had failed to turn up, gone to a wedding or had to work.

Despite this, it only took five minutes for the visitors to burst the bubble, with a goal which once again exposed Bromley's defensive shortcomings. Pat Brown fell over, allowing the Kingstonian centre-forward to make it 1–0. Twenty minutes later, home keeper David Jensen joined the party by inexplicably diving over a weak shot from 30 yards out and it was 2–0. As if the away side weren't finding it easy enough to score, Pat Brown then took it upon himself to try and help them by heading the ball against his own post, with Jensen well beaten.

One spectator, who was sat directly behind me, couldn't take it any more. When former skipper Ian Wigham lost a boot midway through the game he shouted out, 'Don't bother putting it on again, mate. Just hang them up.' The rest of the crowd nodded in agreement.

It wasn't even half-time and people were already starting to file out of the ground. They must have known something, because the second half brought more of the same: another speculative long-range shot left Jensen flapping ineffectually and another piece of comically inept defending led to an easy tap-in for goal number four. But none of this mattered when John Mears scored Bromley's first goal of the season with a superb shot from outside the area. That was the way I saw it, anyway. A more neutral observer might have pointed out that it was almost identical to Kingstonian's second goal.

The final score was Bromley 1 Kingstonian 4. Only about half of the crowd were still there to witness the final whistle.

On the bus home, I was seething with anger. I felt like Captain Hurricane, my favourite character from *The Valiant* comic, who would get so angry every week that he'd fly into what he called a 'ragin' fury' and then destroy entire platoons of enemy soldiers single-handedly.

The focus of my 'ragin' fury' was Dave Ellis, the new Bromley manager. He was to blame for the abysmal start to the season and I was convinced that if he could be replaced, things would be different. Admittedly, this view had been strongly influenced by an article in the local paper, which blamed his lack of tactical awareness and poor selections. I took this to be gospel. After all, if it was in the paper, it must be true. And I've always been a bit suggestible. A few years later, I would formulate my entire political stance on Northern Ireland after listening to a Wings song.

My parents were big on affirmative action and often took me on protest marches, so I decided I was going to take a stand on the Dave Ellis issue.

When I got home, I got my favourite black t-shirt and a paintbrush, and using white watercolour paint, wrote the slogan 'ELLIS MUST GO' on it.

I was going to wear it at the next home game, against Wealdstone on the following Saturday.

# ISTHMIAN LEAGUE HOW THEY STAND

## 15TH AUGUST 1969

|                   | P  | W | D | L | F | A | Pts |
|-------------------|----|---|---|---|---|---|-----|
| Sutton Utd . . . .| 2  | 2 | 0 | 0 | 9 | 2 | 4   |
| Oxford City . . . | 2  | 2 | 0 | 0 | 2 | 0 | 4   |
| Wycombe W . . . . | 2  | 1 | 1 | 0 | 7 | 2 | 3   |
| Tooting & Mit . . | 2  | 1 | 1 | 0 | 7 | 3 | 3   |
| Wealdstone . . . .| 2  | 1 | 1 | 0 | 5 | 2 | 3   |
| Hendon . . . . . .| 2  | 1 | 1 | 0 | 4 | 3 | 3   |
| Hitchin Town . . .| 1  | 1 | 0 | 0 | 4 | 2 | 2   |
| Kingstonian . . . | 2  | 1 | 0 | 1 | 6 | 5 | 2   |
| Barking . . . . . | 2  | 1 | 0 | 1 | 4 | 3 | 2   |
| Leytonstone . . . | 2  | 1 | 0 | 1 | 4 | 4 | 2   |
| Woking . . . . . .| 2  | 1 | 0 | 1 | 2 | 2 | 2   |
| Enfield . . . . . | 2  | 1 | 0 | 1 | 1 | 2 | 2   |
| Ilford . . . . . .| 2  | 1 | 2 | 0 | 1 | 1 | 2   |
| Dulwich Hamlet . .| 2  | 0 | 1 | 1 | 2 | 3 | 1   |
| St. Albans City . | 2  | 0 | 1 | 1 | 2 | 3 | 1   |
| Maidstone Utd . . | 2  | 0 | 1 | 1 | 0 | 3 | 1   |
| Clapton . . . . . | 2  | 0 | 1 | 1 | 3 | 7 | 1   |
| Walthamstow . . . | 1  | 0 | 0 | 1 | 0 | 1 | 0   |
| Corinthian Cs . . | 2  | 0 | 0 | 2 | 1 | 8 | 0   |
| **BROMLEY** . . . . .| **2**  | **0** | **0** | **2** | **1** | **9** | **0**   |

# CHAPTER TWO

I pulled on my 'ELLIS MUST GO' t-shirt, and then, despite it being a sweltering hot summer day, also wore my thickly padded anorak. I wanted to dramatically unveil the protest message when I got to the ground.

As the stand was virtually empty when I arrived, I got the perfect spot to watch from – my seat was right on the halfway line at the front.

There was a small crowd – significantly reduced since the previous Tuesday – and as the teams ran out, the applause was distinctly half-hearted. It was time to take my anorak off and commence my one-boy protest.

Which I would have done, if a familiar figure hadn't chosen that moment to sit down beside me. It was Dave Ellis, who had come to watch the game from a different vantage point. He even asked me if anyone was sitting there and I admitted that there wasn't.

Now I had a dilemma.

The heat was making me extremely uncomfortable. I could feel the sweat making the nylon lining of the anorak cling to me and I was starting to feel light-headed. On the other hand, there was a man under extreme pressure sat right next to me and if I removed my coat, he would see that I wanted him to lose his job.

The anorak stayed on.

Because of extreme discomfort, I can remember very little about the game. Bromley lost, obviously.

The good news was that Roy Pettet scored a great goal from outside the penalty area, to make him Bromley's joint leading scorer with one. The bad news was that Wealdstone got six, each of which was greeted with an anguished murmur by Dave Ellis.

# Bromley reveal weaknesses in all departments

## BROMLEY 1, WEALDSTONE 6

**B**ROMLEY'S sad start to the season has been brought about by weaknesses in all departments. This is obvious following three Isthmian League defeats, the heaviest coming at Hayes-lane last Saturday against a well-drilled, non-stop Wealdstone (writes Tony Flood).

The fact that they have conceded 15 goals and scored only two in those three games underlines what a hard task manager Dave Ellis faces if he is to lift them from the bottom of the table.

Admittedly it has been a blow to have 6ft. 4ins. tall centre-half, Graham Gaston, on holiday, but Pat Brown has done a marvellous job in the "stopper" role considering the poor support offered by his team-mates.

Two players just back from holiday — Willie Proud and Alastair Rhodes — made their league debuts against Wealdstone in place of Mills and Wigham. Proud, although out of position at left-back, showed

adjust himself to this higher class of football.

Bromley's first scare came in the 13th minute when Mitchell netted. Bremer had already fouled Soper, however.

There followed a superb 19th minute goal by right-winger Bremer. Pat Brown failed to cut out a pass by Montague and Bremer raced through to send the ball hard and low into the corner of the net.

Four minutes later the home defence was again split open as John Draper headed in a cross from Hutchinson.

Soper then took a risk in racing out to the edge of his area to dive at Hutchinson's feet, but he succeded in

As it turned out, I needn't have worried about him seeing my t-shirt. When I got home and finally removed my anorak, the sweat had made the paint run, reducing my defiant slogan to a grey smudge.

Once I'd got changed, I received some news that turned a bad day into one of the worst days of my life.

My parents told me that because of my increasingly poor attendance at school and difficulty getting out of bed in the mornings, I would be boarding there.

Although this shouldn't have come as an enormous shock, it did. I was distraught and pleaded my case for carrying on with the existing arrangement, which in theory was my waking at 7.30am, getting the bus to Sevenoaks from the end of the road and getting to school in plenty of time for assembly which started at 9am.

That was the theory.

What actually happened was that I'd leave the house around 8am, wander into Bromley where I would go to the Egg and Griddle and pass much of the day there, drinking tea. I would also spend hours on end at the office of the *Bromley Advertiser*, looking through full-sized prints of photos of Bromley games, occasionally buying one. My other regular place to visit was WH Smith, where I listened to the latest records in their flash new soundproof listening booth.

It was decided that if I boarded at Sevenoaks, my school attendance would be more reliable.

As the new school term dawned, I was beginning to realise the implications of becoming a boarder. The most obvious thing was that I would be forced to miss Bromley's midweek fixtures. The school was a 55 minute bus journey from the ground and I was sure my House Master wouldn't let me go.

Also, as if wandering through the streets in a straw hat wasn't bad enough, I'd have to wear a pink tie. It would have been easier to wear a sign around my neck inviting the town's hooligans to please beat me up.

I really didn't want to leave home and I knew I would miss

everything about it – my mum and dad, my dog Silas, my local park.

Even my sister.

Plus, I'd have to leave my precious Bromley programme collection behind. I felt powerless and went to my room – a room I'd grown up in and would now be leaving behind.

My life was hitting an all-time low. And so was my football team.

●●●

Barking (away) was a fixture I was confident would provide my struggling team with their first point of the season. It was good to finally be playing a middle-of-the-table side after three high-fliers in a row. Judging by the atmosphere on the coach, I wasn't the only one who felt this way.

There was talk of Dave Ellis's new 4–4–2 formation being just what was needed to turn the season around. Graham Gaston, the 6'4" centre-half was rumoured to be making his first appearance of the season, after missing the first three games due to being on holiday.

As usual, things didn't quite go to plan. Gaston couldn't make it as he was too busy working at his printing business. But at least Bromley started the game brightly and the new formation seemed to make a big difference.

When Barking went 1–0 up just before half-time, I was confident of at least a draw.

When they went 2–0 up early in the second half, I still wasn't worried.

When they went 3–0 up with a well-taken penalty, I felt the first stirrings of anxiety.

When they went 4–0 up, I covered my head with the hood of my anorak, as if I could shut out what was happening.

When they went 5–0 up, I turned to my fellow supporters, most of who were looking pale and shell-shocked.

When they went 6–0 up, I glanced at my watch, then at the referee, willing the game to end.

When they went 7–0 up with only a couple of minutes left, I looked longingly towards the exit.

When they went 8–0 up, the Barking fans started singing 'seven nil, seven nil, seven nil, seven nil'.

It was the final humiliation. They'd actually lost count of the score.

# FOUR DEFEATS: 23 GOALS CONCEDED

### BARKING 8, BROMLEY 0

BROMLEY, now bottom of the table with no points, suffered their heaviest defeat of the season—their fourth in four Isthmian League games —, at Barking on Tuesday, and have now conceded 23 goals in those 360 minutes. Yet ironically their new defensive 4–4–2 formation had effectively shut Barking out for 33 minutes (writes Tony Flood).

Bromley, whose worst start was in the 1965/6 season, when they suffered seven successive defeats, seem to crack as soon as they let one goal in. Against Wealdstone they held out 19 minutes before going down 9–1, and against Wycombe they held out 32 minutes before crashing 5–0.

Gaston was expected to play at Barking but was working, and with Pat Brown, Green and Jansen injured, Bromley were again below strength. Wawrzewski was also omitted and his replacement, new sign-ing Dave Clarke, did not turn up.

Loose marking and a failure to move with the man running off the ball cost Bromley dear as Barking, who have taken 13 points from them in their last seven meetings, grabbed four goals in the last 20 minutes.

#### ALL AT FAULT

Bonney, who played a double centre-half role with Bridge, Colin Brown and mid-field men Wigham, Mears and Rhodes were all at fault. Head, who substituted for the injured Rhodes at half-time, made no impression, though he was off the field from the 62nd minute until the 69th minute with a nose bleed.

Off-target shots by Stone-bridge and Head plus a free-kick by Bridge that 'keeper Howard went full length to save, were Bromley's only scor-ing attempts as they slid about on a wet pitch.

Poor Soper saved efforts by Page, Dawson and Fox, but just could not cope after keeping the score down to 1–0 at half-time.

The first goal in the 34th minute came when Fox beat Bridge to the ball and forced it home. The unfortunate Proud, who had played so well until then, had been unable to cut out Page's high cross due to his lack of inches.

#### OFF THE LINE

Bridge cleared off the line from Dawson in the 46th minute, but in the 52nd minute a long-range free-kick by Ford was slotted in by Page. Five minutes later Bonney upended Dawson and Gulver made it 3–0 from the spot kick.

While Head was receiving treatment, Baker held off Bonney's challenge to slam in Page's 65th minute pass. Fox then pushed in a Baker pass in the 70th minute for goal No 5. Baker (72nd minute), Ford (88th minute) and Fox (89th minute) completed the tally.

Barking: Howard, Moore, Guiver, Holman, Soper, Ford, Harwin, Martin, Fox, Page, Baker. Bromley: Soper, Proud, Bridge, Bonney, C. Brown, Petch, Rhodes, Wigham, Mears, Stonebridge, Nottage. Sub: Head.

A week later, I was in Derek Dobson's Morris 1100 on the way to Hitchin for an Isthmian League fixture, since the coach had been cancelled due to 'insufficient demand'. As unofficial leader of the Bromley supporters, Derek had dutifully stepped in to provide us all with a lift to the game. I'd been put in the back with Roy Oliver, the myopic dustman, while Peter sat alongside Derek in the front.

We discussed likely outcomes and none of us any longer thought in terms of winning or even getting a draw. It was now a matter of how many goals the brittle defence would leak. I liked the fact my opinions were taken seriously and that I was treated as an equal. We concluded that if Hitchin won by less than the eight Barking had scored, it would be a good result.

There was a feeling of smug satisfaction on the way home that night. The 6–1 loss that we had just witnessed was being considered a victory of sorts, and Bromley had started to show genuine signs of improvement.

To start with, only two players were missing – Pat Brown with a 'poisoned arm' and Graham Gaston who seemed unable to drag himself away from his printing job.

Also on the positive side, the midfield was looking more cohesive, the Stonebridge/Nottage combination up front was starting to click and the defence were much better than the six goals would suggest. Roy Pettet, too, was running into form. His brilliant goal tonight doubled his total for the season.

Maybe Dave Ellis knew what he was doing after all.

●●●

**'BROMLEY SACK MANAGER ELLIS'** screamed the back page of the *Bromley and Kentish Times*.

The now-former manager had some entertaining reasons to explain his record. Despite using more than 20 players in his five games in charge, and despite missing all the pre-season trials due to being on holiday in Spain, he blamed everyone but himself.

'Nothing went right for me,' he insisted, finishing with 'I signed five players from Carshalton and none came'.

After five games Bromley were now anchored at the foot of the table with no-one in charge of the team. Now, most clubs in this situation would appoint a caretaker manager or even a successor, but not Bromley. They announced that for the foreseeable future, the team would be selected by a committee.

This did not fill me with confidence.

I'd seen members of the committee standing around in their blazers and not one of them appeared to be under 60. Also, there seemed to be rather a lot of them – around ten or eleven.

Their first task was to pick a team to take on lowly Clapton that night.

•••

I had worked out a plan to get into the Clapton game without

# Sixth defeat in a row: 'keeper carried off

## BROMLEY 1, CLAPTON 2

BROMLEY looked set for their first Isthmian League point of the season at Hayes Lane on Tuesday, but a "soft" goal in the 77th minute gave Clapton victory. To make matters worse, goalkeeper Ian McGuire, signed from Carshalton, was carried off with concussion and ex-Romford left-back Leslie Brockman, another new-comer, had to put on the goalkeeper's jersey.

So Bromley, who had dis-missed manager Dave Ellis on the morning of the match, but fielded five of his signings, suffered their sixth successive defeat.

The programme notes by secretary Charlie King refer to the results as being the worst in the long history of the club. But in the 1965-66 season Brom-ley lost their first SEVEN games—though admittedly the goal average was better.

the attack was again unbalanced.

The service from the mid-field men is getting better, and once confidence is restored Bromley's front runners must make full use of their chances.

With rain lashing down throughout the first half, the meagre crowd saw the players struggling to keep their balance. But in the fifth minute Bull showed perfect control in touch-ing home a corner from Ballard.

McGuire made great saves

paying. On a reconnaissance mission during the previous home fixture, I had noticed a ginger-haired youth in a long trenchcoat climbing over the fence on the east side of the ground. It was a good place to do it, because unless you were trying to catch someone in the act, you wouldn't have been able to see him.

I watched as he shuffled to his spot behind the goal, after stopping to collect two cups of tea. He sat down, lit a cigarette and didn't move until the game was over. He got through both cups of tea before half-time.

I vaguely recognised him, because he was going out with a friend of my sister's. I knew people called him The Grubby, but I didn't know why.

I decided that the Clapton game was the perfect opportunity to try out his ground-entry technique. It was pouring rain as I walked past the ground and into neighbouring Norman Park. Throwing my anorak onto the top of the fence to protect myself against any sharp edges, I pulled myself up and over, before falling into a thick grass on the other side.

I was in.

'What's your game, son?' bellowed an angry voice from the top of the bank. I looked up, terrified. It was Charlie King, the club chairman.

There's not much you can really say in a situation like this, so I explained that I didn't have enough money to get in, but loved the team so much I couldn't bear the thought of missing a game.

This was apparently the right thing to say. Mr King not only allowed me to stay and watch, but he also bought me a programme.

It was a nice gesture. But after what followed on the pitch, I remember thinking that he should have paid me to watch the match.

It was the worst game I have ever seen.

Two appallingly inept teams seemingly trying their hardest to avoid scoring goals.

The crowd was officially given as 400, but then again, it always was. I never worked out why this was. It didn't seem to matter whether the ground was packed or empty, the official attendance was always the same. My suspicion was that nobody could be bothered to count.

During this particular game, I was so bored I decided to do a circuit of the ground and do an unofficial headcount, and counted exactly 93 heads.

Because of this, I missed the evening's only moment of drama, when Bromley's latest goalkeeper Ian McGuire, filling in for the injured Jenson, was himself injured and had to be replaced in goal by left-back Les Brockman.

The positive to be gained from this game was that it was the first time all season they had conceded less than four goals. Indeed, when Eric Nottage made it 1–1 on the hour, a draw looked the most likely result. Only a dire piece of luck prevented this happening, as a speculative pass bounced off the hapless Brown and into the path of Clapton's left winger whose sliced shot spun tantalisingly past the fill-in keeper.

I don't know what the committee planned to do to stop this losing streak, but they had to come up with something spectacular – and quick.

# ISTHMIAN LEAGUE HOW THEY STAND

## 29TH AUGUST 1969

|                    | P | W | D | L | F  | A  | Pts |
|--------------------|---|---|---|---|----|----|-----|
| Sutton Utd . . . . | 6 | 4 | 1 | 1 | 16 | 4  | 9   |
| Wycombe W . . . .  | 6 | 4 | 1 | 1 | 14 | 6  | 9   |
| Woking . . . . .   | 6 | 4 | 0 | 2 | 11 | 5  | 8   |
| Hendon . . . . .   | 6 | 3 | 2 | 1 | 17 | 8  | 8   |
| Leytonstone . . .  | 6 | 3 | 2 | 1 | 15 | 8  | 8   |
| Enfield . . . . .  | 6 | 3 | 2 | 1 | 6  | 4  | 8   |
| Tooting & Mit . .  | 6 | 3 | 2 | 1 | 12 | 8  | 8   |
| Barking . . . . .  | 6 | 3 | 1 | 2 | 17 | 9  | 7   |
| Oxford City . . .  | 5 | 3 | 1 | 1 | 5  | 4  | 7   |
| Clapton . . . . .  | 6 | 3 | 1 | 2 | 10 | 13 | 7   |
| Wealdstone . . .   | 5 | 2 | 2 | 1 | 12 | 5  | 6   |
| Hitchin Town . .   | 6 | 2 | 2 | 2 | 13 | 9  | 6   |
| St. Albans City .  | 5 | 2 | 1 | 2 | 8  | 6  | 5   |
| Kingstonian . . .  | 6 | 1 | 2 | 3 | 10 | 11 | 4   |
| Ilford . . . . .   | 5 | 1 | 2 | 2 | 4  | 8  | 4   |
| Walthamstow A . .  | 5 | 1 | 2 | 2 | 5  | 11 | 4   |
| Maidstone Utd . .  | 6 | 1 | 1 | 4 | 8  | 15 | 3   |
| Dulwich Hamlet .   | 6 | 0 | 3 | 3 | 4  | 10 | 3   |
| Corinthian Cs . .  | 5 | 0 | 0 | 5 | 2  | 18 | 0   |
| **BROMLEY** . . . . | **6** | **0** | **0** | **6** | **4** | **31** | **0** |

# CHAPTER THREE

I couldn't believe my eyes.

Bromley were about to pull off the greatest coup in football history and turn their season round with two major signings. A couple of the biggest names in the game, Bobby Charlton and Denis Law, were coming to Hayes Lane! It was there in black and white on the back page of the *Bromley and Kentish Times*.

This would mean the end for Alan Stonebridge and Eric Nottage, but I hoped they would stay and fight for their places. I couldn't wait to tell my friends and rushed down to the park where I knew I would find them kicking a ball about. The news spread like wildfire, and within the next few days, at least ten people told me the news.

It was a shame I was so excited that I hadn't bothered reading the full article. If I had, I would have spotted the clues in phrases like 'Thank goodness the loyal fans have a sense of humour and can laugh off their misfortunes', 'one suggestion is that Bromley should turn semi-professional and approach Manchester United about the possibility of having Denis Law and Bobby Charlton on loan when they are not required by the United first team' and 'just imagine the likely headlines if this actually happened: 'Law and Charlton score five each for Bromley but they lose 11–10'.

When my dad finally managed to convince me that the article was a light-hearted filler, I realised that once again, my hopes had been raised and then cruelly dashed.

•••

The selection committee had made further changes for the visit of Enfield. I was aware of one of these as I stood in the queue to get into the ground. A small band of fans were singing 'One Phil Amato, there's only one Phil Amato'. Actually, they were wrong. There were two. The other one played for Margate and was also swarthy with a turbulent temper. The difference was that their one was a superb striker, who scored spectacular goals with nonchalant ease.

I often wondered if Bromley might have got the Phil Amatos confused and accidentally signed the wrong one.

The signs were bad.

Not only were we playing the champions and easily the best team in the league, but we had Phil Amato, who was widely assumed to be on his way to Gravesend and Northfleet, at right-back.

Jeff Bridge, the left-back, had grown a moustache that really didn't suit him, but he'd vowed not to shave it off until Bromley lost next.

I hoped he'd brought his razor with him.

Once I was in the ground, I did what I always did and bought two programmes. One was immediately sealed in a plastic bag and put carefully into my duffel bag, between the two shin pads to stop it getting creased. It would only be taken out when I got home and added to my collection. The other would be used throughout the next ninety minutes, as I made notes which would help me relive the match at a later date.

These notes would frequently feature the word 'great', as in:

BROMLEY
6. R. Pettet 3.25 PM. Great shot!

BROMLEY
9. J. Wawrzewski 3.56 PM. Great shot, lucky save by goalie.


BROMLEY
10. E. Nottage  4.14 PM. Great shot, nearly a goal.


BROMLEY
1. I. McGuire 4.16 PM. Great save!


I always loved buying programmes, especially ones from home games. I studied them from cover to cover, devouring Charlie King's notes, seeing who had donated the match ball and enviously reading who had won the previous week's £5 Supporters' Club '200 Club' jackpot.

I vowed that I would give all my future business to those who advertised in the Bromley programme. I would eat at the Khush Bhag Restaurant ('Sophistication. Exotic Food') or Viva Maria Restaurant ('First Class Restaurant').

For heating, I'd head straight for Comfort Zones Heating (Heating) Ltd, who I knew I could rely on for my 'home heating comfort'. My first choice of family baker would always be Stanley Wood 'For crusty bread, cakes and pastries of quality and distinction'.

And in the unlikely event of needing floodlights, I'd simply pick up the phone and ring Reid and Barrow Ltd.

The league table on page 5 became a mass of mathematical calculations and arrows, as I incorporated the latest results from the Sunday paper. Sometimes, I would also include projected results for the next few weeks, based on a combination of current form and gut feeling.

But the best bit was the front cover, where Bromley's past successes were proudly listed. Included in the list was winning the FA Amateur Cup on three occasions and the Isthmian

League four times. It was a great comfort to know that I didn't support a useless team, but a good one that was currently going through a bad patch.

●●●

After picking up my programme, I wandered off to the main stand and sat down. I always made sure I had ten minutes to browse through the pages before kick-off, so was shocked to see the Enfield team run out early.

I checked my watch – 2.50pm.

What was going on?

Maybe the dressing-room clock was fast.

But surely the manager had a watch?

Then, as they started a series of exercises, it all made sense.

They weren't the best team in the Isthmian League for nothing – they even warmed up before their warm-up. In stark contrast, Bromley wandered out just before the kick-off, looking as though they'd all rather be anywhere but Hayes Lane.

The game itself started routinely enough, as it took the visitors just four minutes to take the lead with a shot that went in off the post.

But then something strange happened.

They didn't score any more goals, despite having countless chances to add to their slender lead.

And then something even stranger happened. Bromley went on the attack with ten minutes left and a sliced Jan Wawrzewski shot hit an Enfield defender on the arm.

I got to my feet screaming 'Penalty, ref!' – which I did at least three or four times a game with increasing desperation in my voice. On this occasion, the referee (Mr K.A. Duff of West Moseley) agreed and pointed to the spot.

Penalty to Bromley.

I immediately left my seat and ran behind the goal, arriving just as Alan Stonebridge was measuring out his run-up after placing the ball on the spot. He looked calm and composed and I couldn't understand why. Surely this was one of the biggest moments of his career?

In an old *Roy of the Rovers* story in the *Tiger and Hurricane* comic, Tubby Morton, the overweight goalkeeper for Melchester Rovers, had confided to his skipper that he always knew which way the ball would go at a penalty because the taker couldn't resist glancing at the spot he was going to aim at.

I looked at Stonebridge's eyes as he ran in. Sure enough, he looked left. Wolstenholm, the Enfield keeper, must have been a *Tiger and Hurricane* reader too, because that's exactly where he dived. But Stonebridge had been bluffing – the ball headed just inside the right-hand post and it was 1–1.

1–1 against the champions!

I don't think I had ever felt so excited. I ran back to my seat, opened the programme, took a deep breath and, with my right hand shaking, wrote the words:

8. A. Stonebridge 4.31 PM. Great penalty!

I was too nervous to watch the last ten minutes, so I went behind the stands and paced backwards and forwards, relying on the sounds coming from the small crowd (official attendance – 400) to let me know what was happening.

And then I heard it. The long, beautiful, shrill blast of Mr K.A. Duff's whistle that signified full-time. The cheers told me that Bromley had held on.

All the season's disappointments were instantly forgotten as I sprinted round to the players' tunnel to pat them on the backs and offer my heartfelt congratulations as they came off the pitch.

I didn't consider the possibility that the previous 90 minutes had been a case of a below-strength Enfield missing dozens of chances and Bromley getting a penalty that clearly wasn't.

I stopped off at the Supporters' Club hut on the way out of the ground. This was a white garden shed, surrounded by a small picket fence, and was situated parallel to the edge of the penalty area.

It was the inner sanctum of Bromley supporters, where Derek, Roy and Peter worked and then watched matches from a small bench in a fenced-off section outside the hut.

It was my dream to join them one day.

There really was nothing in life I wanted more than to help out in the shop and then relax on the bench with the Hayes Lane elite, getting a close-up view of the game and joining in their analysis. I always felt a sense of longing when I went to the hut, wishing I could be on the other side of the serving hatch, looking out instead of looking in.

I knew they worked hard, but I also knew I could do the job if someone would only give me a chance.

Before and after games, as well as at half-time, they were responsible for selling souvenirs, even though the range was limited to Bromley enamel badges (1/6) and Bromley ballpoint pens (1 shilling).

I owned at least six of each.

Still literally giddy with excitement, I had a look around and treated myself to a another ballpoint pen; but the real reason for dropping in was to discuss what had just unfolded on the pitch.

Derek had gone home to be with his newborn baby daughter, but Roy and Peter were tidying away the pens and badges. I could tell they were as excited as I was, especially Roy. He was flapping his arms around, his eyes blazing behind the thick lenses of his glasses and his hair looking wilder than ever as he released all the season's pent-up frustrations with a garbled summary of what we had just witnessed.

After discussing the highlights, or rather highlight, at least half a dozen times, we went our separate ways.

Instead of getting the bus home, I decided to walk so I would get to my local newsagents around the time the *Evening Standard* football special arrived. This was a paper that came out only an hour or so after the matches had finished, yet somehow had most of the results as well as match reports. I was confident that Bromley's shock result against Enfield would be as newsworthy as whatever happened between Chelsea and Palace, who were also playing that afternoon.

I waited outside, and at five to six the van pulled up and the driver jumped out, hurried into the shop and deposited a bundle of papers onto the counter.

I immediately bought one and went outside to read it, savouring that fresh-from-the-presses smell. The big story was how Palace had snatched a draw at Stamford Bridge, but despite scanning every page thoroughly, there was no mention of Bromley's heroic efforts. It didn't even make the Stop Press section.

I felt a ragin' fury bubble up inside me.

•••

The next day, after a restless night's sleep, I walked up to the newsagent to buy all the Sunday papers, convinced that Bromley's draw would be a major story.

It wasn't.

After ploughing through everything from the *Sunday Express* to the *Observer*, I didn't find a single mention of the match apart from the result. It seemed I would have to wait until Thursday, when the *Bromley Advertiser* came out, and

Friday, when the *Bromley and Kentish Times* appeared, to read about the game.

I bought both of these papers every week and kept a scrapbook of all Bromley match reports, league tables and stories, which I dutifully cut out and pasted every Sunday morning, using a bottle of Gloy glue marked 'To be used for Bromley scrapbook ONLY!!!!'

I was currently on volume 12.

My pocket money was spent on prints of photos which had appeared in the *Bromley Advertiser*, most of which seemed to feature Alan Stonebridge. These were either framed and put up on my bedroom wall, or put in the scrapbook.

At the back of the book, I kept the up-to-date rankings of my favourite player. That morning, Wawrzewski had gone from being fourth on the list to second, displacing Ian McGuire and overtaking Eric Nottage.

Alan Stonebridge was still first.

Phil Amato was still last.

And David Jensen, who had been my goalkeeping idol just a few weeks ago, had disappeared from the list in much the same way as he'd mysteriously vanished from the club after conceding 29 goals in five games.

This book wasn't my only long-term Bromley project. Another was to be able to name all the teams in the Isthmian League in under five seconds.

From memory.

Barking, Bromley, Clapton, Corinthian Casuals, Dulwich, Enfield, Hendon, Hitchin, Ilford, Kingstonian, Leytonstone, Maidstone, Oxford, St Albans, Sutton, Tooting and Mitcham, Walthamstow Avenue, Wealdstone, Woking, Wycombe.

Over the years I had got quicker and quicker. My dad had once caught me practising and while doing it made perfect sense to me, it proved almost impossible to explain to him.

I didn't let that affect me, though. Because after weeks of near-misses, I had finally got under ten seconds.

●●●

Corinthian Casuals were the 'someone else' in the phrase 'However bad things get, there's always someone else worse off than you'.

They were permanently stuck at the foot of the table and rarely managed more than a couple of wins a season. I had a real soft spot for them, probably because they were the one team a Bromley fan could look down on.

Corinthian Casuals were hopeless for a number of reasons.

Firstly, their name didn't exactly strike fear into their opponents.

Then they were resolutely amateur, so didn't pay 'expenses' which most other teams routinely did. They also insisted on 'promoting the game through fair play and sportsmanship'.

This was taken to extreme lengths. After suffering a heartbreaking 1–0 defeat against league-leaders Leytonstone the previous Saturday, thanks to a goal that was reported as being 'several yards offside', the programme notes for the following home fixture pointed out that:

'An excellent feature of the game was a highly competent performance by the referee, Mr K.G. Salmon.'

Other factors preventing them from attracting the cream of footballing talent included the small matter of not actually having a ground of their own and wearing shirts that were divided up into pink and chocolate-brown quarters, which clashed horribly with their blue shorts.

As a result of all this, Casuals teams were generally a mix of the highly principled and the totally inept.

Tonight's game was between the bottom team in the League (us) and the second from bottom team in the League (them). What made it even less likely to attract a sizeable crowd was that it was being played on someone else's ground.

As their current landlords were Tooting and Mitcham, the coach journey to the Corinthian Casuals away fixture was a bit longer than previous seasons, when they shared with Dulwich Hamlet.

But I was glad of the extra travelling time. It allowed me to savour every minute of what was a rare experience – going to a Bromley game confident of getting the points.

The early signs were extremely promising.

Casuals had been forced into fielding a third-choice goal-keeper, which was the equivalent of any other team fielding their fifth-choice goalkeeper.

Goalie Number One was in hospital for a minor operation and Number Two had gone missing. As Number Three ran onto the pitch, Roy and I looked at each other in disbelief.

He didn't look much older than me.

Putting the odds even more heavily in our favour was the recent history. We had come away with the points on each of their last three visits.

Everything was pointing to an easy victory, and it took just three minutes for Eric Nottage to confirm this by scoring after a superb through ball from Stonebridge, whose footballing abilities were starting to become wildly exaggerated in my mind.

Then the game drifted into a stalemate.

It was as though Bromley didn't really know what they should do, now that they found themselves in such an unfamiliar position, while the home team simply weren't good enough to do anything.

Out of the blue, everything changed one minute from half time. Chris Joy, Casuals captain and the son of the *Evening Standard*'s football correspondent, took a free-kick from 30 yards out that sailed past a bemused Ian Mcguire and the scores were level.

It was my turn to get the tea, so I missed out on much of the half-time analysis, but by the time I rejoined the Bromley boys, I noticed a major dip in confidence levels. We decided that a draw wouldn't be so bad after all, as it would still keep us off bottom place. Taking comfort from this, Peter pointed out that Bromley had already equalled their highest score of the season. Plus, we weren't actually losing at half-time, which was a first for the season. By the time the teams came back out, we were all feeling pretty good about life again.

The second half was notable for two things – firstly Postman Pat Brown's glorious header from a perfect Eddie Green corner which gave Bromley a barely deserved lead. And then watching Phil Amato limping from the field, a sight that filled me with conflicting emotions. I expected to feel nothing but pleasure at the possibility of a season-ending injury, but was shocked to find myself also thinking it was a shame and that he'd been playing quite well.

These sympathetic thoughts lasted about a minute, which was how long it took substitute Colin Owen to come on and hit the post almost immediately, with what I described in my programme notes as a 'great volley'.

The game ended shortly after, giving Bromley their first win of the season. Even though it was only against Corinthian Casuals, I felt happier than I had in a long time. A win can do that for you, especially when it's something you hadn't experienced in more than five months.

The glory of victory had completely overshadowed the fact I was off to boarding school in the morning.

The reality of that happening hadn't even begun to sink in.

•••

The next morning, I was sitting on the roof of the house, refusing to come down. The reality of going to boarding school had well and truly sunk in and I was desperately trying to avoid getting in the car and being driven the 15 miles to Sevenoaks, my new weekday home.

I was grateful we lived in a bungalow, otherwise I might well have had to come up with an alternative protest.

Negotiations had pretty much broken down, and my parents were playing the waiting game, knowing full well that I would be down as soon as I got either too cold or too hungry.

They didn't have to wait for long.

Realising the futility and feeling uncomfortable at the small crowd which had gathered outside, I climbed down and sat in the car.

My dad joined me and we drove off in silence. The journey took us past the Egg and Griddle, where I'd spent many a school-day making a cup of tea last for hours. We passed WH Smith, where I had spent much of the rest of the time listening to records by everyone from the Seekers to Bob Dylan in the listening booths. We then drove past Hayes Lane, home of Bromley FC and into the wilds of Kent.

Just over half an hour later, we pulled up outside Johnson's – the boarding house I'd be sharing with 50 other boys.

As I dragged my suitcase inside, I looked out at the perfectly mown back lawn, where several of the boarders were enjoying a game of croquet. In the distance, I could just about make out several rugby fields.

It was like being in another country.

The house itself was all wood panelling, high ceilings and oil portraits of obscure gentry. There was a gong which was sounded at meal times and sweeping stairways leading to three enormous dormitories. An overwhelming smell of bees-wax furniture polish hit you as soon as you stepped inside and it had a cold, impersonal atmosphere.

The house belonged to a different era, when characters like Colonel Mustard or Professor Plum would have scurried furtively from room to room, candlestick or rope in their hands.

I knew as soon as I set foot in the place that I didn't belong there.

•••

Once settled in, I went for a stroll. Johnson's was at the end of a country lane, about a 20-minute walk from the school.

I just wanted to get away, so headed in the opposite direction from where we had driven. After about 15 minutes of aimless rambling, I found myself turning into a small cul-de-sac and was suddenly brought to a standstill by the glorious sight which confronted me.

It was like discovering Shangri-La, Brigadoon and the Lost Kingdom all at once.

Because there, on a small village green, was a set of full-sized goalposts. And around a dozen boys playing a game of football with varying degrees of skill as though their lives depended on it.

I went back to Johnson's in a far better frame of mind, but still just wanted to get the next few days over and done with. There was an important away game against Walthamstow Avenue on Saturday.

# ISTHMIAN LEAGUE HOW THEY STAND

## 4TH SEPTEMBER 1969

|                  | P | W | D | L | F | A | Pts |
|------------------|---|---|---|---|---|---|-----|
| Sutton Utd . . . .8 | 8 | 5 | 2 | 1 | 21 | 5 | 12 |
| Enfield . . . . . .8 | 8 | 4 | 3 | 1 | 9 | 5 | 11 |
| Barking . . . . . .8 | 8 | 4 | 2 | 2 | 2 | 19 | 10 |
| Leytonstone . . . .8 | 8 | 4 | 2 | 2 | 16 | 9 | 10 |
| Wycombe W . . . . .8 | 8 | 4 | 2 | 2 | 14 | 9 | 10 |
| Oxford City . . . .8 | 8 | 4 | 2 | 2 | 7 | 7 | 10 |
| Clapton . . . . . .8 | 8 | 4 | 2 | 2 | 13 | 15 | 10 |
| St Albans City . .7 | 7 | 4 | 1 | 2 | 13 | 7 | 9 |
| Hendon . . . . . .7 | 7 | 3 | 3 | 1 | 19 | 10 | 9 |
| Hitchin Town . . .8 | 8 | 3 | 3 | 2 | 16 | 11 | 9 |
| Tooting & Mit . . .8 | 8 | 3 | 3 | 2 | 13 | 11 | 9 |
| Wealdstone . . . .8 | 8 | 3 | 2 | 3 | 17 | 11 | 8 |
| Kingstonian . . . .8 | 8 | 3 | 2 | 3 | 13 | 11 | 8 |
| Woking . . . . . .8 | 8 | 4 | 0 | 4 | 11 | 10 | 8 |
| Walthamstow A . . .8 | 8 | 2 | 2 | 4 | 12 | 16 | 6 |
| Maidstone . . . . .7 | 7 | 2 | 1 | 4 | 12 | 15 | 5 |
| Dulwich Ham . . . .8 | 8 | 1 | 3 | 4 | 7 | 15 | 5 |
| Ilford . . . . . .7 | 7 | 1 | 2 | 4 | 5 | 12 | 4 |
| **BROMLEY** . . . . .8 | **8** | **1** | **1** | **6** | **7** | **31** | **3** |
| Corinthian Cs . . .8 | 8 | 0 | 0 | 8 | 4 | 26 | 0 |

# CHAPTER FOUR

The supporters' club coach was almost full – testimony to the effect of the tiniest morsel of success on the fair-weather Bromley supporter. Confusingly, the ground wasn't in Walthamstow Avenue, but several miles away in Green Pond Road. Well, half of it was. The other half was in Higham Hill Road.

Luckily the coach driver was up to the challenge and we were dropped directly outside the entrance.

Walthamstow Avenue's ground was my favourite place to visit, with the highest turnstiles and weakest floodlights in the Isthmian League, giving an eerie atmosphere of what I imagined a prison exercise yard would be like at twilight.

This game marked my first awareness of hooliganism filtering down to the lower leagues, albeit in the mildest possible way. The programme rather huffily reported the following story:

> After the match with the Corinthian Casuals, Thursday 28th August, some young hooligan ran off with a ball. The police were called, but, as the ball was later recovered, the Club will not, on this occasion, prosecute.

I found the boy's actions strangely exhilarating (was he acting alone? How did the police find him? Did his mum make him give the ball back?), but kept my feelings to myself and instead joined in the general condemnation.

The topic of conversation soon turned back to the game itself as a very confident-looking home team ran out.

But Bromley, even without the injured Phil Amato and more significantly Pat Brown (his wife was ill), had, in my eyes at least, an air of invincibility.

As if to prove me wrong, there was to be a disastrous start to the match. After just a couple of minutes, injury-prone goalie Ian McGuire dramatically fell to the ground clutching his ankle, even though no-one was anywhere near him. It was as though he'd been struck by a sniper's bullet fired from the terraces.

After lengthy treatment, he painfully limped back to his place between the posts, but it soon became apparent that he had somehow managed to self-inflict a fairly serious injury.

Following frantic hand-waving from the committee, who were sitting together in the stand, John Mears (who had played in just about every other position that season) took over in goal and new signing Jim Watson came on as substitute to take Mears' place.

Both made their marks immediately – Watson handled in the area and Mears could only help the penalty into the net.

1–0 to Avenue.

There then followed a sustained period of attack from Bromley, which was notable for none of the shots being remotely threatening. They went straight to the goalie, wide of the post or over the bar.

It was the latter I had been waiting for, as I stood behind the goal with the rest of the away supporters. As soon as Roy Pettet connected with the ball, I could see it was going to miss the target by several feet. It soared over the bar and kept going over the heads of the fans, finally coming to rest in a ditch behind us.

I set off after it, with a plan in mind. No, I didn't intend emulating the hooligan's efforts by running away with the ball. My plan was to show the committee that I had the necessary skills to take over from the injured Ian McGuire as Bromley's first-choice goalie.

After retrieving the ball, I casually placed it in my right hand and, with a smooth McGuire-esque overarm action, threw it 20 yards or so in the direction of John Mears, somehow managing to not overbalance.

I don't know if he caught it, because I was modestly staring down at the ground after completing the throw. I did, however, permit myself a sly glance in the direction of where the committee were seated.

They showed no signs of having noticed.

The last 20 minutes was the most exciting period of the entire season, or so it seemed at the time. In the 70th minute, Eric Nottage added yet another goal to his impressive tally, with a tap-in after Watson's shot was parried by keeper, Victor Bowley.

Avenue then hit the post.

Then Bromley hit the post.

And then, with time just about up, Bowley the goalie (I had now started giving our opponents nicknames) helpfully repeated his earlier error and again knocked the ball into the path of Eric Nottage, who sealed a 2–1 win.

After the final whistle, I felt elated. I didn't want to leave and almost had to be dragged back to the coach. I stood staring at the now-empty ground, reliving the goals with a real sense of joy and excitement. It wasn't like the win against Corinthian Casuals, which didn't really count. This was a win against a team that had finished near the middle of the table last season. They'd also beaten us twice.

On the journey home, I declined the usual game of cards. I was too busy working out the projected league tables. My conclusion was that if Bromley won the rest of their games, they would not only win the Isthmian League, but would also finish a record 24 points clear of runners-up, Enfield.

When I got home, I took the lime-green Subbuteo box which housed the Bromley team from my cupboard and removed the player with a number two painted clumsily on his back. A small, plastic version of Jeff Bridge.

I then got the thinnest paintbrush I could find – one of the benefits of having an artistic dad – and painted what was meant to be a luxuriant moustache over the right-back's upper lip.

It was an acknowledgement that Bromley had turned the corner and the moustache was a permanent fixture.

Sadly, the delicate touch needed for this was absent and the Subbuteo version of Jeff Bridge ended up with a large brown smudge covering the lower part of his nose, lips and chin.

He looked as though he'd tried to stuff an entire chocolate cake into his mouth and missed.

●●●

I hadn't missed a game all season. In fact, I hadn't missed one since Leytonstone (away) on Valentine's Day in 1968, when I was in hospital with appendicitis.

I hated the thought of missing watching Bromley play, so I had no idea what I was going to do about the next midweek fixture, which was the Ilford match in ten days time. I knew I wouldn't be allowed to go – I'd already asked. So the only options were to miss it or run away from school.

The latter had recently been done successfully by another boarder called Daniel Day-Lewis, whose dad was a famous poet. Daniel was a year or two below me and had decided to take off with a couple of friends, for the understandable reason that he hated Sevenoaks School and everything about it.

He had evidently been forgiven, because I'd seen him around since then. And if he had managed to get away with it, I probably could as well.

I promised myself that if Bromley won on Saturday against Woking, I would walk out of school on the following Tuesday and take the bus to Hayes Lane without telling anyone. It seemed a perfectly reasonable thing to do.

●●●

Bromley Football Club were clearly not familiar with the philosophy of never changing a winning formula. As part of their seemingly compulsive need to overcomplicate things, they effectively formed one-man sub-committees to report to the committee, by appointing a coach (Alan Basham) and a trainer (Frank Morris).

I knew this because I'd saved the *Bromley and Kentish Times* for the Sunday evening journey back to Johnson's and was reading it on the bus.

There was also news of injuries to goalie/defender/half-back/forward John Mears and winger Eddie Green, whose recent good performances had forced him into third place in my favourite players list.

They would both miss Saturday's game against Woking, as would recent signing Bobby Lennox, who was attending a P.E. course at Loughborough College. Unfortunately, this was not the Bobby Lennox who scored in the European Cup Final when Celtic became first British team to win it.

But such was the team's form currently, that it no longer seemed to matter if players had to miss games. I was confident that replacements would be found who would slot in without having any negative effect.

My faith in the committee was absolute. They had turned

around a season that was heading for disaster and the team were nearly unbeaten since they had taken over.

They could do no wrong in my eyes.

●●●

Back at Johnson's, I was really trying to fit in, even to the extent of joining in an early Sunday evening game of croquet. But my heart just wasn't in it and I soon found myself wandering off to the village green, in the hopes I would find someone playing football.

On this occasion, my luck was in.

A group of five or six boys were practising shooting – and the really good thing was that the one in goal was complaining loudly about it being someone else's turn. No-one was volunteering to take his place.

I stood nervously on the sideline, hoping I would be invited to join in. I did everything short of sticking my hand in the air and jumping up and down to attract their attention. I think it was my loosening-up exercises (which consisted of rotating one shoulder, then the other – like Ian McGuire did before a game) that finally got me noticed.

I was asked if I wanted to play. After modestly telling them I was a goalkeeper, I took my place between the posts and for the next 40 minutes dived around, making a few saves and letting in a lot of goals.

It was the perfect way to make new friends. I got back to Johnson's late, happy and covered in mud.

●●●

Sevenoaks, unlike just about every other school in the universe, had school on Saturday mornings. Double maths, chemistry and Latin. I hated all these subjects with a passion, but Latin more than anything.

Being a Saturday, all I could think about was getting back to Bromley and watching the game against Woking, so as soon as the bell went I rushed for the door. It was imperative that I went home before going to the ground, so I could dump the straw hat, change into less formal clothes and pack my duffel bag.

In my hurry, I managed to collide with another boy, who was also keen to make a quick escape. 'Oi, watch where you're going,' he muttered. 'No, YOU watch where you're going', I replied, slightly disappointed that this was the best I could come up with.

It was a trivial incident which would have major repercussions in the weeks and months to come.

# ISTHMIAN LEAGUE HOW THEY STAND

## 12TH SEPTEMBER 1969

|                    | P | W | D | L | F | A | Pts |
|--------------------|---|---|---|---|----|----|-----|
| Sutton Utd . . . . | 9 | 6 | 2 | 1 | 23 | 5  | 14  |
| Leytonstone . . . .| 9 | 4 | 4 | 1 | 17 | 9  | 12  |
| Oxford City . . . .| 9 | 5 | 2 | 2 | 12 | 8  | 12  |
| Clapton . . . . . .| 9 | 5 | 2 | 2 | 19 | 17 | 12  |
| Barking . . . . . .| 9 | 4 | 3 | 2 | 19 | 10 | 11  |
| Enfield . . . . . .| 8 | 4 | 3 | 1 | 9  | 5  | 11  |
| Wycombe W . . . . .| 9 | 4 | 3 | 2 | 14 | 9  | 11  |
| Hendon . . . . . . | 8 | 3 | 4 | 1 | 19 | 10 | 10  |
| St. Albans City . .| 8 | 4 | 1 | 3 | 14 | 9  | 9   |
| Hitchin Town . . . | 9 | 3 | 3 | 3 | 16 | 13 | 9   |
| Tooting & Mit . . .| 8 | 3 | 3 | 2 | 13 | 11 | 9   |
| Wealdstone . . . . | 8 | 3 | 2 | 3 | 17 | 11 | 8   |
| Woking . . . . . . | 8 | 4 | 0 | 4 | 11 | 10 | 8   |
| Kingstonian . . . .| 9 | 2 | 4 | 3 | 13 | 12 | 8   |
| Maidstone Utd . . .| 8 | 3 | 1 | 4 | 14 | 16 | 7   |
| Walthamstow A . . .| 9 | 2 | 3 | 5 | 13 | 18 | 6   |
| Dulwich Ham . . . .| 9 | 1 | 4 | 4 | 17 | 15 | 6   |
| **BROMLEY** . . . . .| **9** | **2** | **1** | **6** | **9** | **34** | **5** |
| Ilford . . . . . . | 8 | 1 | 2 | 5 | 7  | 18 | 4   |
| Corinthian Cs . . .| 9 | 0 | 0 | 9 | 5  | 31 | 0   |

# CHAPTER FIVE

At 14, when your football team is going well, life is going well.

And it wasn't just me who was feeling the psychological benefits of Bromley's successful mini-run.

Roy and Derek were going about their work at the Supporters' Club hut with smiles on their faces. Sales of pens and enamel badges were really taking off and the recent addition of rosettes had proven to be a shrewd business decision, even if they weren't strictly in the right colours. Most supporters seemed to be wearing them.

I had three.

But it was something in the recent Bromley programmes that had got me very excited indeed.

There had been an announcement that the Supporters' Club were looking for someone to work in the tea hut on the far side of the ground. I often helped out, collecting cups and saucers after games and returning them to Peter, who was in charge of the hut.

But this was something far more desirable. If I could get the job, it would get me into the inner circle of supporters. Not only would I be able to serve tea and watch games from a superior vantage position, but it would be a step towards my ultimate dream – working in the Supporters' Club hut itself.

I tentatively asked Derek for an application form, but he just laughed and pointed out John Self, the secretary of the Supporters' Club, and said I should ask him.

I decided to do it later, once I'd worked up the courage.

●●●

I took the same seat in the stand that I'd sat in for the Enfield game. I was pretty big on superstition and since my attempts at growing a Jeff Bridge moustache had fallen frustratingly short of being noticeable, I had decided to do my bit by sitting in the same place every home game throughout what I was convinced would be a lengthy unbeaten run.

The seats in the stand weren't so much seats as a narrow wooden bench, with wobbly white lines painted on to separate you from whoever was sitting next to you.

I was in Seat B8. And B8 was where I was determined to stay all season. The only bad thing about this position was that it was directly underneath the tannoy speaker, which played badly scratched records by military marching bands for half-an-hour before kick-off.

For the second game running, I had my programme reading drowned out by crackly renditions of 'Colonel Bogey', 'The Dambusters' March' and 'Those Magnificent Men in their Flying Machines'.

When the team changes were announced, it was like having them shouted directly into my ear by a very loud Charlie King, who doubled up as Chairman and Ground Announcer. The news he gave was mixed. Pat Brown's wife was clearly feeling better, because he would be playing. Ian McGuire hadn't recovered from his mystery injury, so would be replaced by the great Alan Soper in goal. And the possibly-no-longer-useless Phil Amato had got over his stubbed-toe problems.

Woking were a mid-table team – not as good as Enfield, and not as bad as Corinthian Casuals. A win today and Bromley would join them on eight points.

The home team started well. A ridiculous back pass almost let Jim Watson in and Eric Nottage ruined a brilliant piece of play when he flicked the ball over the full-back's head, ran around him and volleyed the ball directly into the corner flag.

Woking's answer was pure comedy. The winger, McCormack, ran down the left and, with the choice of five colleagues in the penalty area, completely miscued and fell over, injuring himself so badly he was carried off and replaced.

The applause from the Bromley fans as he left the field was sympathetic. We were no strangers to witnessing self-inflicted injuries, having seen Ian McGuire's efforts a few days earlier.

Ironically, it was McGuire's replacement who would be Bromley's hero today. Alan Soper had the game of his life and somehow kept a clean sheet despite a barrage of shots, headers and ill-advised back passes on his goal. As a fellow goalie, I felt I had an expert's understanding of just how well he was playing. His decision making was excellent – he seemed to know exactly when to catch the ball and when to tip it over the bar. And his distribution was, in my opinion, even better than McGuire's.

The game was decided 22 minutes from the end, during a forgettable 60 seconds for the Woking centre-half Edwards. First he was booked for a late tackle on Wawrzewski. Then, from the resulting free-kick he headed the ball straight to Jim Watson, who gratefully accepted the chance and it was 1–0 to Bromley. And that was the way it finished. We now had three wins in a row and were just seven points away from the current league leaders, Sutton United.

Soper had been so good, I ran out of space in my record of his saves in the programme (most of which were 'great' though one was 'amazing') and had to continue on the opposite page, writing over the Cracker Southland Coaches Ltd advertisement.

The 1953 Cup Final between Blackpool and Bolton Wanderers had been so dominated by Stanley Matthews that it had become known as 'The Matthews Final'. This game, to me, would always be known as 'The Soper Match'.

●●●

I found John Self helping Peter out with the washing up at the tea hut. Thinking that a good way to ingratiate myself would be to collect the empty plates, cups and saucers from around the ground, I took a tin tray with 'A Double Diamond works wonders' on it and stacked it with all the used crockery I could find on the terraces and in the stands.

By the time I got back, John Self had gone. I decided to talk to him on Tuesday during the Ilford game.

I think I'd always known I'd be there. I was pretty sure Johnson's wouldn't even notice I'd gone. Especially if I left the ground early and got back before bedtime.

My plan wasn't particularly well thought-out. It was basically this:

1. Leave Johnson's after supper at 5.30.
2. Get bus to ground,
3. Watch game,
4. Get bus back,
5. Sneak in to dormitory,
6. Go to bed.

I had thought of stuffing a dummy made of pillows and wearing pyjamas into my bed, like I'd seen in a war film on TV, but decided it was an unnecessary complication which probably wouldn't fool anyone.

The first part of the plan went smoothly, in that I left Johnson's after supper. This wasn't that unusual – I often went for a kickabout on the village green, so no-one would have realised anything was amiss.

As I was coming from Johnson's I'd had the chance to change into something a bit more suitable. I didn't have my anorak – that was at home – but neither did I have the straw hat or pink tie.

I hadn't told anyone what I was doing. I didn't know any of the other boys well enough to trust them with my plans, so I just took off.

By the time I got to the ground at 7.15pm, all I could think about was the match. The excitement I got from walking up the long path to the ground entrance and getting the first glimpse of the blazing floodlights was intensified by Bromley being on a winning streak.

The game started brightly enough. With 'Colonel Bogey' still ringing in my ears, Pat Brown's fourth-minute free-kick was completely missed by the flapping Ilford goalie and Eric Nottage headed the ball into an unguarded net.

In the Bromley goal, Alan Soper was once again on great form, with a series of great saves. He looked unbeatable.

But just when Ilford appeared to have given up on ever finding a way past him, Postman Pat Brown showed them how with a spectacular own-goal.

An innocuous cross from their right-winger Johnny Clark was headed with such power and precision past a startled Soper that it would have been one of the goals of the season, had it happened at the other end.

With the scores level at half-time, I went in search of John Self and found him serving at the tea hut. The only way I could think of to talk to him was to join the queue, so I patiently waited my turn. Unfortunately, I lost my nerve at the last minute and ended up asking him for a cup of tea and an egg sandwich instead. I then trudged back to Seat B8, no nearer to getting my dream job. The fear of rejection had been too overwhelming, especially as it would have happened in front of a small queue of parched Bromley fans.

It was to be that kind of night. Nothing turned out quite

as well as I imagined it would.

The second half was another example. When Eric Nottage soared above the defence to head home his sixth goal of the season, it was perfect timing. If I left immediately, I'd just have time to catch the 8.40 bus which would get me back at Johnson's before lights out.

I checked my pocket for bus fare. And realised, to my alarm, that I didn't have enough. I'd spent too much buying a cup of tea and sandwich that I didn't really want. I was going to have to hitch back.

While the full horror of this was sinking in, Jeff Bridge decided to attempt a back pass which went straight to the Ilford inside-forward, who beat Soper from a tight angle to make it 2–2.

The night was going from bad to worse. A feeling that was confirmed when Eric Nottage limped off with what looked like a serious injury just before the end.

I left the ground demoralised. The draw, which a month ago would have been cause for celebration, was now a wasted opportunity.

And I had around 20 minutes to get back to Sevenoaks before I would be missed.

It was dark, so I decided to stick to the main roads where I would have a better chance of getting a lift. The fact that it was basically the same route as the 704 bus, which I had travelled on several hundred times, meant I wouldn't get lost.

But as it was the kind of night where everything was going wrong, I wasn't too confident.

I started walking, thumb held out. However, cars were few and far between and by the time I got to Farnborough, a couple of miles away, it had gone 10pm.

By the time I got to Green Street Green, which wasn't even

half way, I was starting to feel tired and cold. My school blazer was no match for a freezing Autumn night and being overweight meant I was ill-prepared for the exertion of a long walk.

As I got deeper into the countryside, there was less and less street lighting and more and more open fields.

Just before getting to Pratt's Bottom, I became aware of the owls hooting – a sound which took on a sinister air to an impressionable 14–year-old. I looked at the luminous dial on my watch – 12.25am. For once, I wished I was in bed at Johnson's.

I even thought of sleeping in the Badger's Mount bus shelter and getting the first bus in the morning, but realised that would be too late. Someone would have noticed I wasn't in my bed. Besides, it was far too cold to sleep.

I went through my pockets, trying to find something to eat and found some Opal Fruits and a bag containing a few boiled sweets that were shaped like peanuts and tasted nothing like them. The plan to ration these didn't work as I stuffed all of them into my mouth at the same time.

I then carried on walking. All the places that whizzed by when you were on the bus seemed to be enormous distances apart when you were on foot and I was getting increasingly tired.

But I was determined to get back before morning, even though traffic was virtually non-existent apart from a couple of long-distance lorries, both of which ignored my thumb.

Finally, at 3.15am, just outside Riverhead and only a few miles from Sevenoaks, a car pulled up. I was on the brink of exhaustion, scared and hungry. The driver wound down his window and called my name. It was my dad. He'd been driving around for hours trying to find me. Apparently there were cars searching everywhere. The police were involved as were friends of my parents and several concerned teachers from school.

I got into the car and promptly burst into tears.

# ISTHMIAN LEAGUE HOW THEY STAND

## 25TH SEPTEMBER 1969

|                   | P   | W | D | L  | F  | A  | Pts |
|-------------------|-----|---|---|----|----|----|-----|
| Sutton Utd        | 11  | 8 | 2 | 1  | 29 | 9  | 18  |
| Wycombe W         | 11  | 6 | 3 | 2  | 19 | 9  | 15  |
| Clapton           | 11  | 6 | 3 | 2  | 25 | 20 | 15  |
| Leytonstone       | 11  | 5 | 4 | 2  | 22 | 9  | 14  |
| Enfield           | 9   | 5 | 3 | 1  | 12 | 5  | 13  |
| Wealdstone        | 11  | 5 | 3 | 3  | 22 | 13 | 13  |
| Barking           | 11  | 5 | 3 | 3  | 16 | 13 | 13  |
| Oxford City       | 11  | 5 | 3 | 3  | 16 | 13 | 13  |
| St. Albans City   | 11  | 6 | 1 | 4  | 18 | 15 | 13  |
| Hitchin Town      | 12  | 4 | 4 | 4  | 20 | 17 | 12  |
| Kingstonian       | 12  | 4 | 4 | 4  | 16 | 15 | 12  |
| Hendon            | 9   | 3 | 4 | 2  | 19 | 11 | 10  |
| Tooting & Mit     | 9   | 3 | 4 | 2  | 14 | 12 | 10  |
| Woking            | 11  | 5 | 0 | 6  | 12 | 13 | 10  |
| Maidstone Utd     | 10  | 3 | 2 | 5  | 16 | 21 | 8   |
| Ilford            | 11  | 2 | 4 | 5  | 11 | 21 | 8   |
| **BROMLEY**       | **11** | **3** | **2** | **6** | **12** | **36** | **8** |
| Dulwich           | 12  | 1 | 5 | 6  | 10 | 23 | 7   |
| Walthamstow A     | 12  | 2 | 2 | 8  | 15 | 24 | 6   |
| Corinthian Cs     | 12  | 0 | 0 | 12 | 6  | 38 | 0   |

# CHAPTER SIX

I was allowed to spend the next day in bed, where I caught up with my Agatha Christie reading. It had been a late night, explaining where I'd been and promising I wouldn't do anything like it again.

I meant it, too. I felt really guilty about what I'd done and had vowed to make a fresh start. From now on, I was going to throw myself into life at Sevenoaks. I planned to play rugby and croquet, study and be a perfect student.

It had been made very clear to me that if I ever got into trouble again, I would be expelled. This was my last chance and I was determined to take it. My behaviour was going to be perfect from now on.

I was even going to miss Bromley's midweek matches and only go to their Saturday games.

I threw myself into school life, vowing there'd be no more standing on the sidelines.

I put my name down for the inter-house rugby competition, even though I'd never played a game in my life. I entered the Upper Fourth-form Monopoly tournament and got through to the second round. I studied harder than I'd ever studied before, spending over five hours one night writing an imaginary interview with Xerxes, King of Persia, on how he felt after his fleet had been destroyed by the Athenians.

I even asked about taking up wrestling. This was a sport I had a keen interest in, not least because one of the greatest wrestlers of his generation lived a few doors down from me in Bromley. His name was 'Judo' Al Hayes and just about every time I went down to the park, I would pass his house and see him washing his Jaguar in the driveway. His toughness had made a huge impression on me. A few months ago, he had taken a terrible beating at the hands of Honey Boy Zimba, 'the sweetest wrestler of them all', in a televised bout from a provincial town hall.

The commentators questioned whether he would ever be able to walk again after Zimba put him in a trademark Boston Crab and refused to let go, even though Hayes had submitted and was screaming in pain. The crowd were on their feet booing, but Zimba took no notice. There was madness in his eyes.

The next day, I was expecting to see an ambulance outside his house – but instead, there he was, miraculously unmarked, cleaning his car. It was an incredible recovery.

While I was still at primary school he had become British heavyweight champion after defeating his former trainer (and mentor) Sir Athol Oakley for the title. More recently, he had adopted the identity of 'The White Angel', a mysterious masked mauler who claimed to be from France. His nemesis was another man in a mask – Dr Death. The end came when The White Angel challenged Dr Death to an unmasking match at the Granada Cinema in Tooting. The loser would have their mask ripped off and their identity revealed to a world.

Dr Death's underhand tactics cost Hayes the fight and led to the end of The White Angel. He had since carved out a successful career under his own name.

To say I worshipped 'Judo' Al Hayes would be an understatement. I had his autograph eight times, often walked past his house just so I could see him and firmly believed that if I took up wrestling, he would be able to give me tips.

But even if I wasn't able to wrestle, there were plenty more activities I would be happy to take up, including cricket, chess and cross-country running.

I was going to put my name down for all of them. But just because I was considering doing all these things didn't mean I wasn't constantly thinking about football.

In particular, the FA Cup.

●●●

It isn't just supporters of the bigger league teams who dream of FA Cup glory.

And with Bromley due to take the first steps towards Wembley on Saturday in the first qualifying round, I had worked out that with a mixture of a kind draw and a few upsets, we could go a long way. Maybe all the way.

There were signs everywhere. The five-game unbeaten run, to start with. Another thing was the knowledge that Bromley had come desperately close to beating West Ham a couple of months ago, a team who had not only lifted the trophy in 1964, but also won the European Cup Winners' Cup a year later.

Then there was the fact that the FA Cup was littered with upsets – in one of the biggest footballing shocks of the decade, 4th Division Crewe Alexandra had held Spurs, who were the best team in the country, to a 2–2 draw and almost beaten them.

The replay didn't go quite so well as they lost 13–2.

What really captured my imagination about this wasn't just the astonishing amount of goals they managed to concede, but also discovering (according to my copy of *The Topical Times Football Annual*) that Crewe had left Euston from platform 13 after the game and arrived home on platform 2.

The final factor in my current FA Cup optimism was the brilliance of Alan Soper and Alan Stonebridge, the in-form players in an in-form team.

Soper was, in my mind, easily the best goalie in the Isthmian League. But it was Stonebridge I really idolised. Even though Eric Nottage was scoring more goals Stonebridge was the more glamorous figure. He was younger, and looked like a cross between John Lennon and Paul McCartney. He always scored the flashier goals – of his 23 the previous season, many had been thrilling. There were cavalier efforts from impossible angles, audacious penalties and even a couple of thunderbolts from breathtaking distances. Nottage was more of a centre-forward in the traditional mould – a solid converter of crosses, a finisher of moves. If Nottage was Bromley's Bobby Charlton, Stonebridge was the local George Best.

My growing optimism was tempered by one unavoidable statistic – Bromley hadn't actually scored a goal in the FA Cup in four years.

Our opponents on Saturday were Aveley Town, who were currently near the top of the Athenian League, which was of a slightly lower standard than the Isthmian league.

If Bromley could beat them, we would be just ten games away from Wembley. I wanted to make sure I watched them throughout their entire cup run, so decided that I would be the best-behaved boy in the whole school.

●●●

I didn't rush out of my Latin class when the bell went at 12.30pm on Saturday. I made sure I finished my work first, carefully packed my books away and walked to the bus stop.

I even thought about doing some revision on the bus back to Bromley, but decided that would be going too far. So I stared out of the window, daydreaming of that afternoon in May when I would watch skipper Roy Pettet get hoisted onto the shoulders of his team-mates, proudly holding the trophy – just as Manchester City's Tony Book (a former non-league player himself) had done a few months ago.

When I got home, I made sure I spent time with my parents, impressing upon them my new attitude.

I then left to meet the coach which would take me to Aveley.

Aveley was an hour away, so I settled down next to Peter and we immediately started talking about the big match. It had attracted so much interest that the Supporters' Club had laid on two coaches – something I hadn't seen before.

I suspected Peter of having a contact on the committee, because he always had the very latest team news and gossip.

He gave me the double-dose of good news that Amato had failed his fitness test and Nottage had passed his.

But then he casually dropped a bombshell – Jan Wawrzewski had been left out of the team because he'd missed training. Apparently the new coach, Alan Basham, had said that fitness was going to have to be improved – he'd noticed players 'hiding' during recent games and part of his masterplan was a strict 'No training, no selection' policy. This applied to everyone except Pat Brown, who played for the Post Office on Thursday afternoons, which was considered to be the equivalent of a training session.

Peter always seemed to have connections. If you wanted a ticket, he would somehow get his hands on one. If you needed a lift, he'd arrange it.

I was planning on bringing up the subject of the job in the tea hut. If anyone could help me get it, Peter could.

But just when I was about to ask him, I saw a road sign reading 'Dartford Tunnel 3 miles' and a feeling of total panic welled up inside me.

I always hated going through the Dartford Tunnel. In a school science project, I had learnt about how much water pressure there was on the structure of the tunnel and, ever since, was convinced it would cave in whenever I went through it.

To make matters worse, I could actually see water dripping down the sides of the walls.

Despite it only taking a couple of minutes to get through, I shut my eyes and felt an enormous sense of relief when we came out the other side.

By the time my heart rate had got back to something approaching normal, it started to speed up again as I got my first glimpse of the Aveley floodlights. It was an indication the ground was nearby, and the familiar feeling of excitement had set in.

The coach drove into the official Aveley car park. We got out, paid our shillings at the gate and walked into the ground just as the teams were running out.

We waited for the toss of the coin so that we would know which goal to stand behind and then took up our places behind Tony Wiseman, the Aveley goalkeeper.

We weren't alone there.

If it was a bit odd seeing the home fans join us at the end their team was defending, it was completely bizarre hearing them talk of a possible giant killing. Even I, with my inflated view of the team, had never really seen Bromley as giants. Maybe Aveley were worse than I thought, but I felt strangely proud.

The game kicked off, and the home team, playing in all blue, went straight onto the attack. Alan Soper was soon in action, saving from centre-half Wimpory and the inside-left, Berrecloth, who was causing Les Brockman (deputising for the injured Phil Amato) so much trouble, I actually wished Amato was playing instead.

Inevitably, Aveley took the lead. Berrecloth beat Brockman yet again and crossed for someone to head home. I was sulking too much to care who scored and didn't bother writing it down in my programme.

When Aveley almost doubled their lead a few minutes later, I looked over at coach Alan Basham with a 'Well, I hope you're happy' look, which was intended to convey my displeasure at the dropping of Wawrzewski, a misjudgment that was clearly responsible for the current scoreline. If a football team is losing, fans can usually find an excuse.

But then Bromley settled down and, with one fatal mistake, were back in the match. The fatal mistake was made by the home goalie, Tony Wiseman. He caught an optimistic John Mears lob and then foolishly dropped the ball at the feet of Alan Stonebridge.

1–1.

The relief amongst the Bromley fans was immense. Roy and I shook hands, congratulating each other, as though we were personally responsible for the equaliser. Peter was beaming and even Derek looked cautiously optimistic.

Cup games are even more nerve-wracking than league games because of their sudden death nature. In the league, there's always next week, even if you're 7–0 down. But in the cup, one slip and that can be it for the season.

So even at 1–1 with ten minutes left, I was far from confident. Aveley were playing well and a giant-killing was still a possibility. But just as thoughts were turning to a replay, Roy Pettet over-hit a long ball and it bounced safely into the arms of their goalie, Wiseman. And then, inexplicably bounced out again. Before he had the chance to realise what was happening, the ball was nestled in the back of the net courtesy of the quick-thinking Alan Stonebridge, and Bromley were through. We shook hands with the Aveley fans and made the journey home, happy and relieved.

The draw for the second qualifying round would come out

on Monday and would be in Tuesday's paper. I didn't really care who we got, although another Athenian League team would be good, especially if it was at home.

Last season, the cup run came to an abrupt halt before it had even started when Bromley were drawn away to Hillingdon Borough from the Southern League and lost 7–0.

I was hoping for a kinder draw this year.

# CHAPTER SEVEN

The draw had been made for the second qualifying round of the FA Cup. Hillingdon Borough, away. For the second season running.

What made my heart sink most about this was Jimmy Langley.

He was the Hillingdon player/manager but, a few years ago, he had reached even greater heights. He had been England's left-back and also had a League Cup winner's medal from his time at Fulham.

The previous season, apart from having that big win over Bromley, Hillingdon had missed out on promotion to the Football League by just one place.

If Bromley were going to beat them in a fortnight's time, it would be a true act of giant-killing.

But more immediately concerning was Tuesday's game against Leytonstone. I had pretty much accepted that I would have to miss it due to my newfound exemplary school behaviour, although there was just a tiny part of me that was still hopeful of making the trip to east London.

•••

My superstition seemingly had no bounds. I'd been listening to *Pick of the Pops* on Sunday afternoon before going back to Johnson's and my latest theory was that since the record 'Bad Moon Rising' had just gone to Number One, it was a sign that Bromley's good run would now be over.

It really did feel like a bad moon was on the rise,

especially as it was now 6.15pm on Tuesday evening and I was going to have to do my maths and French homework while Peter, Derek and Roy would be watching Bromley without me. Life had never seemed less fair.

Leytonstone (away) was shaping up as being the game of the season. Both sides were playing really well and only six points separated them.

By 7.30pm, I had lost all interest in my homework. I went to the Common Room and switched on the radio, jumping from station to station in the desperate hope of finding commentary on the game, even though I knew full well I wouldn't succeed. In all the time I'd been supporting Bromley, they had never been on the radio and weren't likely to start now.

By 7.45pm, I couldn't take it any more. And that was when I had a brilliant idea. I would sneak out to the phone box on the village green and phone the Leytonstone ground. They would be able to tell me the score.

I climbed out of the window and ran all the way to the phone box. I rang Directory Enquiries and was given the number. Putting the four pennies in the slot, I dialled the Leytonstone ground and soon heard the ringing tone. I pressed Button B and was through.

'Leytonstone FC,' said a man's voice.

'Hello, can you tell me the score please?' I asked.

'Hang on', he said. 'I'll go and ask someone.'

After a tense wait, I was given the news I had being fearing. Leytonstone were winning 1–0 and it must have been half-time.

I thanked him and ran back to Johnson's, where I climbed back through the window and sat back down to my homework.

But concentration was impossible. I managed to hold out for just over ten minutes before I headed for the window again, climbed through and ran back to the phone box. After waiting for what seemed like an eternity for a young woman to finish her conversation and let me have my turn, I finally stepped into the box, which now smelled of Polo Mints, and urgently dialled the number which I had already memorised.

'Hello, can you give me the score please?', I asked breathlessly as soon as the phone was picked up at the other end.

The man sounded less friendly this time, but said he'd go and find out. When he got back, he told me that it was still 1–0 to Leytonstone.

I tried to get a bit more information, asking how Bromley were playing, if they'd had any good scoring opportunities and who were their best players, but he wasn't being particularly helpful.

'Couldn't tell you, mate. All I know is it's 1–0 Leytonstone.' And with that, he put the phone down.

The next time I rang, at 8.30pm, he sounded a lot less friendly.

'It's 2–0 to Leytonstone' was all he had to say.

I tried ringing again at 9.10pm, which was around fulltime, but nobody picked up.

It was several days before I discovered that 2–0 was the final score. The unbeaten run was at an end. And I hadn't even been there to see it happen.

At least I had Saturday to look forward to and the return fixture with Wycombe Wanderers. We had lost to them heavily in the first game of the season, but this was a different Bromley team.

I was convinced that the loss to Leytonstone was just a blip and in my imagination, it had been two lucky goals that were responsible for Bromley's defeat.

•••

There was a decent-sized crowd for the Wycombe game – for once, the official figure, which would doubtless be 400, would be accurate.

I was at the Supporters' Club hut talking to Roy, who was filling me in on what really happened at Leytonstone. He wasn't able to answer all my questions in as much detail as I would have liked, because he hadn't been able to commit the full 90 minutes to memory, nor had he made any notes in the programme he'd got for me.

But he did tell me what I was hoping to hear – that Bromley deserved to win, the first goal was definitely offside, Stonebridge had been robbed by a biased referee and Bromley's team was missing five first-choice players.

There had also been a moment of huge drama when John Mears had fallen over and apparently broken his arm. He'd been carried off on a stretcher and it was thought he'd be out for at least six weeks.

It turned out that he was only out for about 15 minutes as he returned for the second half, much to the relief of the Bromley faithful.

Roy's expert opinion was that Wycombe Wanderers were about to feel the full fury of the Bromley backlash. And as soon as I saw the determination on the clean-shaven face of Jeff Bridge, I sensed he was right.

Bromley were all business as they went about their warm-up, raining shots in on Alan Soper's goal. But as I surveyed the pitch from my usual position in the stands, I couldn't help but notice that there were two glaring absences.

Pat Brown wasn't there.

And neither was the entire Wycombe team.

As 3 o'clock came and went, I could see the players looking at each other, not quite knowing what to do.

In a moment of excitement, I considered the possibility of

Bromley kicking off without the other team being there. Surely it was their responsibility to get to the ground on time? If that was so, we'd only win 1–0, because after we scored, they wouldn't be able to kick off.

But then I remembered reading about such a scenario in the *Guardian*, my parents' newspaper of choice. It had a weekly feature called *'You are the ref'*, which illustrated various unlikely football scenarios (frequently involving a burst ball) and asked you to decide what action to take. A typical question was 'A striker catches the ball in his turban and runs 20 yards into the net. Do you award a goal?' You decided what action you'd take if you were the referee then turned the page upside down to reveal the answer.

In the case of the missing opposition, the rules clearly stated that the match would be unable to start because a team constituted a minimum of seven players. It would be called off and either played at a later date or the points would be awarded to Bromley.

So the best possible scenario would be for seven Wycombe players to arrive and for the game to take place, allowing Bromley to run up a huge score.

But there was also another scenario to consider. What if the entire Wycombe team turned up but Bromley only had 11 players, including the substitute? Surely they would need someone else. Someone who had their boots and shin pads.

I was ready.

My thoughts were rudely interrupted by Charlie King coughing loudly on the tannoy to get our attention. Was he going to ask if anyone would be able to fill in for Pat Brown? No, he wasn't. He was announcing that Wycombe had been stuck in traffic and had only just arrived. The match would now kick off at 3.10.

Minutes later, I felt a huge sense of disappointment when

I saw Pat Brown, still in his postman's uniform, scurry past the stand and disappear through the tunnel towards the changing rooms. I later learned that he had also been held up in a traffic jam, but had got away with it thanks to the late arrival of our opponents. I wasn't sure I believed his story, though. Every time I'd seen him out and about, he was on his Post Office bike.

When the 12 missing players finally took the field, the match was able to get under way. Having missed the previous game, I was even more excited than usual to see Bromley in action. The training regime that had been established by coach Alan Basham had clearly made a difference to the players' fitness. There seemed to be a lot more running, although much of it appeared to be aimless, as if they were trying to show the coach how fit they were and therefore not risk getting dropped for being unfit.

Wycombe played the game at a more leisurely pace, content to let the ball do the work. The closest they came to scoring in the first half was when Bromley's centre-half Alan Bonney kicked the ball out of Soper's hands into the path of a Wycombe forward, who was so surprised he fluffed his shot.

I would have been really happy with a 0–0 draw. Wycombe were third in the table and had an England amateur player in winger Len Worley, who had been happy to sign my autograph book after the 5-0 defeat on the opening day of the season.

He had been a constant threat that day. But now, he was being so well marked by Les Brockman that he hadn't had a look-in. I felt a surge of pride, thinking of how our reserve left-back had completely defused the threat of an international who was known as 'the Stanley Matthews of amateur football'.

The surge promptly vanished when Worley left Brockman trailing in his wake and coolly slid the ball past Soper from an inch-perfect cross for the winning goal ten minutes from time. It was Bromley's second loss in a row.

As I collected the empty cups and saucers, I glanced up and noticed the moon rising. A few months previously, the moon had symbolised hope and optimism as man took his first steps on it. Now, it had become a harbinger of doom.

•••

Peter and I were having a post-match cup of tea, when he asked me if I still liked to play football. It was the continuation of a conversation we'd started on the coach back from Aveley, when I confided in him how frustrating it was not to find a team to play for, since the school team I had started at Sevenoaks managed to attract just three boys to the first and only practice.

He told me that the Bromley supporters had a team in the Orpington and Bromley District Sunday Football League and their first game of the season was tomorrow. How would I like to play?

This was about as near as I had ever got to true happiness. Although I shrugged and said something like 'Yeah, OK', I felt as though I had won the big £100,000 pools jackpot.

When teams were being picked at primary school, I had always been the last one chosen. Even after the kids with glasses, the asthmatics and the ones even fatter than me. Now, here I was, a first-choice player in a team which was sort of representing Bromley FC.

Our team was called Hayesford Park Reserves. As Peter explained, we weren't actually the reserve team for Hayesford Park, but calling ourselves that had somehow made it easier for him to enter us in the league.

I knew I wouldn't be able to play in goal because Derek

was the established goalie, so I told Peter that my preferred position was centre-forward. That was the most glamorous place to play – centre-forwards were always making headlines and being transferred for huge amounts of money. Allan Clarke had recently gone from Leicester to Leeds for an unbelievable £165,000. Other great centre-forwards included Derek Dougan, Peter Osgood and Alan Stonebridge. These were the born goalscorers and I wanted to be like them. The trouble was that surely everyone would want the number nine shirt. Did I really stand a chance? Especially since I was about as far away from being a born goalscorer as it was possible to be.

The game was against Forresters FC and it would kick off at 10.30am. I decided to go home and get an early night so I would be fresh for my debut.

I was in bed by 8.30pm, happy to sacrifice *Match of the Day* for the greater good of the Hayesford Park Reserves team.

# ISTHMIAN LEAGUE HOW THEY STAND

## 29TH SEPTEMBER 1969

| | P | W | D | L | F | A | Pts |
|---|---|---|---|---|---|---|---|
| Wycombe W . . . . . .13 | 7 | 4 | 2 | 21 | 10 | 18 |
| Clapton . . . . . . .13 | 7 | 4 | 2 | 28 | 22 | 18 |
| Sutton Utd . . . .12 | 7 | 3 | 2 | 27 | 9 | 17 |
| Leytonstone . . . .14 | 7 | 3 | 4 | 26 | 13 | 17 |
| St. Albans City .14 | 8 | 1 | 5 | 20 | 16 | 17 |
| Enfield . . . . . .10 | 6 | 3 | 1 | 14 | 6 | 15 |
| Barking . . . . . .12 | 6 | 3 | 3 | 28 | 14 | 15 |
| Hitchin Town . . .14 | 4 | 6 | 4 | 22 | 19 | 14 |
| Oxford City . . . .13 | 5 | 4 | 4 | 16 | 17 | 14 |
| Tooting and Mit .11 | 5 | 4 | 2 | 23 | 14 | 14 |
| Wealdstone . . . .11 | 5 | 3 | 3 | 22 | 12 | 13 |
| Kingstonian . . . .14 | 4 | 5 | 5 | 17 | 20 | 13 |
| Hendon . . . . . .10 | 4 | 4 | 2 | 23 | 11 | 12 |
| Maidstone Utd . .12 | 4 | 3 | 5 | 18 | 22 | 11 |
| Woking . . . . . .13 | 5 | 0 | 8 | 13 | 19 | 10 |
| Ilford . . . . . .12 | 3 | 4 | 5 | 14 | 21 | 10 |
| Dulwich Hamlet . .15 | 1 | 6 | 8 | 13 | 31 | 8 |
| **BROMLEY** . . . . .13 | **3** | **2** | **8** | **12** | **41** | **8** |
| Walthamstow A . .11 | 2 | 2 | 7 | 14 | 22 | 6 |
| Corinthian Cs . .13 | 0 | 0 | 13 | 7 | 40 | 0 |

# CHAPTER EIGHT

I arrived at Derek's house at 9.30am the next morning, having spent the previous half-hour cleaning my boots, which now smelt heavily of Chelsea Dubbin polish. This seemed to be suspiciously similar to ordinary Dubbin, but since it had been advertised in *Charlie Buchan's Football Monthly*, I assumed it was a superior product.

Derek's kit was neatly packed, in stark contrast to my overstuffed duffel bag. We were playing at Norman Park, which was right behind Bromley's ground and it only took ten minutes to get there on the empty Sunday morning roads.

Peter and Roy were already there, together with four or five scruffy, unshaven characters who I didn't recognise. I later learnt they were all binmen who worked with Roy.

Peter was dressed in a dark-blue tracksuit, the bottoms of which were tucked into yellow football socks. He was wearing football boots and holding a bucket that contained a sponge in one hand and a huge blue laundry bag in the other. He had decided he would be more use as our trainer than as a player.

Once the groundsman had come along and unlocked the changing rooms, Peter opened his bag and removed a pile of slightly worn red football shirts with white cuffs and threw one to each of the players. It was never explained how he had acquired these but I later learned they had once belonged to Hayesford Park, who were, in theory, our first team. I caught mine and looked to see what number I had been given. It was the number nine – Alan Stonebridge's number. Although I was trying to appear calm, I was deeply excited. It meant I would be leading the attack, possibly based on the exaggerated claims made concerning my footballing abilities at the tea-hut the previous day.

I proudly put my shirt on, hoping no-one would notice the fabric stretching uncomfortably over my midriff.

We then set off to put the nets up. I had never played a game with proper nets before, which only led to increase my anxiety and feeling that I didn't really belong there.

During our warm-up, three things were immediately apparent. Derek was, indeed, an outstanding goalie. Roy, however, was a terrible full-back. He wore his glasses and stumbled around the field like a newborn foal, swinging wildly at the ball with his long, skinny legs and usually missing it. The other thing was that I was completely out of my depth. These were grown men I was playing with, who were faster, fitter and, with the exception of Roy, far more skilful.

Peter had decided we would play 4–3–3. I would be upfront alongside Cavan, an Irish dustman, and Raymond Arthur Smart, a plumber, whose middle name and occupation I knew because they were written in large letters on his van, which was parked on the side of the pitch.

No-one had turned up to watch. I had been half-hoping that one or two of the Bromley players would come along to support their supporters, but it seemed they had resisted the temptation.

I touched the ball only a few times in the entire game, usually when we were kicking off after conceding yet another goal. If it wasn't for Derek, we wouldn't have found ourselves only 6–0 down with a couple of minutes left and with the interest having long gone out of the game.

He'd been outstanding, making save after save once the Forresters winger had worked out he had pretty much got a free ride down Roy's side of the field and put over a succession of crosses.

But now it was our turn to mount a rare attack. A Forresters goal kick found me midway between the half-way line and penalty area. I kept taking the ball towards the goal and the defenders kept backing away.

The nearer I got to goal, the more panic I felt. I was desperately trying to find someone to pass to, but they were all being tightly marked. Eventually, as I was only about ten yards from the goal, I decided I might as well have a shot. From that moment on, everything seemed to be happening in slow motion.

I mishit the ball with the inside of my right boot and it spun away from the goalie, who had been wrong-footed. He and I watched in disbelief as it trickled towards the goal line and then kept on going over the line, before nestling in the net. I went berserk, charging around as though I'd got the winning goal in a Wembley cup final.

I replayed the goal in my mind literally hundreds of times in the hours following the game and made sure I'd never forget it by drawing a detailed diagram in my scrapbook as soon as I got home.

I then asked my mum to wash the shirt straight away so I could wear it back to Sevenoaks, under my school shirt. It would be several days before I could be persuaded to remove it.

There was to be a perfect end to my perfect week. When I got the *Bromley Advertiser* the following Saturday, there was a small match report on the inside back page, which Peter had undoubtedly contributed. The final paragraph of three finished with the words 'David Roberts struck a consolation goal for Hayesford Park Reserves just before the final whistle'.

I cut it out and stuck it alongside the diagram in my scrapbook.

●●●

My first proper game of football was followed a day later by my first proper game of rugby.

It was the 4th Form inter-house competition and I was playing for Johnson's against another boarding house, Lambardes. It wasn't really fair as we had several boys who played for the school and we won comfortably.

The highlight for me was scoring a try to go with my goal the previous day. I'd been passed the ball just out from their line. Picking out the smallest boy, I closed my eyes and launched myself at him. His skinny frame was no match for my 12-stone bulk and when I opened my eyes again, I was over the line, touching the ball down.

The first thing I did when I got back to Johnson's was to find a blank page in my autograph book and sign it with a slightly bored flourish. Then underneath, I printed the words:

D.A. ROBERTS. HAYESFORD PARK RESERVES
AND JOHNSON'S RUGBY TEAM.

In the space of a week I had uncovered a previously undetected sporting prowess, scored a goal and a try as well as getting my name in the paper. That was the good news. The bad news was that Bromley had lost two in a row.

I hoped it wasn't about to become three.

Alan Bonney, who had come so close to scoring an own goal on the previous Saturday finally succeeded in a re-arranged fixture at Ilford on the Tuesday. But his contribution was unnecessary. They still would have won without him.

Once again, I was stuck at Johnson's and once again, I had to rely on furtive visits to the phone box. Having sensed some hostility when I'd repeatedly rung Leytonstone the week before, I decided to try and disguise my voice every time I rang the Ilford ground, in case whoever answered got fed up with the same person always ringing and eventually stopped answering.

Firstly, I attempted a sort of Scottish accent, which was based on Dr Cameron, a character from the TV series *Dr Finlay's Casebook*.

'Halloo, I was wonderin' if ye could tell ma the score?' I asked.

'Ilford are 3–0 up,' said a man who sounded quite pleased with the way things were going.

I was shocked. This was not what I was expecting. Conceding three first-half goals was an abysmal start, even by Bromley's recent standards.

'Oh NO,' I said, completely forgetting about the Scottish accent. 'How long have they been playing?'

'About half an hour.'

I thanked him and rang off. By my calculations, Ilford were scoring a goal every ten minutes. If they kept that up, they would end up winning 9–0.

I was immediately plunged into a deep depression. I felt powerless. My team was disintegrating and I couldn't even be there to support them.

I didn't ring again. I didn't even want to know what the final score had been, so I just assumed my calculations were correct and we had lost 9–0 to fourth-from-bottom Ilford. When I later found out that it had only been 3–0, I was irrationally happy.

Bromley were drifting back down the table and now only had Walthamstow Avenue and Corinthian Casuals below them, with Ilford and Woking just above.

I slowly realised that games against these lowly teams had provided all of Bromley's points for the season and that they still had to play most of the good teams.

●●●

It took me several attempts to read the team news for the upcoming FA Cup game against Hillingdon Borough, because there was a huge hole in the sports page of the paper where I had cut out the Hayesford Park Reserves match report, which had been on the other side.

Alan Bonney, who had managed two own-goals in recent matches was thankfully going away on holiday to Greece, but this had come too late to save the great Alan Soper, who had been dropped for the return of Ian McGuire.

Bonney's replacement would be Graham Gaston, who I had given the nickname 'Gasmask' confident that all the Bromley fans would soon be calling him that. It hadn't really caught on, though.

It seemed Gasmask's printing business would be able to spare him, after the special contract that had kept him busy had almost been completed.

There was another signing which had me very excited. Although Bromley were seemingly keeping it low-key, I was sure that the news of Dave Clark joining the club would soon get out. It had been tucked away at the end of a preview of the weekend's game, but I suspected this was deliberate.

The boys I played football with at the park had assured me that it was *the* Dave Clark, drummer and leader of the Dave Clark Five, who had been on *Top of The Pops* a few months ago with a rock'n'roll medley, which I didn't like as much as their earlier stuff.

The best thing about him playing for us was that the Crystal Palace fans would be really annoyed – their theme tune was 'Glad all Over' by the Dave Clark Five and it was played before every home game.

Anyway, Clark wasn't in the team to play at Hillingdon, but I couldn't wait for him to make his debut. Maybe it was just as well he wouldn't be playing on Saturday. It was going to be our toughest test so far this season and the local press were already conceding defeat.

I wasn't, though. In fact, I was encouraged that Tooting and Mitcham, a middle-of-the-table Isthmian League team, had held Hillingdon to a draw in the previous round before losing the replay. But every time I started thinking that we might have a chance, my mind went back to last season's debacle.

The truth was, we had been lucky to escape with a 7–0 defeat.

# ISTHMIAN LEAGUE HOW THEY STAND

## 8TH OCTOBER 1969

|                    | P   | W | D | L  | F  | A  | Pts |
|--------------------|-----|---|---|----|----|----|-----|
| Wycombe W  . . . . | 14  | 8 | 4 | 2  | 22 | 10 | 20  |
| Sutton Utd . . . . | 13  | 8 | 3 | 2  | 31 | 12 | 19  |
| Leytonstone  . . . | 15  | 7 | 4 | 4  | 27 | 13 | 18  |
| Clapton  . . . . . | 13  | 7 | 4 | 2  | 28 | 22 | 18  |
| St Albans City . . | 15  | 8 | 2 | 5  | 21 | 17 | 18  |
| Enfield  . . . . . | 11  | 6 | 4 | 1  | 15 | 7  | 16  |
| Barking  . . . . . | 13  | 6 | 4 | 3  | 29 | 15 | 16  |
| Hitchin Town . . . | 15  | 5 | 6 | 4  | 24 | 19 | 16  |
| Oxford City  . . . | 15  | 6 | 4 | 5  | 22 | 21 | 16  |
| Wealdstone . . . . | 13  | 6 | 3 | 4  | 24 | 15 | 15  |
| Kingstonian  . . . | 15  | 5 | 5 | 5  | 21 | 20 | 15  |
| Tooting and Mit  . | 11  | 5 | 4 | 2  | 23 | 14 | 14  |
| Hendon . . . . . . | 10  | 4 | 4 | 2  | 23 | 11 | 12  |
| Maidstone Utd  . . | 12  | 4 | 3 | 5  | 18 | 22 | 11  |
| Woking . . . . . . | 13  | 5 | 0 | 8  | 13 | 19 | 10  |
| Ilford . . . . . . | 13  | 3 | 4 | 6  | 14 | 24 | 10  |
| Dulwich Hamlet . . | 16  | 1 | 7 | 8  | 13 | 31 | 9   |
| **BROMLEY** . . . . | **14** | **3** | **2** | **9** | **12** | **42** | **8** |
| Walthamstow A  . . | 13  | 2 | 3 | 8  | 15 | 24 | 7   |
| Corinthian Cs  . . | 14  | 0 | 0 | 14 | 7  | 44 | 0   |

# CHAPTER NINE

The confidence that had been so apparent on the journey to our first qualifying round match was more subdued on the journey to our second qualifying round match.

Hillingdon were in a different league.

Literally.

They were in the Southern League that was just one step away from the Football League. They were professional footballers. They had a former England full-back.

They also hadn't lost at home for 18 months and 40-odd matches, while Bromley's away form had been artificially boosted by a win against Corinthian Casuals, which didn't really count. There was also the small matter of losing the last three games in a row.

So why was I so confident about an upset? Because the Bromley team was now at full strength. I felt the return of Gasmask (I was determined to persevere with the nickname) was crucial. He was freakishly tall and was virtually unbeatable in the air. Since most non-league attacks were built around long balls into the area, a big centre-half was vital. Preferably one who didn't have a habit of scoring own-goals, like the man Gasmask was replacing, Alan Bonney.

The first thing we noticed when we got to the ground was the size of the crowd. It was huge. There must have been at least a couple of thousand spectators and the noise was noticeably louder than we were used to. It was like being at a proper big game and not a Bromley one.

The programme provided some amusement to break the tension. The Bromley team had presumably been dictated over the phone to a hard-of-hearing person who was putting the programme together – thus our goalie had become 'A. Foper' instead of Soper and our left-back was now known as 'L. Brahnan' instead of Brockman.

Hillingdon took the field to applause that was so loud and enthusiastic, we were momentarily confused and looked around to see what had caused the excitement. The home team's support put our efforts to shame. We realised that that moment that we needed to do more than just watch our team – we needed to support them.

It felt good to really get behind the players, shouting encouragement and cheering when they did something good.

'Tackle him, Brahnan' I shouted as the Hillingdon winger bore down on Les Brockman and was delighted when one or two of the travelling supporters actually laughed at my witticism.

It inspired me to try another one later, loudly praising Foper after a great save, but this didn't get the same reaction – probably because I'd forgotten that Soper wasn't playing and McGuire had been recalled in his place.

We were never going to beat them, of course. But there was a moment at the start of the second half, when Alan Stonebridge scored a great goal (it wasn't just me who thought so – everyone did) and brought it back to 2–1, that a replay was an outside chance. But Hillingdon scored again and then added a last-minute goal to give them a slightly flattering 4–1 win.

I don't think I had ever felt so proud over a losing per-formance. McGuire had been magnificent and I had to grudgingly concede that Soper couldn't have done any better. Stonebridge and Pettet were brilliant.

Yes, I was disappointed to go out of the cup – but I was also proud that Bromley had come so close to causing a huge upset and, more importantly, played so well. It had been 3–1 going into the last minute, which was highly respectable. If Gasmask hadn't gone off injured after half an hour, it might have been even closer.

We might have been out of the FA Cup and the league was only a distant possibility. But there were plenty of other trophies we had a chance of winning.

Plus, I'd have another chance of some football glory the next morning at 10.30am.

●●●

There comes a time in just about every boy's life when he realises he's simply not going to be good enough to play football professionally.

In my case, the time was around 12.15 the next afternoon, following the match-up between Hayesford Park Reserves and Chelsfield.

I went into the game on a high, believing it would be simple to repeat last week's scoring, conveniently forgetting it had been a total fluke. I couldn't do anything right – my passes were over-hit, I ended up losing the ball every time I tried to dribble and my one attempt at goal went way over the bar. After the referee mercifully blew his whistle for full-time, I trudged off a dejected figure. I had contributed nothing. Once again, Derek had kept us in the game and we had got our first point with a 2–2 draw.

As football was my whole life, I found the double disappointment of Bromley's FA Cup exit and my abysmal display for Hayesford Park Reserves ruined what was left of the weekend.

Before going back to Johnson's, I tried watching the first episode of a new programme called *Monty Python's Flying Circus*, but it was stupid so I did some homework instead.

At school the next day though, boys were talking about nothing else. *Monty Python's Flying Circus* had been a huge hit.

People were quoting the 'Genghis Khan' sketch, reciting the German joke and telling anyone who would listen that their name was Arthur 'Two Sheds' Jackson. I was horrified. How had I managed to miss out on this? I was pretty sure it had been a load of rubbish, but maybe I was wrong.

I wasn't going to be accepted by my classmates if I didn't join in. So I started asking people if they'd seen it and wrote 'I love Monty Python' and 'I am Arthur "Two Sheds" Jackson' on one of my exercise books. I soon picked up a few of the catchphrases and repeated them, despite never having seen them performed on TV.

This was exactly the kind of thing that can lead to acceptance at school. And since no-one else liked football, it was my best chance.

•••

One of the very worst aspects of going to public school was cross-country racing. But it was unavoidable. Once a year, the whole school had to take part.

The last time I had been to Knole Park, which was right next to the school and where the course was, it had been to see the Beatles. They were making a film to go with their single 'Strawberry Fields Forever' and word spread around the school like german measles.

The bell for lunch had signalled a mass exodus to the park and soon the Beatles had been joined by hundreds of boys in straw hats. Ringo and John in particular were quite friendly, coming over and chatting with us between takes.

When asked to sing something, John burst into 'Hey, hey, we're the Monkees'. It was one of my best times at Sevenoaks.

Taking part in the cross-country race was one of my worst.

I started out fast and went into the uphill part of the course in about 40th place. At that point, I remember thinking that it was much easier than I'd thought and that a top 30 place was within my reach. I had begun to see myself as someone who was good at sport, following a couple of minor recent successes.

Buoyed by this, I increased the pace, with thoughts turning to a top 20 place. I was sprinting flat out. But it was a pace I could never keep up and it wasn't long before I realised I was going slower and slower, falling further and further down the field.

Boys I'd passed with ease not so long ago were now overtaking me just as effortlessly. I was moving further towards the back. My breathing had suddenly become incredibly hard and my legs were barely strong enough to stand on.

I walked the last mile and a half, finishing in the last group and hating my body for not being more sporty and hating Sevenoaks even more than I had ever hated it.

•••

Despite Bromley's poor recent cup record (the previous season they had lost 0–9 and 0–7 in the two major trophies), the team would be taking part in a total of six different cup competitions during the season.

Most of these were variations on a theme. There was the Kent Senior Cup, the Kent Floodlit Cup, the London Senior Cup, the South Thames Cup, the FA Amateur Cup and the FA Cup.

This list was well down on recent years, when Bromley had also fought unsuccessfully for the Kent Amateur Cup, Bromley Hospital Cup, London Charity Cup, Hastings Charity Cup, Flushing Cup or London Challenge Cup.

Despite these countless opportunities to add to the trophy

cabinet, Bromley hadn't won anything since 1964 when four goals from Postman Pat Brown helped them beat Cray Wanderers in the Bromley Hospital Cup, a competition which seemed to exist purely so Bromley could play a random weaker team – sometimes Cray, sometimes, Beckenham Town – at home.

Embarrassingly, the weaker teams frequently won, despite the odds being heavily stacked in the hosts' favour. Perhaps this was why the Bromley Hospital Cup had vanished from the fixture list.

The philosophy seemed to be that the more cups you enter, the better your chances of actually winning something.

And now that the FA Cup was out of the way, Bromley were free to concentrate on the Kent Floodlit Cup.

The Kent Floodlit Cup – a Cup that appeared to have been invented by a mad professor. To start with, it seemed a dubious honour to want to win – being the best amateur team in Kent at playing football under floodlights.

But what really got fans of all teams scratching their heads was the experimental nature of the point-scoring system. Ten points were awarded for a win and five for a draw. Each goal was worth an additional point, the flawed theory being that it would encourage high scoring – despite it being obvious to most that it would have the opposite effect, since a 0–0 draw was worth more than a 5-4 defeat.

Bromley were in a group with Gravesend and Northfleet, Bexley United, Erith and Belvedere, Dartford and, bizarrely, Grays Athletic.

Grays' presence in the competition made no sense, since they were in Essex and therefore nowhere near Kent. They couldn't have been there to make up the numbers, since our group had one more team in it than the other three groups. Still, they did fit the other essential criteria of playing football and having floodlights.

But the trip to Essex was still several weeks away.

First up for Bromley was an away fixture against the hopelessly out-of-form Gravesend and Northfleet. The exciting thing about this was the name of their ground, which was surely a sign.

It was called Stonebridge Road.

•••

There can be no more depressing place to be than Gravesend and Northfleet's ground on a cold, wet and dark Wednesday night in October, soaked to the skin by the relentless rain, watching the team you love being torn apart by a much better side and knowing that you've got into so much trouble at school that your whole life was about to change completely.

This is how I came to be there . . .

I was queuing for lunch in the canteen the day before, when I was tapped on the shoulder and heard a sneering voice behind me say 'Are you a homo?'

I looked round. It was a boy known as 'Four eyes'. He wore glasses and all boys who wore glasses were known as 'Four eyes'. He was the boy who had collided with me after Latin class on that Saturday morning.

I was aware that other conversations had stopped and silence had fallen over the canteen.

'Say that again and I'll beat you up,' I said, desperately hoping he wasn't going to say it again. I had never had a fight in my life and didn't really want my first one to be in front of dozens of boys against someone who was bigger than me.

'Are you a homo?' he repeated, this time a little louder.

'No,' I said, hoping that would be the end of the matter.

'Yes, you are. You're a homo!'

Although I wasn't certain, I didn't think I was a homo. I

was also fairly sure I was being insulted. I had to do something.

I didn't want to hit him in case he hit me back.

So I put him in a 'Judo' Al Hayes-style headlock.

He struggled to get out and failed. But he did somehow manage to get me in a headlock at the same time.

We were standing there, in the lunch queue, arms around each other's necks, bent forward and grunting with effort like a couple of Olympic weightlifters. We were temple to temple and I could feel his greasy hair against my face.

Eventually, momentum forced us to leave the queue and stagger around the room, joined together and bumping into tables like a drunken two-headed hunchback.

After about ten minutes of this and with the other boys bored of chanting 'fight, fight, fight', we manoeuvred our way to a bench on the side of the cafeteria and sat down together, headlocks still applied, as if by an unspoken agreement. We were both getting exhausted, taking it in turns to say:

'Do you submit?'

'No, do *you* submit?'

I was determined not to give in and so was Four Eyes. The minutes ticked by, with neither of us willing to concede. The bell went for the end of lunch break, but we didn't move – although there was a touch more desperation in the 'Do you submits?'

I then became slowly aware of a silence.

The encouraging shouts had gone. Something had changed.

A cough made me look up. The cougher was our Form Master and the look on his face indicated that I was in really, really big trouble.

Even then, I didn't release my grip on Four Eyes' neck. And neither did he let me go.

We had to be physically separated and were then told to wait outside the Form Master's office.

# CHAPTER TEN

When I was called in to the Form Master's office, I had a pretty good idea what was in store for me. He had a large cane and, with a grim expression, told me to hold my hand out.

I did.

'You have to be punished for fighting,' he informed me.

'I do?'

He then said that I would receive six strokes of the cane. I held my hand out and watched the cane move towards it in a downward arc.

The pain was intense. A lingering, stinging agony made even worse by repetition.

I bit my lower lip, determined not to cry. I was shaking with fear, but still the punishment continued. It was far, far worse than I ever imagined. At least he didn't say that it was hurting him a lot more than it was hurting me.

It was my first-ever experience of deliberately inflicted violence. And it wouldn't be my last for the year either.

From then on, things for me seemed to move quickly. My parents were summoned to the school and in a behind-closed-doors meeting, it was agreed that I would be leaving Sevenoaks. As half-term was about to start, now would be the perfect time for the school and I to part company. Collecting my clothes and belongings from Johnson's was the last act of my Sevenoaks era. I didn't have many goodbyes to say and there was no-one I would miss.

I was told I'd be going to a Langley Park Grammar School, news that was music to my ears. It was the school most of my primary-school friends had gone to and they were all football-mad, even though rugby was mostly played there.

I couldn't wait to start. It would be a new beginning, a fresh start. It was a shame Bromley FC couldn't have had the same sort of opportunity.

●●●

The day I left Sevenoaks was the day John Mears left Bromley. This was a massive shock. There had been a steady stream of dissatisfied players leaving, but none had been regular first teamers. Some, I'd never even heard of. But Mears was different. He had been one of the best all season and was being replaced in the team by Doug Head, who was being rushed into the starting line-up for a game I was expecting to miss, but would now be attending.

The final piece of good luck came when Derek said that there was room in his car. In fact, there was plenty of room – no-one else had fancied the trip. Not even Roy.

The Gravesend game had ended in a 5-1 defeat but at least I'd been able to go to a game I had been resigned to missing.

Doug Head, who had the unenviable task of following in the footsteps of John Mears, had put Bromley into the lead and if the game had stopped there, I would have gone home happy. But it didn't. Gravesend, helped by a couple of penalties and countless chances could still only manage five goals, when they really should have had at least ten.

Chairman Charlie King was showing the first signs of strain at Bromley's ineptitude. In his programme notes for a later game, he sounded off about the loss at Gravesend, blaming, in no particular order:

- Bobby Lennox's flu
- A whistle-happy referee

- Gasmask's problems with double vision
- Eric Nottage's knee
- Alan Bonney's Greek trip
- Eddie Green's wrist
- A bone-hard pitch
- Inferior floodlighting
- Two penalties, one extremely harsh

All things considered, maybe 5-1 wasn't such a bad result.

Derek and I talked a lot on the way back. I told him about my recent school troubles and hinted that they might have been to blame for my poor Hayesford Park Reserves performances of late. We were doing even worse than Bromley. They had managed a couple of wins, at least.

Talking to Derek definitely helped. He felt that the new school would be perfect – he hadn't gone there himself, but had friends who'd really liked it. For once, I was looking forward to half-term being over.

I spent the next day revisiting my old haunts. I walked to the park, noticing that, for once, 'Judo' Al Hayes wasn't cleaning his car. But the soapy water on the gravel surrounding the Jag suggested that he'd done it fairly recently.

I went to the shop behind the park and got a Mr Kipling blackberry and apple pie, a Cornish pasty, a bottle of lemonade and a copy of the *Bromley and Kentish Times*, then sat down to watch my friends kick a ball around in the park and read the latest football news.

The main story stopped me in my tracks. One of my past favourites, Johnny Warman, was returning to Bromley after a short spell with an obscure Athenian League second division side.

Despite being one of the most outstanding players of

recent years he did not look remotely like a footballer. No taller than 5'3", he had thinning red hair and, apart from when he was on the pitch, was never seen without a roll-up cigarette between his nicotine-stained fingers. His age seemed to be a closely guarded secret, although he was probably somewhere between his early thirties and forty. His build could only be described as scrawny with a podgy belly.

He was the type of winger that had gone out of favour with the England manager, Alf Ramsey. He liked to go on mazy jinking dribbles, much like Jimmy Johnstone of Celtic and Scotland, before delivering wonderful crosses for the likes of Eric Nottage to coolly slot home. These runs often ended with him leaning on his haunches having a coughing fit.

The only flaw in his game was a petulant streak that led to frequent disciplinary problems. It was a given that in every ten matches he played, he'd be booked a couple of times and sent off once.

He would then serve his suspension (usually a fortnight or so), return to the team and the cycle would start all over again.

My nickname for him was Ginger. This was also everyone else's nickname for him including, I imagined, his famous brother Phil. Phil Warman played for Charlton Athletic and still lived in the same house as Ginger. I know this because I looked them up in the telephone directory.

Like Pat Brown, Ginger was a postman, but I think he worked in a different district. He played for his Post Office team, which meant he was exempt from training.

Was it a coincidence that two of our best players were both postmen? Yes, I think it probably was. Although if all the current problems were being put down to lack of fitness, I thought that having a job which entailed lots of walking had to help.

By the time I'd digested all the Bromley news, as well as

my pie and pasty, I was ready to play football.

I decided to play on the right wing and pretend to be Bromley's new signing.

●●●

Just about the first thing the real Ginger Warman did on his return was to score a magnificent goal against high-flying Hitchin to level the score at 1–1.

The game, like the previous home fixture in the Isthmian League, had started late because the visitors hadn't got to the ground on time. Hitchin's excuse was that they were held up by the fog and consequently kick-off was moved to 3.20pm.

At 3.55pm, Hitchin took the lead when Phil Amato wandered upfield, forgetting his marking duties and a man called Giggle headed home.

Half an hour later, Ginger Warman was on the spot to tap the rebound from a stunning Stonebridge shot, which had hit the post, into the empty net. Unfortunately, he took a wild swing and missed the ball completely. But as the defenders were still wondering how he'd managed to not score, Ginger recovered his composure and slammed it home at the second attempt.

And 1–1 was how it looked like finishing until a couple of late, late goals gave Hitchin a flattering 3–1 win and condemned the late-fading Bromley team to extra training and me to another night of misery.

The improved fitness promised by Alan Basham hadn't yet materialised.

●●●

The first day at my new school was much like my last day at my last school, in that I loved every minute.

Everything about Langley Park was better. The buildings were much more modern, as though they actually belonged in the 20th century. The boys seemed far more normal to me. Some, I recognised from primary school.

And there was no Latin. Just French, which was taught in the language laboratory – a place that utilised headphones and tape recorders. It sounded incredibly exciting.

I was also thrilled by the tuck shop, which sold all my favourite sweets and crisps, including Acid Drop Spangles, which had a kind of tangy bitter-lemon favour and hadn't been available anywhere in Sevenoaks.

The boys were much friendlier here, with several saying hello and one or two even asking me about my previous school.

There was a group of four or five skinheads who didn't look so welcoming. They were hanging around in a corner of the playground and all wore Arsenal scarves around their wrists. A couple of them were huge, like full-grown men. Other boys were keeping their distance.

It was difficult to look intimidating while wearing a maroon blazer, but they managed it effortlessly. I noticed them talking to a boy I'd known since I was five. His name was Morrie and I immediately realised he could be my ticket into the hardest clique in the entire school.

He'd already said hello to me when we first saw each other and seemed quite friendly. I remembered a few photos I'd taken when we were at primary school, when Morrie was much fatter. In the pictures, he was lifting up his shirt to reveal a large belly. His hair had been a basic short back and sides, nothing like the severe crop he now sported.

I thought that if I showed these pictures to his skinhead friends, they'd immediately accept me. What I failed to take into account with this plan was what Morrie's reaction might be.

Energised by my idea, I picked one of the many kick-abouts happening in the playground and asked if I could join in. They not only let me, but also said I could play in goal. Fitting in seemed far easier than I had ever imagined.

I even passed The Grubby, who was in the year above me, on my way to the canteen for lunch. He was the only other person I'd seen who wore the black, white and gold Bromley enamel badge in the lapel of his maroon blazer.

Our eyes met and we solemnly nodded at each other.

●●●

I'd been looking forward to the Kent Floodlit Cup fixture at home to Bexley with a feeling of excited anticipation that was way out of proportion to the actual event.

I carefully packed my autograph book, even though both teams had signed it the previous season.

But one man was playing tonight who didn't play in that fixture. And now I was determined to land the prized signature of the Bexley United substitute.

It was Dave Clark, formerly of Bromley.

I arrived at the Hayes Lane ground early and looked around, to see if I could see the other four of the Dave Clark Five, but soon realised I didn't know what they looked like.

For once, I had more interest in watching the opposing team run out than Bromley.

I didn't have to wait long.

The visitors ran out purposefully but were wearing tracksuit tops, preventing me from identifying the player with the number 12 on his back.

From a distance, none of them looked like the Dave Clark Five front man. I didn't know for certain that I had been the victim of a cruel practical joke until after the coin toss, when the players stripped down to their red shirts and one of them trotted off to the bench.

It was definitely not the same Dave Clark.

Making the best of a bad job, I tapped him on the shoulder and asked him for his autograph anyway. He was happy to sign.

It hadn't been the first time I'd been fooled into thinking a footballer and pop star with the same name were the same person. I'd long been convinced that Neil Young of Manchester City was also Neil Young of Crosby, Stills, Nash and Young. It wasn't until I saw a photo of the footballing Neil Young in *Shoot!* magazine that I realised his hair was considerably shorter than the singing Neil Young and that he was a different person altogether.

It explained certain inconsistencies – how a Canadian hippie came to be playing for the FA Cup holders for instance – and I felt embarrassed for ever thinking they were one and the same.

# ISTHMIAN LEAGUE HOW THEY STAND

## 17TH OCTOBER 1969

|               | P   | W  | D | L  | F  | A  | Pts |
|---------------|-----|----|---|----|----|----|-----|
| Wycombe W . . . .| 16 | 10 | 4 | 2  | 28 | 10 | 24  |
| St. Albans City | 18 | 9  | 4 | 5  | 28 | 21 | 22  |
| Sutton Utd . . . | 14 | 9  | 3 | 2  | 33 | 12 | 21  |
| Enfield . . . . | 13 | 8  | 4 | 1  | 22 | 8  | 20  |
| Leytonstone . . | 17 | 8  | 4 | 5  | 30 | 14 | 20  |
| Wealdstone . . . | 15 | 8  | 3 | 4  | 29 | 16 | 19  |
| Hitchin Town . . | 17 | 6  | 6 | 5  | 28 | 22 | 18  |
| Clapton . . . . | 15 | 7  | 4 | 4  | 31 | 28 | 18  |
| Kingstonian . . | 17 | 6  | 5 | 6  | 25 | 24 | 17  |
| Oxford City . . | 17 | 6  | 5 | 6  | 24 | 27 | 17  |
| Barking . . . . | 14 | 6  | 4 | 4  | 29 | 17 | 16  |
| Tooting and Mit | 13 | 6  | 4 | 3  | 26 | 18 | 16  |
| Hendon . . . . . | 12 | 5  | 5 | 2  | 26 | 13 | 15  |
| Ilford . . . . . | 16 | 4  | 5 | 7  | 18 | 30 | 13  |
| Maidstone Utd . | 13 | 4  | 3 | 6  | 19 | 24 | 11  |
| Woking . . . . . | 14 | 5  | 1 | 8  | 15 | 24 | 11  |
| Dulwich Hamlet . | 17 | 1  | 7 | 9  | 13 | 34 | 9   |
| **BROMLEY . . . .** | **15** | **3** | **2** | **10** | **13** | **45** | **8** |
| Walthamstow . . | 14 | 2  | 3 | 9  | 15 | 27 | 7   |
| Corinthian Cs . | 15 | 0  | 0 | 15 | 7  | 47 | 0   |

# CHAPTER ELEVEN

I'd decided to watch Bromley matches from a different position, beginning with tonight's game. To start with, I was fed up with loud marching music and the sound of Charlie King at full volume. The other thing was superstition. I'd sat in the same place during Bromley's recent decline and wondered if a change might benefit the team as well as myself.

I saw The Grubby sitting alone behind the goal Bromley would be attacking. As always, he had a couple of cups of steaming hot tea on the bench beside him and an Embassy cigarette between his lips.

I decided to join him.

The whole move was carried out without words. I got myself a cup of tea and wandered over to the bench where he sat. I then indicated the place next to him with a nod of my head and he nodded slightly, his unspoken way of saying that he had no objection to me sitting there. I sat down and we both gazed out into the night, waiting for an end to the torture our team had been putting us through.

The committee had sprung a couple of surprises. Gasmask Gaston was making one of his rare excursions outside his printing business and Postman Pat Brown had been pushed up front to play alongside Alan Stonebridge.

It didn't seem to make much difference. Bexley, despite being bottom of the Southern League, were much the better side and took an early lead, which resulted in The Grubby angrily throwing his almost-finished cigarette to the concrete floor and grinding it violently with his heel.

'Rubbish,' he growled.

I nodded in agreement.

When Bromley got an unexpected equaliser 15 minutes later The Grubby's face burst into a broad smile. He got to his feet and, with his arms raised above his head and cigarette hanging from his mouth, applauded the goal scorer, Bobby Lennox. He turned to me and said 'Beautiful'.

My new friend's mood had visibly lifted.

It didn't last long, of course. Bexley scored again and held on until the end, despite a great late effort from Ginger Warman. There was also a brief cameo from the other Dave Clark, which demonstrated why he had made the starting line-up of neither team that season.

As the players walked off, I turned to The Grubby and saw him hunched despondently over his empty cup of tea, taking the final drag of the eighth cigarette he'd smoked since I'd been sitting next to him.

He looked the way I felt. He was clearly experiencing the same pain that I was. I turned to him, shook my head and said 'Rubbish'. He shook his head too, looking downcast and got to his feet.

We then wandered off in different directions, lost in our thoughts.

●●●

The next day at school I was determined to discuss the match with him. I found him sitting on his own in the canteen and sat down with him. The shocking thing was how talkative he was. It seemed that he got so involved in football, so focused on the game, that he was unable to communicate and watch at the same time.

I understood this. It was exactly how I felt. But away from Hayes Lane, he was a different person. We found plenty of common ground. We were both goalkeepers, both liked music and both drank a lot of tea.

Our favourite player was the only area we differed. Mine was Alan Stonebridge, of course. His was Johnny Warman – a man who, like The Grubby himself, was ginger-haired with a fragile temperament.

The Grubby had just turned 16 and didn't seem to fit in at school. When everyone else had a number one, two or three crop, he wore his hair parted in the middle and halfway down his back. He complemented this with an unfashionable moustache, which I suspected had been started around the same time as Jeff Bridge's. The full-back had shaved his off when Bromley's unbeaten run had come to an end; The Grubby's remained.

He was different in other ways, too. While others walked around with Trojan or Motown records tucked ostentatiously under their arms, The Grubby carried a copy of *Those Who Are About To Die Salute You* by Colosseum, an awful jazz-rock LP, which he played me many times over the next few years. However many times I heard it though, it always sounded as bad as it had the first time.

His passion, apart from Bromley FC, was drumming. But not in the Dave Clark sense. That was 'too commercial'. He idolised Colosseum's drummer, Jon Hiseman, and was in a local band called Monolith, who sounded identical to Colosseum.

They were not hugely successful, which delighted him as any form of success would have been seen as selling out.

The Grubby also seemed uninterested in the academic side of school, which was its main purpose. I gathered that his parents had bribed him to stay at school and so he turned up every day and went through the motions. I was shocked to learn that he had eight 'O' levels. But the more I found out about him, the less surprising it was to know he was a Bromley supporter. He didn't seem to fit in.

I was beginning to see a theme emerging. The big clubs like Arsenal attracted the masses, those with normal social skills who had no problem being accepted by society at large. People at ease in large groups.

The small amateur clubs like Bromley were for the rest of us. The Grubby, I learnt, was absolutely fanatical about Bromley. But while he would never miss a home game, he resolutely refused to travel to away games for reasons that never became clear.

•••

There were mixed omens for the Oxford City away game and I wasn't sure which one was the more meaningful.

It was definitely our unlucky ground. In the last nine seasons, Bromley had lost all nine games at the White House Ground, scoring just seven goals and conceding a miserable 38.

On the other hand, the referee was Mr KA Duff of West Moseley, our lucky ref, who had been in charge when we held Enfield to a draw earlier in the season.

I decided to go with the talismanic Mr Duff and looked forward to an exciting, close game, despite it being the longest coach trip of the season.

My confidence was tested by Peter's news of today's absences from the Bromley line-up. Gasmask couldn't make it for reasons that weren't clear but probably had something to do with printing. Roy Pettet, Colin Owen, Bill Hennessey, Eric Nottage and Phil Amato had all visited hospital for various reasons during the week and were likely to miss the trip to Oxford. Eddie Green was still injured and Alan Bonney was still on holiday. Pat Brown was working, although I wasn't sure I believed it since there was no post on a Saturday afternoon. Maybe he was just fed up with losing.

As I had only discovered a week or so ago, Dave Clark had mysteriously left for Bexley without playing a game. If you also included the recently departed John Mears, that there was an entire team of Bromley players who wouldn't be playing for Bromley today.

I suddenly wondered if the presence of Mr KA Duff could really make up for the much-weakened team Bromley would be forced to put out.

My worries were well founded. In the next hour and a half, everything that could go wrong did go wrong. Mr KA Duff's habit of giving dubious penalties continued – except this time it was Bromley on the receiving end. Twice. And twice Oxford scored from the spot. He then booked Doug Head in an act of gross injustice.

Oxford scored five more goals through a variety of means, ranging from a lob that was completely misjudged by Ian McGuire to a gift-goal donated by Chris Sellens, our latest centre-half who was a former England youth international.

The final score was Oxford City 7 Bromley 0.

I later heard that Bromley chairman/ground announcer/ programme seller Charlie King was apoplectic with rage at the result. He conceded that the long coach journey from Bromley had given the Oxford team an advantage, but was deeply unhappy about the lack of effort from the players. At first, I laughed, thinking that these were desperate excuses from an old fogey.

Then I realised that I agreed with him. The team really didn't appear to have been trying and that was wrong. Myself and a coach-load of supporters had made a six-hour round journey to support them and they had simply gone through the motions.

At least I had learnt that an unlucky ground easily outweighed a lucky referee.

By kind permission of Oxford Mail and Times

OXFORD CITY
FOOTBALL CLUB
WHITE HOUSE
GROUND

**OXFORD CITY**
*versus*
**BROMLEY**

N? 85

Sat., 18th Oct., 1969
Kick-off 3.0 p.m.

ISTHMIAN LEAGUE    Official Programme    Price 6d.

By now I was starting to sense that this was a bit more than an unlucky run where results were going against us.

Games were taking on a predictable pattern. The Grubby and I would sit with perhaps a dozen other spectators behind the goal at the Norman Park end of the ground.

We would go through anguish as the team continued to plumb new depths. One game blended into another. The opposition was different but the result was always the same. Another defeat.

The contest was generally over by the half-hour mark. Tonight's Kent Floodlit Cup game against Grays was the perfect example. Grays, who were third from bottom of the Athenian League, were completely dominating their supposedly more illustrious opponents.

Within 30 minutes, they were 3–0 up and that was the way it stayed.

None of the Bromley players seemed to be making any effort. They just looked relieved to get through 90 minutes.

The sense of feeling let down, that had started at the Oxford game, was now growing. It was Bromley's ninth successive defeat and my programme notes consisted of just one sentence:

9. P. Brown 8.30 PM consolation goal

The next game for Bromley was another one that hadn't attracted enough interest for the Supporters' Club to run a coach.

It was easy to see why. Sutton were league leaders and were also in the middle of a brilliant FA Cup run. Bromley were second from bottom and had already been knocked out of the FA Cup.

The odds were stacked against Bromley.

Despite this, Derek, Roy and I were in high spirits as we made the short journey from Derek's maisonette to Sutton's ground in Gander Green Lane. We all believed an upset was possible. When top teams played bottom teams, the scores were often closer than people thought they'd be. The top teams relaxed a bit too much and the bottom team lifted their game.

And that's what looked like happening in this match, until

something happened that typified Bromley's tendency to be architects of their own misfortune.

The seeds for the inevitable defeat had been planted the week before, when the Isthmian League had voted to introduce Bromley's suggested rule change, with immediate effect.

This meant that substitutes could now be used for any reason, instead of just for injuries – a rule that had been used in the Football League since the 1967/1968 season and had inexplicably taken two years to drift down to the lower leagues.

It made me feel good that my team had been responsible for such a radical piece of legislation. It had all come about because of the incompetence of previous manager Dave Ellis, who hadn't been aware of the existing 'injuries only' law and had substituted Graham Farmer for tactical reasons in the opening game of the season at Wycombe. The club received a formal warning and this prompted them to lobby for change.

The first team to take advantage of the new law was Sutton United in tonight's game at their Gander Green Lane ground, my third-favourite ground to visit after Walthamstow Avenue and Clapton.

They were a goal down to Bromley well into the second half, after Ginger Warman had put us ahead with a glorious effort just before half-time and a real shock result was on the cards.

Or at least it was until Sutton brought on their history-making substitute, Ken Grose, to replace former Bromley forward Ray Hutchings, who was having a nightmare against his old club.

There was an air of inevitability amongst the more seasoned Bromley supporters about what was about to happen next.

Grose scored a quickfire hat-trick and Sutton ran out easy

3–1 winners. If only Bromley hadn't proposed the rule change, they probably would have won.

Charlie King was surely close to breaking point. He'd seen his team lose because of inferior floodlighting, incompetent refereeing, bumpy pitches and now through a rule change that he himself had forced through.

The stress must have been enormous.

And it was.

Charlie King announced that he would be taking a two and a half month cruise around the world, starting in early January.

His trip would take in South Africa, Australia and America and he would be returning in time for the final six games of the season – but, and this was probably a good thing for his health – he would miss at least ten games.

Several lower-profile committee members would share his workload.

According to Peter, Mr King would be receiving telegrams with the results and goal scorers while he was away.

I wished someone had done that for me when I was at Sevenoaks. It would have saved me a small fortune in phone calls.

•••

The crisis at Hayes Lane was building.

Apart from the massive amount of injuries, players were regularly walking out, sometimes without bothering to notify anyone.

At a time like this, the last team you'd want to play would be St Albans, a strong, attacking side who were currently second in the table and were the form team.

In contrast, Bromley were second from bottom and had the worst defensive record in the league. A loss today would be their eleventh in a row. Even Crystal Palace, who were being held up by the press and boys at school as an example of a team in crisis, were doing better. And they hadn't won any of their last nine league games.

Bromley had made some new signings to cover all the injuries and resignations, but none fired the imagination. There was Ray Ransom, the General Manager's son, John Sullivan, described in unexciting terms as 'a midfield player from Crawley,' and John Somerville, who 'played for Southborough on Sundays and West Wickham on Saturdays'.

There was also a rumour that Jim Roberts, one of our better centre-forwards in recent years, was rejoining the club. If it was true, this was good news. But I was also a bit scared of being found out about my claim that he was my uncle. I'd told Peter this in my early days of following Bromley, when I was desperately eager to impress him.

The injuries, according to Peter, were even worse than was thought. Alan Stonebridge was having to play through the pain barrier every time he took the field due to boils on his leg, which explained why he hadn't scored in the past six matches. Eric Nottage's knee had swollen up like a balloon and was why he'd gone 11 games without a goal.

The Grubby and I sat together for 90 gloomy minutes, the rain pelting diagonally under the roof of the terrace behind the goal, soaking us to the skin. It was so bad that it rendered several of his cigarettes unsmokable and he had to keep lighting fresh ones. He cleverly stopped the rain getting into his tea by placing the saucer over the cup.

Bromley's tactics appeared to be the standard response to any crisis. Revert to safety first. Defenders passed the ball back to Ian McGuire at the slightest hint of danger. Even the midfield sometimes saw going backwards a better option than going forward.

The theory being that if St Albans didn't have the ball, they couldn't score. I felt this was a risky strategy, especially with own-goal specialist Alan Bonney back in the side after his recent holiday.

It worked for about half an hour, when a bizarre piece of goalkeeping handed St Albans the opening goal on a plate. McGuire advanced out of his goal to meet the winger who had broken through the feeble Bromley defence. Despite being out of his area, he tried to dive at the feet of the bemused attacker who then rounded his prone body with ease and walked the ball into the empty net.

It wasn't just McGuire who was going through the horrors. Phil Amato, after his brief spell of looking like a half-decent player, reverted to his more familiar uselessness. This peaked with a succession of passes which went into empty spaces and stayed there until a grateful St Albans player retrieved the ball.

But the expected avalanche of goals didn't materialise. Instead, Eric Nottage dribbled into the area in an almost exact replica of my run for Hayesford Park Reserves against Forresters.

He was just in the process of rounding the goalie when he was tripped. The referee (Mr AH Cooper, hometown not specified) decided to award a penalty and the sense of excitement that had been missing for the past few home games was back.

The Grubby and I didn't move. We didn't need to as we already had the perfect view.

Alan Stonebridge picked the ball up, placed it on the faded white spot, most of which had been washed away by the unrelenting rain.

I knew exactly what Stonebridge was going to do. But did Mackie, the visiting goalie?

I held my breath as my idol ran into take the penalty. I

glanced over as The Grubby was taking a deeper than usual drag from his cigarette, causing the end to glow a bright orange against the fading daylight.

Alan Stonebridge was nonchalant. With a subtle sway of the hips, he sent the hapless goalie one way and the ball firmly into the roof of the net.

My heart felt as though it was about to burst with joy. I wanted to hug The Grubby, but decided I didn't really know him well enough just yet.

It was just like the old days. The whole team seemed to lift as a result and Bromley were actually looking the most likely to win. The only blemish in this period came when Postman Pat Brown stopped a defender by rugby tackling him.

The Grubby tutted in disapproval. He was a purist and didn't like to see that kind of thing on a football pitch.

Then, in a heartbreaking few minutes, Ian McGuire gave St Albans two goals. The first was when he dribbled the ball to the edge of his penalty area and then allowed the number ten, John Butterfield, to take it off him with laughable ease and slotted the ball in easily.

The next act was even more generous. Butterfield headed a corner straight at him. This time McGuire, his confidence visibly shattered, stood paralysed as the ball passed inches over his head and into the net.

At least Bromley showed a bit of fight. First Ginger Warman and then Eric Nottage both came close. A Stonebridge header skimmed the bar before bouncing off the corrugated iron at the back of the stand and into The Grubby's arms. I noticed that he took it well, getting his chest right behind the ball.

When the final whistle went, neither of us was too downcast. It was a greatly improved performance, making me think that we were about to turn the corner.

I leapt to my feet to give Bromley a well-deserved standing ovation, my heart beating rapidly with excitement. A season ago, this kind of thing was reserved for a good win, but times had changed. Signs of improvement were now enough to prompt seemingly undeserved displays of approval.

I felt that my knowledge of football gave me an insight into the significance of Bromley's performance that others wouldn't have seen. Most of the spectators filing out seemed to have taken the game at face value and looked dejected. But I knew that our team were on the way back, despite the fact that I had just witnessed yet another 3–1 defeat.

Bromley's third in a row by that scoreline.

●●●

As soon as I got home that night I dug up the photos of Morrie and put them in the inside pocket of my blazer, so I wouldn't forget them on Monday morning. I was hoping they would be my ticket to acceptance with the scariest boys in the whole school.

The start of the new week came around and at morning break I tentatively approached one of the skinheads and said, 'Wanna see what Morrie used to look like?'

He looked at me and took the photo, which caused him great amusement. He passed it around and soon they were all laughing. We were all laughing.

This was what I had dreamed about. I left them with the photo still enjoying what they were seeing.

A few minutes later, as I was waiting to go into chemistry class, I heard a commotion.

Coming towards me at great speed was a red-faced Morrie, breathing heavily, eyes blazing with fury. He stopped in front of me and, without saying anything, drew his head back and then propelled it forward with great force, landing his forehead smack on the bridge of my nose. He then walked off.

I was stunned.

The pain was intense. My eyes started to water. Everyone who was milling around was pretending to look the other way. I was sure my nose had been broken.

I somehow stopped myself collapsing to the ground by holding onto the coat rack. Keeping the tears from my eyes was just as hard.

I didn't realise until much later how lucky I'd been. There was no blood and nothing had been broken. But I knew that from then on I would be known as the boy who had been headbutted by Morrie.

I walked into the chemistry class, my head held as high as possible under the circumstances and tried to act as though nothing had happened.

# ISTHMIAN LEAGUE HOW THEY STAND

## 25TH OCTOBER 1969

|  | P | W | D | L | F | A | Pts |
|---|---|---|---|---|---|---|---|
| Wycombe W . . . . | 17 | 10 | 5 | 2 | 30 | 12 | 25 |
| St. Albans City . | 20 | 10 | 5 | 5 | 32 | 2 | 25 |
| Sutton Utd . . . . | 17 | 10 | 4 | 3 | 37 | 16 | 24 |
| Leytonstone . . . | 19 | 9 | 4 | 6 | 32 | 18 | 22 |
| Enfield . . . . . | 14 | 8 | 5 | 1 | 24 | 10 | 21 |
| Wealdstone . . . . | 17 | 9 | 3 | 5 | 31 | 20 | 21 |
| Oxford City . . . | 19 | 8 | 5 | 6 | 32 | 27 | 21 |
| Barking . . . . . | 16 | 8 | 4 | 4 | 35 | 19 | 20 |
| Hitchin Town . . . | 18 | 7 | 6 | 5 | 32 | 22 | 20 |
| Kingstonian . . . | 19 | 7 | 5 | 7 | 29 | 27 | 19 |
| Clapton . . . . . | 17 | 7 | 5 | 5 | 31 | 30 | 19 |
| Tooting & Mit . . | 14 | 7 | 4 | 3 | 29 | 18 | 18 |
| Hendon . . . . . . | 14 | 5 | 6 | 3 | 28 | 18 | 16 |
| Ilford . . . . . . | 18 | 4 | 7 | 7 | 19 | 31 | 15 |
| Woking . . . . . . | 16 | 5 | 2 | 9 | 17 | 25 | 12 |
| Maidstone Utd . . | 13 | 4 | 3 | 6 | 19 | 24 | 11 |
| Walthamstow A . . | 16 | 3 | 4 | 9 | 19 | 29 | 10 |
| Dulwich Hamlet . . | 19 | 1 | 8 | 10 | 16 | 39 | 10 |
| **BROMLEY . . . . .** | **18** | **3** | **2** | **13** | **15** | **58** | **8** |
| Corinthian Cs . . | 17 | 0 | 1 | 16 | 9 | 58 | 1 |

# CHAPTER TWELVE

The Morrie incident had had a serious effect on my campaign to be accepted at Langley Park School.

*Everyone* knew about it.

And soon people were asking me for details. I wisely declined to show anyone else the photo, but was happy to give the impression that it hadn't really hurt and, besides, I was no stranger to that kind of thing.

I decided to lower my sights. Trying to get in with the truly hard boys had been a mistake. It would be much smarter to make friends with the less scary ones. The kind of boys who wouldn't headbutt me.

Dave, who sat next to me in English, seemed promising. I liked the fact that while he was meant to be writing about *Animal Farm*, he was gouging the words 'Eddie Kelly is King' into his desk with the sharp point of a compass.

This impressed me because it meant he took his football seriously and that he didn't necessarily follow the crowd – Eddie Kelly was a fringe Arsenal player – not one of their big stars. Not only did he look more like a labourer than a footballer, but he wasn't even a regular selection. He was in and out of the team.

If I had been an Arsenal supporter, he was exactly the kind of player I would have adopted as my favourite.

I wondered if I might be able to persuade Dave to come along and watch Bromley sometime. It would need to be the right game – preferably against one of our fellow strugglers that Bromley had a chance of winning. A quick glance at the forthcoming fixtures showed no matches with any real potential for Bromley to break the losing sequence. I decided it would be better to wait.

•••

The Hayes Lane ground was virtually deserted for the fixture against Gravesend and Northfleet the following Tuesday. I sat behind the goal, staring at the brown leaves caught up in the net – a feature of many non-league grounds in Autumn, as, unlike the big Football League grounds, a lot of them were surrounded by trees.

It seemed that local interest in a meaningless Kent Floodlit Cup fixture was low, especially as it followed a humiliating run of 11 losses. I felt saddened looking over at the sparsely populated terraces, and found it hard to imagine there was a time when the ground was packed with 10,798 (a figure that was embedded in my memory) people – a ground record.

Yet that's what happened on a late September day in 1949 as Bromley had taken on Nigeria in a friendly. It was a game I'd read about and even talked about with one or two of the older supporters who had been there that day.

I wished I could have seen it.

The visitors, who played in bare feet, apparently possessed skills never witnessed before, or since, at Hayes Lane.

There was 'Big Kicker' Chukura, whose nickname was self-explanatory. Salamo 'The White Ant', who had earned his title through his capacity for hard work. And the solid, reliable 'Experienced' Ottun, a calm head at the heart of the defence.

The Nigerians lit up Hayes Lane with a display of football virtuosity and gave a rare treat to a crowd more used to seeing the likes of Tooting and Mitcham or Leyton.

'Thunderbolt' Balogun sealed the victory for the visitors after they had come back from being 1–0 down at half-time to win 3–1.

Both teams received a standing ovation after the final whistle and the game was still being talked about today, a little over 20 years later.

I had promised myself that if ever the Tardis on *Dr Who* became a reality – and the moon landing showed that anything was possible – the first thing I would do would be to travel back in time to watch Bromley v Nigeria on September 24th 1949.

But right now I was watching Bromley v Gravesend and Northfleet on October 28th 1969 and it was doubtful this game would be talked about in 1989.

If it was, however, the biggest talking point would be that Postman Pat Brown had been sent home before the game had even started – he had got to the ground late only to find that a replacement, Colin Brown, had already got changed.

Despite the loss of one Brown for another, Bromley started with a surreal ten-minute burst, which featured some of the best football I'd seen all season. They just seemed to click from the kick-off, with Eric Nottage at his best and Alan Stonebridge his usual brilliant self.

The two of them combined in the 10th minute for Nottage to thump home a superb Stonebridge cross and each could have had a hat-trick before the visitors equalised just before half-time.

Bromley then fell to pieces as Gravesend scored four second-half goals for their second 5–1 victory over Bromley in the space of three weeks.

The home team looked exhausted as they trudged off afterwards. Their fitness regime didn't seem to be working and they had another match just 48 hours later against Clapton, one of the better teams in the Isthmian League.

•••

Clapton's main claim to fame was the name of their ground, which must have made them a difficult opponent to take seriously.

It was called The Spotted Dog ground. And as if that wasn't bad enough, they had a typically useless Isthmian league nickname of 'The Clap'. But despite these handicaps, they were in the top half of the table.

Somehow, the fixture had attracted enough interest from Bromley supporters to merit running a coach and the journey was just long enough for me to lose all my matches, including some I'd borrowed from Derek, at gin rummy, our usual card game

As always, I looked for an omen, but the only one I could come up with was bad news for Bromley. If they lost today, it would be their 13th defeat in a row.

The nearest thing to a good sign came with the news that Postman Pat had been spotted arriving at Hayes Lane and boarding the team coach. It was pleasing to hear he'd got somewhere on time.

Roy Pettet and Eddie Green were back from injury. This was very exciting news – both were key players and I convinced myself that their absence had been at least partially responsible for the pathetic recent performances. Of my optimum Bromley line-up, only Jeff Bridge was missing today.

For 85 minutes, a good result seemed possible. In all that time, Bromley had only conceded one goal and had come close to scoring several times, including hitting the post once.

Then Clapton made use of Bromley's substitution rule, by bringing on Pamplin who predictably set up the goal that sealed the match.

I wondered if every game from now on would be settled by a tactical substitute coming on and finishing Bromley off.

I also wondered why our substitutions seemed to be so ineffective, considering we invented the rule.

●●●

The greatest day of my young life started routinely enough – up at 8am, Marmite and butter on Weetabix for breakfast, on my bike by 8.15am arriving at school in plenty of time for the register at 9am. The rest of the schoolday passed without incident.

As soon as the bell went to end the day's lessons I dashed home in record time, so I could dump the bike and start hitching to Grays, for the Kent Floodlit Cup game.

It took around three hours to get there in a total of six

different cars, but not once did I question the rationality of what I was doing.

To me, anything was worth going through to watch Bromley. Even though they had now lost 13 in a row, conceding 44 goals in the process and scoring just 8, I always felt we were about to turn the corner.

So if it meant I had to hitchhike to the wilds of Essex for a Kent Floodlit Cup game, then that was what I was prepared to do.

Predictably, the effort wasn't worth it as the 0–0 draw made a mockery of a points system that was meant to encourage attacking play. But at least it put an end to the losing streak and, technically, formed a one-match unbeaten run.

The game was every bit as dreary as the score suggested and five points and a booking for Phil Amato was all Bromley took out of the fixture.

The Lillywhites also managed to spoil Grays' 100% record, but such was the unimportance of the competition, the handful of home supporters didn't seem to care. Most of them had drifted off long before the end.

After the final whistle, I saw Tony Flood, the *Bromley and Kentish Times* football reporter, hovering by the players' entrance. I asked him if there was any chance of a lift home since I'd hitched there.

He apologetically explained that his car was full, but he'd ask around and see if anyone could find room for me.

He then asked if we could have a chat as he'd like to do a story on me for the paper.

Me?

A story?

I was suddenly full of self-importance, but gracefully acquiesced to his request.

He was impressed by my devotion to the team and asked

me a few questions, such as how many matches I'd been to, how long I'd supported Bromley and where I went to school. I took an inordinate of time answering, carefully considering each response.

He jotted my answers down in his notebook and told me to get the paper on Friday as I would be in it. He couldn't promise anything, but thought it might make the back page.

I felt as though the whole season had been worthwhile. I was going to be in the paper for the second time in a few months – this time in an article that would probably be read by some of the Bromley players.

Mr Flood then told me to wait by the car-park entrance and he'd see what he could do about getting me a lift home.

I stood there for ages, watching car after car drive past until the car park was almost deserted. Finally a green Triumph Herald stopped and the driver wound his window down.

'Are you the lad looking for a lift back to Bromley?'

'Yes'

'Jump in then.'

'Are you sure?'

'Yeah.'

'Really?'

'Yeah.'

I was stunned.

It felt as though I was in a dream. Barely able to believe what was happening, I opened the door and sat down in the passenger seat of Alan Stonebridge's car.

My breathing had become shallow. He even asked me if I was alright and I assured him I was.

I then offered my congratulations on a great game tonight and started firing questions at him.

My questions were based on *Shoot* Magazine's weekly profiles of footballers, in which they would be asked their favourite meal, what car they drove, their favourite ground, most difficult opponent, most memorable match, best goal ever scored. That kind of thing.

I didn't ask about his car, as I was sitting in it. But I did ask all the rest. We even discussed some of his goals and it seemed to me that I could remember more of them than he could.

He was really nice and not stuck up like some famous people can be. I'd once tried to get an autograph from Geoff Boycott, the England cricketer, at a charity match and he'd just ignored me. Alan Stonebridge was nothing like that.

Alan even asked me about school and told me it was important to work hard and get qualifications. He was a teacher, so he probably felt he had to say that.

The journey passed all too quickly and he kindly dropped me off right outside my house.

'Thanks, Alan,' I said, a little too loudly just in case anyone was watching and recognised him. 'See you on Saturday.'

# CHAPTER THIRTEEN

The next week passed in a bit of haze.

In my mind, I was still in Alan Stonebridge's car, reliving every second. I did have one or two regrets. Some of the questions I'd asked him were a bit embarrassing. I wished I could take back the one where I asked him if he had a girlfriend.

Also, if I had the chance to do it all again I probably wouldn't stare at him so much. I knew he'd caught me a few times just gazing at his profile when he was concentrating on the road.

But all in all, I felt we'd got on pretty well. I had pretty much decided to invite him to my 15th birthday party in March, hoping that he might bring a few more players along.

The article had appeared on the back page of the *Bromley and Kentish Times*, as promised. It was headed 'FOUR HOUR TRIP WAS WORTH WHILE' and praised the fact I wasn't a young troublemaker. However, I had been misquoted. Mr Flood had said that I hadn't missed a game all season, when I had clearly told him I had missed the away games at Leytonstone and Ilford.

He had also downplayed my lift home by saying it had been from 'a Bromley official'. I couldn't believe it. I wanted the whole of Bromley to know I'd been driven home by Alan Stonebridge.

It seemed I would have to spread the word myself.

When I went to the Supporters' Club hut before the Oxford game on the following Saturday, I casually mentioned that I'd got a lift back from Grays with Alan Stonebridge, expecting an outpouring of envy and questioning over what he was like.

Instead, they seemed pleased that I'd managed to get a lift and started talking about our chances in today's game.

Only a few weeks ago, Oxford had beaten us 7–0 in a game that was every bit as one-sided as the scoreline suggested. But on that day Bromley were without several key players. Today we were at full strength.

The good news from the Oxford team was that Woodley, who had scored four times the last time the teams had met, was missing. The bad news was that Morton, who had got a hat-trick in the same game, was in today's line-up.

I saw The Grubby, hunched over a cup of tea as usual, and went to join him behind the goal. I deliberately hadn't mentioned the Stonebridge lift during the week, preferring to find a more dramatic moment to reveal all; perhaps just after the great man scored a goal. That would be when my achievement should have maximum impact.

The game kicked off in cold, swirling wind that made life difficult for both players and spectators. The Grubby and I sat shivering, drinking endless cups of tea to stay warm.

Bromley made the much better start and Ginger Warman deserved at least two goals in the opening ten minutes. On one occasion, the goalie made a brilliant save and on the other Ginger fell over with the goal at his mercy.

It was all Bromley. So it was a huge shock when Oxford undeservedly took the lead with a diving header from Oram, who until that moment had done nothing.

Bromley seemed to somehow know then that it wasn't going to be their day. Perhaps losing had become a habit because everything they tried failed.

A rare Ginger Warman header (you don't win much in the air when you're 5'3") produced a miraculous save from the Oxford goalie. The same man then thwarted Alan Stonebridge, thus depriving me of a premium name dropping opportunity.

# FOUR-HOUR TRIP WAS WORTH WHILE

A FINE example that not all young soccer supporters are would-be trouble-makers is 14-year-old Langley Park Grammar School boy David Roberts.

Although Bromley had lost their previous 13 games, David, of 7, Grasmere Road, Bromley, who has watched all their matches this season, was determined to see them at Grays on Tuesday.

The supporters club did not have enough bookings to run a coach, so David hitch-hiked his way to Grays—a journey that took him four hours. He was rewarded by seeing Bromley draw and was driven home by a club official.

It was getting more and more frustrating. Shots were going just wide or producing great saves.

The Grubby was suffering. Really suffering. The final whistle failed to put him out of his misery.

'That's it. No more,' was all he had to say as he gathered up his half-empty pack of Embassy and lighter before storming off.

•••

I found The Grubby in the canteen at school on the following Monday, sitting alone and scowling.

Something was missing.

I slowly realised it was his Bromley Supporters' Club enamel badge.

He was serious. He'd had enough.

In an outpouring of emotion he told me that the loss to Oxford had been the final straw.

'I just couldn't take any more,' he said, before going on to explain how he had gone home after the game and played his drums until the early hours of the morning, trying to release some of his anger and frustration.

During this frenzy, he had come to the conclusion that Bromley would never win another game and that the pain of watching them twice a week was one he no longer wanted to suffer. He had gathered all his programmes together and thrown them into the dustbin. His badge had suffered the same fate.

He wouldn't be switching to another team. No-one could replace Bromley. He was thinking of getting a Saturday job – he'd heard that Debenhams were looking for someone in their carpet department and he was going in for an interview after school.

I was shocked. I'd often felt like stopping watching Bromley, especially during this disastrous run. But I knew I'd never be able to carry it out.

I almost envied The Grubby.

●●●

Walking through the turnstiles for the Erith and Belvedere game in the Floodlit Cup, I wondered what it was going to be like watching a game without The Grubby. It wasn't like we said a lot to each other during games – but it was nice just being with someone who understood how much it all meant.

I bought a couple of programmes and made my way to the bench behind the goal, ready to take up my lone vigil.

Looking up, I saw a sight I wasn't expecting to see.

Sitting there, the sleeves on his green corduroy jacket rolled up, his fingers drumming a nervous rhythm on his thighs, was The Grubby. He was smoking furiously, cigarette clenched tightly between his teeth, and he had three cups of steaming hot tea beside him.

He greeted me with a curt nod and handed one of the cups to me. We never spoke of his about-turn and I never mentioned it again.

After four minutes, his resolve was put to the test when Erith opened the scoring. A speculative shot squirted out of McGuire's hands and trickled over the goal line.

The Grubby was expressionless. He also seemed unaffected when Eric Nottage equalised. It was as if he'd decided his only hope of coping with watching Bromley was to suppress all emotion.

But when Phil Amato was brought crashing to the ground with only the goalie to beat and the linesman raised his flag, The Grubby leapt to his feet and punched the air. I was slightly more restrained, contenting myself with a celebratory whooping sound.

Then it all went wrong.

The referee, Mr GM Campbell (hometown not specified, but probably Erith or Belvedere) waved play on.

Someone in the main stand offered the referee his glasses. The Grubby sat down, defeated. I was in shock.

Then it got even worse as Eric Nottage limped off with what looked like a serious injury. This was quickly followed by Erith and Belvedere taking an undeserved 2–1 lead with a fluke goal. It was soon 3–1, when a mix-up in the Bromley defence led to a tap-in from a yard out.

There was to be a bright spot amidst the gloom. With 20 minutes left, Ginger Warman took advantage of some appalling defending to bring it back to 3–2.

But that was as close as it got. My anger towards the referee was matched only by The Grubby's anger towards the referee.

He had clearly cost us five points, which somehow seemed more serious than if it had happened in an Isthmian League game and only cost us one point.

But while everyone who had been at the game would know the real story, the bare facts were that Bromley had now gone 16 games without a win.

●●●

The next day, I finished school early. It was The Grubby's idea. His dad was away and his mum was at work – so we could take the afternoon off, go round to his house and kick a ball about in the back garden.

It was the first time I'd been to his place and I was surprised to find that he lived in one of the posher parts of Beckenham. I soon discovered where his voracious appetite for tea came from – the teapot was so large, it dominated the kitchen.

His garden wasn't a perfect garden for football. Not only was it quite narrow, but also small with a concrete path running through the penalty area. There were several flower-beds, which would have to be avoided. The goal posts were two silver-birch trees, which were only about four feet apart and the crossbar was a rolled-up garden umbrella perched between the branches, from one tree to the other. The net was a compost heap behind the trees.

There was a penalty spot painted on to the lawn precisely 12 yards from the goal.

It is a cliché that many back-garden games of football end with the shattering of glass as the ball is miscued in the direction of a greenhouse, going through a pane and leaving broken glass all over someone's prize lettuces.

It shouldn't, therefore, have come as any great surprise

when this happened to me.

What was meant to be a swerving, dipping volley into the top corner spun off my foot and straight through the glass. The Grubby and I both reacted in exactly the same way – we put our heads in our hands and looked pained. Then ran.

I later heard that we were both banned from playing football in his back garden. Next time, we would have to go to the park.

In our world of football, not much was going right.

●●●

I had a huge football day ahead. It would start with Bromley at home to Dulwich Hamlet, who were having a terrible season. Not as bad as Bromley's, but still terrible.

Then, about five hours after that finished, I would witness the first ever *Match of the Day* in colour. This was tempered slightly by the fact we only had a black and white TV, so I wouldn't be able to appreciate the full effect, but it was still exciting. It felt like the dawning of a new era.

I had similar hopes for the Bromley match. Even though the last 16 games hadn't really gone to plan, Dulwich would be the weakest team – on paper, at least – that we had faced in months.

The only fresh absence was Ginger Warman, who had been sent off during the week while playing for his Post Office side. Otherwise, it was a strong line-up.

I was pleasantly surprised Bromley had managed to put out a near full-strength team. The previous game against Erith had seen a succession of leg injuries, with Nottage, Green, Pettet, Lewis and Amato all requiring treatment. I put it down to dirty tactics from Erith and Belvedere, but Charlie King had a different theory. 'It is the opinion of many top league managers and trainers,' he thundered in his programme notes, 'equally shared by many in the amateur field including the writer, that many ankle injuries sustained by players nowadays are the result of the "Dancing Pump" type of football boots generally worn, which offer no protection whatsoever to the ankles.'

I didn't know what 'Dancing Pump' meant, but took my boots out of my duffel bag. He was right – If they were 'Dancing Pump' boots, which they probably were, they offered no ankle protection.

The Grubby was unusually relaxed, relishing the prospect of a win to break the barren spell. He sipped his tea slowly, relishing every mouthful and lit another cigarette with the glowing remnants of the previous one before flicking it to the ground.

He had a lazy smile on his face. One that didn't last for long. I have never seen a man fall apart so quickly and so completely as The Grubby that day.

Bromley struggled from the start. All the improvement they had shown over the past month was suddenly gone as they reverted to utter uselessness.

Dulwich were too fast, too skilful, too good. Only Alan Stonebridge seemed able to match them, as he carried the attack on his own. One blistering 'Stonebridge Special' was touched on to the post by the goalie.

But it was nowhere near enough. At the other end, goals were going in with alarming frequency, each triggering a fresh smoking frenzy from The Grubby.

Dulwich were scoring goals every ten minutes or so, starting just before half-time. Some were good, some lucky and a few were the results of poor defending.

Their 5–0 win was their biggest away win in two years and our biggest home defeat in even longer. I hated the team for building up my hopes and then crushing them.

I went to bed early, too depressed to even watch *Match of the Day*.

## Bromley crash to another sad defeat

**BROMLEY 0, DULWICH HAMLET 5**

BROMLEY slumped to yet another dismal defeat at Hayes Lane last Saturday—their 16th in 17 games. Dulwich, also struggling near the bottom of the table, were made to look like champions by the demoralised home side.

It was only Dulwich's third win of the season and their biggest away victory in two years—which all goes to emphasise how poorly Bromley played.

Bromley, however, were weakened by the absence of Eddie Green, who is still not fit, and Roy Pettet, who has an injured ankle. Johnny Warman, who has started a three-week suspension for an offence while playing in midweek for his Post Office side, was also missed in attack.

Bromley, struggling from the start, bravely held the visitors to a one goal lead at half-time, but twice missed great chances to draw level and pull themselves back into the game.

When these chances were missed—one by Dave Hall just before the interval and the other by Bob Lennox early in the second half—it seemed to quench all Bromley's spirit and they conceded four second half goals.

Bromley were soon under pressure from the nimble Dulwich forwards and conceded a series of corners. Dulwich, however, were unable to press home their advantage due to their own poor shooting and the safe handling of McGuire.

In attack, Bromley showed little punch and Noltage was often the only player upfield as hopeful passes were punted into the Dulwich half. The deep-lying Dulwich defence were rarely troubled and centre-half Firmin had an outstanding game.

Lennox and Brown often swapped wings in a vain bid to upset the rhythm of the visitors' defence and Stonebridge, although working hard, was unable to penetrate.

Dulwich took a deserved lead in the 30th minute when Hugo lobbed a soft shot over McGuire after centre-forward Heasman had easily dispossessed a Brom-

Bridge and Asquto both keeping, it was no surprise when Dulwich increased their lead through O'Connell, who appraised McGuire with a sharp shot when everyone expected a cross.

Dulwich's talented centre-forward Heasman made it 3 in the 65th minute when he slammed straight back into the net McGuire's badly taken goal kick.

Seven minutes later Bromley's defence was exposed by a great Firmin pass down the middle and substitute Wyatt, who came on for Major in the 64th minute, slotted the ball home.

The fifth goal came in the 84th minute when Hugo had all the time in the world to number five from Sampherd's cross.

Bromley—1 McGuire; J Brady, W Lewis; P Brown, A Bonner, P Amato; J Brown, D Hall, A Stonebridge, F Noltage, B Lennox, Sub J Sullivan.

F.W.T.

### Hockey

## LANGLEY PARK'S BEST DISPLAY OF THE SEASON

**WALLINGTON G.S. 1.**
**LANGLEY PARK II 1**

Langley Park II, with a much weakened side, put up their best display of the season holding Wallington to a 1—1 draw last Saturday.

Good defensive work by Langley Park prevented any score during the opening exchanges and soon the roles were reversed with only the fine play of the Wallington backs keeping out the sweeping attacks of the visitors.

• • •

The 17th defeat in 18 games was at Bexley, a ground that held memories so strange, I had to wonder if they were really some kind of trick of the mind.

I had first visited their ground a few years back for a friendly against Bromley. The pitch was on a dramatic slope, which was even more pronounced than the one at Wycombe.

Less than a year later, I went back for another friendly only to find the surface was now perfectly level. The only problem was that it was covered in sand, creating a giant grey sandpit.

Someone had apparently had the bright idea of filling in all the sloping bits with sand to level out the playing surface. This meant that at one end, you would be playing in about three feet of sand, which worked well in dry weather, but could be disastrous when it rained. The other end just had a light coating.

Today there was no trace of sand or slope, so I assumed someone had found a better solution to the slope problem.

If there was such a thing as a Kent Floodlit Cup local derby, this was it. Bexley wasn't quite near enough to go on my bike, but it was easy to get there by bus.

Alan Stonebridge once again showed how valuable he was by stylishly steering the ball home after a defender's miskick landed just short of the goalie. It was his sixth goal of the season – something that was put in perspective later that day by news of Pelé scoring the 1000th goal of his career. But at least it was enough to give the travelling faithful (me, Peter and Roy) hope of escaping with a draw.

It was not to be. By way of retaliation, Bexley simply mounted another attack, scored another goal and then settled back into their pattern of seemingly toying with Bromley.

It ended 2–1 to Bexley. Under the weird scoring system, they got 12 points for the result and we got one.

●●●

On the way back, Peter told me to watch for big changes. The committee were going to hold a crisis meeting in a couple of days' time and Alan Basham was going to have to explain the recent run of pathetic results. I was glad they were reacting. It just seemed to be a bit late.

At least we still had Alan Stonebridge who had proved once again that he was the one (and only) reason to keep watching Bromley.

# ISTHMIAN LEAGUE HOW THEY STAND

## 20TH NOVEMBER 1969

|                     | P   | W  | D | L  | F  | A  | Pts |
|---------------------|-----|----|---|----|----|----|-----|
| Sutton Utd . . . .  | 22  | 12 | 6 | 4  | 44 | 24 | 30  |
| St Albans City . .  | 25  | 11 | 8 | 6  | 37 | 31 | 30  |
| Wycombe W  . . . .  | 19  | 12 | 5 | 2  | 36 | 14 | 29  |
| Barking   . . . .   | 20  | 11 | 5 | 4  | 48 | 22 | 27  |
| Enfield   . . . .   | 17  | 10 | 6 | 1  | 33 | 11 | 26  |
| Hitchin Town . . .  | 21  | 9  | 7 | 5  | 37 | 24 | 25  |
| Wealdstone . . . .  | 19  | 10 | 3 | 6  | 33 | 23 | 23  |
| Oxford City  . . .  | 20  | 9  | 5 | 6  | 33 | 27 | 23  |
| Tooting & Mit  . .  | 16  | 9  | 4 | 3  | 36 | 18 | 22  |
| Leytonstone  . . .  | 21  | 9  | 4 | 8  | 32 | 20 | 22  |
| Kingstonian  . . .  | 21  | 8  | 5 | 8  | 31 | 28 | 21  |
| Clapton   . . . .   | 20  | 8  | 5 | 7  | 35 | 36 | 21  |
| Hendon . . . . . .  | 17  | 6  | 7 | 4  | 34 | 25 | 19  |
| Ilford . . . . .    | 22  | 5  | 9 | 8  | 24 | 38 | 19  |
| Woking . . . . .    | 20  | 7  | 2 | 11 | 19 | 31 | 16  |
| Dulwich Hamlet  . . | 22  | 3  | 8 | 11 | 24 | 40 | 14  |
| Maidstone Utd  . .  | 18  | 5  | 3 | 10 | 25 | 34 | 13  |
| Walthamstow A  . .  | 21  | 4  | 4 | 13 | 23 | 42 | 12  |
| **BROMLEY  . . . . .** | **21** | **3** | **2** | **16** | **15** | **66** | **8** |
| Corinthian Cs  . .  | 20  | 0  | 2 | 18 | 12 | 57 | 2   |

# CHAPTER FOURTEEN

Even though the headline was staring at me in black and white, my brain refused to accept it.

Bromley without Alan Stonebridge would be like the Beatles without Paul or *Coronation Street* without Ena Sharples.

Unthinkable.

At least Alan Soper would be a decent replacement for McGuire. But Stonebridge was irreplaceable. I wondered if he could be persuaded to change his mind. I also felt a bit let down that he hadn't mentioned anything to me in the car.

For three seasons he had been my hero. He was the one player who always seemed to play well, no matter how badly the rest of the team played.

My bedroom wall was covered with pictures of him scoring

goals, frozen in mid-air heading the ball or just posing for the camera. These pictures were all signed.

He and McGuire had decided to return to Carshalton Athletic who I had briefly considered switching to as well. But since that would mean a couple of hours travel time for home games, I decided against it.

While I was trying to come to terms with the enormity of that news, there was more.

There had been an emergency committee meeting and big changes were in the wind.

Alan Basham, who had overseen a period of disastrous decline, had been rewarded by being given full control of team selection as well as fitness and training.

He'd even been given an assistant.

Inevitably, there were new sub-committees. A three-man panel headed by Charlie King, who was on just about every committee and sub-committee, would handle all matters regarding the team.

According to 'a spokesman' (I suspected this was Mr King), this would cover things like what players were eligible, and arranging training times and meeting places.

Oddly, the selection sub-committee would continue to meet, despite having no powers whatsoever.

The other big decision made at the crisis meeting was to contact Graham 'Gasmask' Gaston to see if he was now free from his business commitments and was able to play regularly.

He declined.

His job, apparently, was more important than the future of Bromley FC.

But all of this was only a momentary distraction from the incredible Alan Stonebridge bombshell. I found I was still shaking with shock as I tried to take in the full significance of the great man's announcement.

Phil Amato had been threatening to leave all season, but he was still at Bromley. This gave me hope that things weren't quite as dark as they seemed.

I had to go and lie down, and soon found myself staring at the pictures of Alan Stonebridge on the wall. Everywhere I looked, there seemed to be something to remind me of him.

I thought of removing the pictures, but not yet. The pain was still too fresh.

By now, my Bromley-induced misery was starting to seep into my everyday life. The full horror of what was happening had finally filtered through my veil of optimism.

I still went into every game thinking Bromley were going to win. But it was becoming clear that unless something changed dramatically, the losing streak could stretch into the following year or the following season.

And if Bromley weren't as infallible as I had believed, what about my ability to fit into the new school?

I was about to find out.

Trials were about to be held for the school football team. Thanks to me giving everyone exaggerated descriptions of my Hayesford Park Reserves exploits, it was assumed I'd walk into the team. I had a feeling that I was getting way out of my depth.

●●●

I had agonised over whether to continue my support for Bromley, but had recently read that Don Revie, the Leeds manager, had said that no player should be bigger than the club.

I agreed. Although Bromley would always be my first love, if the worst came to the worst I had plenty of 'other teams' from around the globe.

Raith Rovers were my Scottish team as we'd once been

on a train that went past their Starks Park ground on the way from Kirkcaldy to Edinburgh. They were playing at the time, but I couldn't make out their opponents. It was the only time I'd ever seen them in action, but it was enough for me to form an unbreakable bond. I also was a big Dynamo Moscow fan. This was because of Lev Yashin, their legendary goalie and the original 'Black Cat' whom I idolised. He inspired me to insist on getting a black goalie's jumper for my 9th birthday and try to change my nickname to 'The Black Cat'.

In Australia, one name that stood out for me on the Summer Pools coupon was South Coast United. I knew nothing about them apart from their location, but considered myself a fan. I was also a loyal follower of Eintracht Frankfurt, because I felt sorry for them after they lost the European Cup final by a huge score when I was six.

Then there was Young Boys of Berne, who had won the Swiss League ten times. I'd started supporting them many years before, when I was under the impression that they were a team of young boys playing in a men's league. When I discovered, in *Charles Buchan's Football Monthly*, that the team had got their name to avoid confusion with the other big Berne club, Old Boys of Berne, it was too late. My passion for them was already too well established.

All in all, I had about seven foreign teams, all of whom used to play in a sort of Subbuteo Super Cup, which Bromley always won.

●●●

The post Stonebridge-era was given the toughest possible start. Away to St Albans, who were a point clear at the top of the table and had gone 12 games without defeat.

I felt a surge of hope when I saw the familiar figure of Mr

KA Duff of West Moseley trot out, flanked by his smiling linesmen.

St Albans' Clarence Park ground was yet another sloping pitch. I often wondered how hard it could be to actually build a level playing surface.

Bromley were playing downhill in the first half but it was Alan Soper, who I always preferred to McGuire, who was the busier keeper.

He made a couple of impressive saves and this seemed to breathe confidence into the Bromley team and supporters.

David Wise, who had replaced Alan Stonebridge started brightly, but he was no Alan Stonebridge.

After ten minutes, Eric Nottage stunned everyone, probably including himself, by giving Bromley an unlikely lead. He nearly made it two a few minutes later and suddenly the travelling supporters found themselves absorbed in a close game. I could tell by Roy's agitated state that he sensed an upset.

Unbelievably, Bromley were outplaying the League leaders. Nottage, in particular, was playing brilliantly. But when you're down, things don't go your way.

The St Albans equaliser came from John Butterfield, his third against Bromley for the season, in a scrappy goalmouth scramble, which should have seen Bromley awarded a free-kick. Instead, St Albans were awarded a dubious goal. Roy, Peter, Derek and I were aghast. The referee *must* have seen the pushing that was going on.

Mr Duff made up for it on the hour mark by turning down one of the most obvious penalties I had ever seen. The St Albans left winger had broken clean through when Colin Brown dived at his feet, taking his legs from underneath him and bringing him tumbling to the ground. To everyone's astonishment, Mr Duff waved play on.

The reprieve was only temporary. Vic Lucas got the winner

a few minutes from time. I think we all knew that Bromley would lose, even when the scores had been level.

Close defeats can sometimes hurt more than big losses, because the hope is still alive until the end. But in this game, I felt that defeat was always going to happen.

I just couldn't imagine a Bromley team winning a game without Alan Stonebridge. I still couldn't believe they'd let him go. It was just the latest in a long line of disasters and I felt I had to do something to stop the slide. John Lennon had just returned his MBE to Buckingham Palace in protest at something or other. I wanted to make a stand that was just as powerful.

I decided that when I got home, I would write a letter to the editor of the *Bromley and Kentish Times* outlining my thoughts on what had gone wrong with Bromley's season and what I thought the club should do about it.

The editor would probably recognise my name – I had appeared in his paper twice already that season. For good measure, I would say that I knew Tony Flood, his sport reporter.

Some of my ideas were radical; others were plain commonsense.

Top of the list was persuading Carshalton to give back Alan Stonebridge. I was convinced he had somehow been forced to join them against his will.

I also wanted all powers to be returned to the committee. The team were much fitter under Alan Basham, but they were also much worse. The Isthmian League had to share some of the blame for the club's decline, as the refereeing had been substandard and we had conceded too many goals that were clearly offside and blatant penalties had been ignored. No-one was spared as I addressed a wide range of issues. I felt the supporters (apart from the three which I named) weren't supporting the team properly.

My other big idea was to get a board made up with the words 'THIS IS HAYES LANE'. It would be placed in the players' tunnel so the teams could see it as they were running out onto the pitch. I'd got the idea after reading about the 'THIS IS ANFIELD' board at Liverpool's Anfield Road ground, which was there to intimidate opposing teams. I also felt that a suitable tune should be found to greet the appearance of the Bromley players at home games. Something that would become as well known as Palace's 'Glad all Over' and Everton's 'Z Cars'.

My suggestion was to use 'Bend Me, Shape Me' by Amen Corner. I even offered to lend them my spare copy of the single.

The marching music, I told them, was too old fashioned.

And finally, I put forward the radical theory of approaching the Isthmian League and suggesting a mid-season injury break. This would allow players to rest for a couple of weeks, allowing them time to shake off those niggling little aches and pains that had accumulated over the first few months of the season.

If our twin strike force hadn't been affected so badly by leg boils and swollen knees, things would surely be different. Thinking about this topic had dredged up the memory of our ten-man injury list for the Oxford away game that we'd lost 7–0. It had me seething at the injustice of being forced to play with such a weakened side.

I typed the letter up on my dad's typewriter, making a carbon copy, which I sent to Charlie King (his address, which was 'Rosings', Falcon Avenue, Bickley, was on the front cover of home programmes).

I then posted both envelopes and eagerly awaited that Friday's *Bromley and Kentish Times*, particularly the controversy I knew my words would stir up.

●●●

If one game summed up all that is wrong with Bromley, it was their final Kent Floodlit Cup fixture, away to Erith and Belvedere.

I went into Erith's Park View ground knowing that Bromley could still, technically at least, finish top of the group. It required an unlikely sequence of events – we needed to win tonight's game by approximately 30 goals, while Gravesend and Northfleet had to lose by ten goals or more. But where there's life, there's hope.

Bromley didn't even look interested in giving it a go.

The game was an embarrassingly one-sided affair and the first time I had ever seen Bromley go an entire game without having one single shot. The home goalie literally did not have a save to make.

Alan Soper had a far busier night, including picking the ball out of his net three times.

It was a terrible, *terrible* performance and I couldn't understand why Alan Basham had decided to rest Eric Nottage and Bobby Lennox, our two best forwards.

It was as though he'd decided the game didn't matter and was happy to lose. I couldn't imagine the committee having that attitude.

Mercifully, the end of the game also signalled the end of Bromley's participation in the Kent Floodlit Cup for the season. The first phase was over and Bromley's group, Group 'D', was incredibly close. Erith and Belvedere's 3–0 win was enough for them to finish in first place with 69 points, just ahead of Gravesend and Northfleet on 67. These two teams qualified for the quarter-finals, with Bexley United on 65 just missing out, together with Grays who had a mere 52 points.

But the team that stood out at even the most casual glance at the table was Bromley. In their eight games, they had managed a grand total of 12 points, the lowest of any of the 17 teams in the competition.

This made them undisputedly the worst amateur team in Kent at playing football under floodlights.

•••

The big story on the back page of the *Bromley and Kentish Times* was Johnny Warman's return from suspension. I was a bit disappointed that my letter hadn't had priority over that, but could accept that this was newsworthy.

My feeling of understanding turned to full-blown anger when I looked through the rest of the page and saw no mention of my letter. I hurriedly opened up the paper, assuming it had been relegated to the inside, but all I saw was reports of various hockey matches, Sunday league results and news of the official opening of Eric Fright's Bromley Sports Centre.

My letter had not made it.

The feeling of powerlessness was greater than ever. Not only did I have to suffer appalling decisions, bad luck and injustice, but my thoughts were being ignored.

I tried to concentrate on reading the preview of the upcoming game against Woking, but was distracted by the sounds of hail crashing against the window. I gazed outside and thought that the bad weather could easily mean the match would have to be postponed and provide the break Bromley so desperately seemed to need.

•••

When snow is falling heavily, the early afternoon sky is dark and threatening, and ice has formed a skating rink-thick layer over the ground, it's the perfect Saturday to sit around at home with the heater on watching the wrestling on TV.

Unless your team's game is one of the few that hasn't been called off, that is.

Woking v Bromley was one such fixture. I rang their ground and was told that the game was on. They had a bit of snow on the pitch, but not enough to cause a postponement. This was exciting news. I'd already prepared myself for the blow of having no football and the news felt like a reprieve.

My next phone call was to Peter. He, too, had heard the game was still on and would be picking me up after he'd got Roy. I got ready for the journey, carefully packing my boots into my duffel bag, confident that the chances of at least one Bromley player having a non-fatal road accident in these conditions was high.

When Peter announced his arrival by tooting his horn, I ran out of the door and immediately slipped on the icy pathway. I picked myself up and walked slowly and tentatively towards the car, unable to see how a football match could possibly take place in such conditions.

The drive was a nightmare right from the start, the car crawling along at under 30mph, the tyres with a tenuous grip on the road and a flurry of thick snow being constantly swept aside by the windscreen wipers.

It all brought out the worst in Roy, who was a born worrier. His concerns ranged from being convinced the game would be called off, to us not making it on time to Bromley losing heavily because they'd be tired after their nerve-wracking journey.

It took the best part of an hour to get to Raynes Park, which was about half-way to Woking. By this time conditions had deteriorated so much we decided to find a phone box so that Peter could put in another call to Woking's ground, unable to believe that the match could possibly take place. He came back to the car with astonishing news – it was definitely on, although the kick-off had been delayed because none of the Bromley players had arrived yet.

By the time we got to Esher, it was already dark despite being only 2.45pm. By now, driving was next to impossible and there was a long hold-up due to an accident. I immediately felt overwhelming guilt – what if it was one of the Bromley players?

Peter decided to ring the ground again for another update. Surely no game could possibly go ahead in this?

He was told that the referee was stranded in Streatham, but that the senior linesman had arrived and declared the pitch playable. Bromley were still stuck in traffic, but kick-off had provisionally been scheduled for 3.30pm.

Eventually, it got under way at 3.45pm. We weren't there to watch it, though. Peter had decided to turn back. We had no hope of getting to Woking in time. I volunteered to find out the score if Peter could stop at some phone boxes on the way home.

Peter agreed and the news that Bromley had lost 2–0 only added to the general air of misery in the car.

I was finally dropped off at home around 7.30pm, thankful that the next game was at Hayes Lane.

●●●

The Woking game was the last time I ever took my boots with me when I went to watch Bromley play.

I heard a few days later that Graham Farmer, who had made his debut in the first game of the season at Wycombe Wanderers, had been fatally injured in a car crash.

I couldn't help but feel partly responsible, as the reason I always packed my boots in my duffel bag was in case any players had been involved in an accident on the way to the game.

I felt guilty.

Guilty for ever wishing for accidents (even though I always made sure to specify that they were to be non-fatal), guilty for never including him in any lists of my favourite players and guilty for being so selfish in thinking only of what would benefit me.

I didn't know much about Graham Farmer. He only ever played in the Wycombe game, but he was still registered as a Bromley player. I could only vaguely recall what he looked like, but I was still deeply upset by what had happened.

The only games I took my boots to after that were ones involving Hayesford Park Reserves.

●●●

The four-mile bike ride to school at the start of the week was every bit as difficult as Saturday's car journey.

The weather was still atrocious. Our Sunday league game had been mercifully called off after an hour, with Hayesford Park Reserves trailing 6–0. The excited chatter in the changing room afterwards was down to Roy's theory that we might be awarded a draw since we hadn't played the full 90 minutes.

Following a frantic phone call to the Orpington and Bromley District Sunday League later the next day, Peter discovered that the game had been awarded to our opponents, Chelsfield Colts. Apparently it was felt unlikely that we would score a minimum of six goals in the remaining half-hour.

I felt that we should appeal, citing Portugal's remarkable comeback in the last World Cup, when they went 3–0 down to North Korea and then came back to win 5–3.

No-one seemed to think this would help sway the League and the matter was quietly dropped.

But while football continued to provide disappointments in my life, school was going brilliantly. The skinheads seemed to treat me with benign amusement and Morrie hadn't followed up with any further assaults, despite having several opportunities to do so. It was as if he considered justice to have been metered out and was content for the status quo to return.

While I hadn't actually made any friends yet, there were several boys who I enjoyed talking to. Just about all of them seemed to like football and it definitely helped my credibility when I told them I played in a men's Sunday league. I gave the impression that I was a goalkeeper and also hinted that my team were better placed than they actually were.

This led to me being approached by one of the boys, who ran a team in a local Beckenham league. He wanted to know if I'd consider playing on Saturday mornings for his team, which was made up of the best players in the school.

They badly needed a goalie. My immediate instinct was to agree. But then, I wisely told him that unfortunately I wouldn't be able to do it. The official reason was that I wouldn't have time. The truth was that I had finally realised that I was a terrible goalie.

I felt as though I'd had a close escape. If I'd played for them, I probably would have humiliated myself so much, I'd never be able to live it down.

Then I remembered I had a trial for the school team coming up. And I couldn't see a way out of it.

●●●

The trial didn't go as badly as I imagined it would, but that was only because what I'd imagined had been so horrific, it would have been impossible in real life.

There were positives to be taken out of it. While it was soon obvious to everyone that I wasn't a good enough goalie to play at that level, I did make a few good saves.

And despite my fears, no-one had laughed at me. I was replaced at half-time and asked if I wanted to play up front, like I did in my Sunday league team.

I wisely declined.

## ISTHMIAN LEAGUE HOW THEY STAND

### 4TH DECEMBER 1969

|                    | P   | W  | D  | L  | F  | A  | Pts |
|--------------------|-----|----|----|----|----|----|-----|
| St. Albans City . . | 26  | 12 | 8  | 6  | 39 | 32 | 32  |
| Wycombe W  . . . . | 20  | 13 | 5  | 2  | 40 | 14 | 31  |
| Sutton Utd . . . . | 23  | 12 | 7  | 4  | 44 | 24 | 31  |
| Enfield. . . . . . | 19  | 12 | 6  | 1  | 37 | 11 | 30  |
| Barking  . . . . . | 21  | 12 | 5  | 4  | 52 | 22 | 29  |
| Hitchin Town . . . | 22  | 9  | 8  | 5  | 37 | 24 | 26  |
| Oxford City. . . . | 22  | 10 | 5  | 7  | 37 | 30 | 25  |
| Wealdstone  . . . . | 20  | 10 | 3  | 7  | 33 | 27 | 23  |
| Clapton. . . . . . | 22  | 9  | 5  | 8  | 38 | 39 | 23  |
| Tooting & Mit. . . | 16  | 9  | 4  | 3  | 36 | 18 | 22  |
| Leytonstone  . . . | 22  | 9  | 4  | 9  | 32 | 22 | 22  |
| Hendon. . . . . . . | 19  | 7  | 7  | 5  | 36 | 27 | 21  |
| Kingstonian  . . . | 22  | 8  | 5  | 9  | 31 | 31 | 21  |
| Ilford . . . . . . | 23  | 5  | 10 | 8  | 26 | 40 | 20  |
| Woking. . . . . . . | 22  | 8  | 3  | 11 | 23 | 33 | 19  |
| Dulwich Hamlet  . . | 23  | 4  | 8  | 11 | 27 | 42 | 16  |
| Maidstone Utd. . . | 19  | 5  | 3  | 11 | 25 | 36 | 13  |
| Walthamstow A . . . | 22  | 4  | 4  | 14 | 25 | 45 | 12  |
| **BROMLEY**  . . . . . | **23** | **3** | **2** | **18** | **16** | **70** | **8** |
| Corinthian Cs . . . | 20  | 0  | 2  | 18 | 12 | 57 | 2   |

# CHAPTER FIFTEEN

I had a love/hate relationship with snow.

I loved sitting at my window at home, watching it fall onto the garden in the orange glow of the streetlight.

But I hated how it sometimes put Bromley's games at risk of being called off, after I'd been looking forward to them all week.

Today's game was a game very much at risk. Heavy snowfall had led to a procession of postponements being announced on *Grandstand* and if I wanted to see Bromley take on Wembley in the London Senior Cup, I knew I had to play my part.

Wrapping up in my Hayesford Park Reserves shirt, two jumpers and my anorak, I took the bus to Hayes Lane, where a small party of volunteers were already hard at work, clearing the snowfall and pouring salt on the ice.

After changing into my wellington boots, I was handed a shovel and got to work clearing the touchline on the Main Stand side of the ground. It was hard work, but I was driven by the prospect of seeing my heroes in action later that afternoon and knowing that I was at least partly responsible for the game taking place.

After about 20 minutes, Roy came over and said that everyone was going to go to the canteen under the stand and get a cup of tea.

I joined them, enjoying the feeling of a hot cup warming life back into my hands.

But when everyone else got up to get back to work, I stayed behind. I wanted to have a look around and see what was under the stand.

I wandered up the corridor, my heart beating fast as I smelled stale liniment coming from the dressing room with a handwritten sign saying 'HOME' on it. I checked no-one was around and then pushed the door slightly ajar. It was where Bromley changed. The pegs they hung their clothes on, the bench they sat on while the committee delivered the team talks and the baths where they washed the mud away before changing back into their everyday clothes.

I stood there, allowing it all to sink in. This was it, the club's inner sanctum.

I sat down on the bench and closed my eyes, rubbing imaginary liniment into my thighs, fantasising I was part of the team about to take the field for an important cup game. It was almost a disappointment to open my eyes and see empty pegs and unoccupied benches.

Somehow, I managed to drag myself away and back to the corridor.

Opposite the changing rooms was another door. I couldn't help myself and let myself into a tiny room, the size of a large cupboard. It was where Charlie King sat and made his matchday announcements. I was a bit disappointed. I was expecting some kind of high tech set-up, straight out of *Tomorrow's World*, but instead found an old mono record player with a huge 1950s-style microphone dangling over it.

There was also a pile of marching LPs scattered across the tiny desk, although one of them looked a lot more dog-eared than the others. I wasn't surprised to see that it featured the familiar recordings of 'Colonel Bogey', 'The Dambusters' March' and 'Those Magnificent Men in their Flying Machines'.

Taking the record from the sleeve, I could see that it was badly scratched. Why didn't they just play one of the other LPs?

In the next room down the corridor, I found the nerve centre of Bromley Football Club. The boardroom.

Here, I imagined, the committee met to discuss team selection, where members took it in turns to put forward their ideas. The furniture was noticeably more opulent than anywhere else, giving the room an aura of power – an impression that was heightened by the ashtrays stuffed with cigar stubs.

In contrast, at the end of the corridor was the supporters' bar. I had never been in there as I was too young. But I'd walked past on many occasions and glanced inside where I'd seen a few wooden chairs and tables, with open packets of Sovereign and Number 6 cigarettes, where men drank beer under a cloud of thick smoke.

I slowly jogged up the players' tunnel, soaking up what it was like to make the short journey from changing room to the pitch, imagining the fans calling out my name.

I then picked up my shovel and carried on clearing the touchline.

●●●

It was a tense time as the referee, Mr AC McGuire, inspected our handiwork before deciding that the ground was in good enough condition for the game to take place.

My big hope was that it was also in bad enough condition to turn the game into a farce and earn Bromley a replay at Wembley in ten days' time.

For many years, I had assumed that Wembley played their home games at Wembley Stadium, but over the last few years had realised that this was unlikely.

Unlikely, but still possible. One of my favourite football facts was that Queen's Park, a useless Scottish Second Division team, played all their home games at Hampden Park, one of the world's biggest stadiums.

This fact was in just about every football book I owned.

So if a replay was to be needed, it wasn't out of the question that it would take place at the same ground England won the World Cup. Which is why I was hoping for a draw, although a win would have been even better. I just found it best to have downgraded expectations these days.

The crowd was pathetic. Even Charlie King admitted that it was 'around 300', which was the first time he'd publicly admitted to anything less than 400 spectators being in attendance. It was officially the worst gate of the season. The truth was even worse. There were only 85 people at the game. It didn't take long for me to count them.

I later found out from Peter that the poor gate had meant the club had lost money in staging the match. It cost Bromley and Wembley £4 each to cover the loss.

Bromley played with absolutely no confidence. It was painful to watch. No-one seemed to want the ball. And when they did get it, they got rid of it as soon as possible.

Eric Nottage was a lone figure up front, demonstrating that the gap left by Alan Stonebridge was a large one. I doubted it would ever be filled.

The Wembley goal – their only goal and the goal that won the match for them – was offside. Glaringly, blatantly, obviously so. I was beseeching the referee to change his mind but he ignored me. The frustration filled me with a rage I hadn't known since my sister got more cake than me at my 9th birthday party. I felt distraught. After all I'd done to get the pitch ready, I got to see my team lose to a goal that should never have been allowed.

To make things worse, the ball was clearly handled during the movement leading up to it and Alan Soper was booked for the unique offence of getting kicked in the face.

The feeling of injustice was overwhelming and over-shadowed the obvious signs of a team in terminal decline that were there for all but me to see – slack marking, bickering, indecision and poor positioning.

I yearned for more. And watching Bromley trudge off after yet another defeat in front of a handful of people led me to think that I should seriously consider doing something drastic.

●●●

I took the decision on the following Monday.

Demoralised by the Wembley loss, a feeling that was compounded by an 8–1 defeat suffered by Hayesford Park Reserves the next day, I was pushed beyond breaking point.

So when Dave, the boy I had befriended at school, asked me to go and watch Arsenal against Burnley with him the following Saturday, I agreed.

The thought of watching a successful team, packed with household names like Radford, Wilson and Graham was an exciting prospect.

My new friend had a connection with the team. He had once almost been Bobby Gould's babysitter when Dave lived in Hornchurch. Eager to outdo him, I told him about the time I got a lift home from Alan Stonebridge.

When that failed to get a response, I quizzed him about his Bobby Gould story. It seemed that he'd read in *Goal* magazine about how Bobby and his wife were looking for a babysitter so they could start going out again after their son Jonathan had been born. Dave immediately wrote to the magazine, offering his services, even though he was only 12 and lived over 100 miles away.

They didn't take him up on it. Dave reckoned they must have found someone who lived nearer.

And that was by no means his only brush with the Gunners' star players. When Dave and several friends started their own team in Hornchurch, Dave decided that they needed an Arsenal player as coach. He found a George Armstrong in the Dagenham telephone directory and called. His mum answered. George came to the phone and said yes, he played for the Gunners.

A few days later he was surprised to find about a dozen boys on his doorstep trying to persuade him to manage their team. The boys had taken the tube and then walked for several miles to get there. They left the Armstrong household still manager-less.

Like me, Dave had regularly sent his club Christmas cards with his address helpfully printed in huge letters on the back in the hopes of getting one in return.

Like me, he had failed to get a response.

This was someone who must surely understand the nature of my Bromley obsession. He had done the same kind of things that I'd done. And was still doing them.

The only condition I made about going to Arsenal was that he had to come and watch a Bromley game with me. I earmarked the Corinthian Casuals home game in early January.

I wanted him to see Bromley win and that was as near to as dead cert as it got in the Isthmian League.

He agreed. And we also decided that if it was OK with my mum, he would stay for dinner and possibly the night.

●●●

I actually felt guilty about not watching Bromley's next game, so was relieved when I heard that Saturday's FA Amateur Cup game had been called off for the kind of thing that only ever happened to Bromley.

Seven Oxford players had gone down with the flu. Charlie King wasn't sympathetic and announced that unlike the Oxford management, Bromley had taken the anti-flu precaution of naming 14 players for the game, which meant a couple could be bedridden and the game would still have taken place. As it turned out, Jim Roberts was the only flu victim leaving 13 players raring to go.

Mr King's petulance had no effect. The game was postponed until the following Saturday.

Knowing that I wouldn't be missing a Bromley game and clear of conscience, I met Dave at Bromley South station and we took the train to Victoria before getting on the underground to Arsenal, the nearest station to Highbury Stadium.

Everything about going to watch First Division football was on a bigger scale. Instead of a half-empty 47 bus, we were packed into a tube crammed with red and white scarves. When we emerged into the chilly North London night, the floodlights towered over the massive stadium, making Bromley's look like something out of a Subbuteo set. Despite being early, we had to queue for 15 minutes to get into the famous North Bank, a vast expanse of concrete terracing where the home supporters stood. It was soon packed.

As I turned round to survey the mass of bodies, a man towards the back raised his scarf and started to sing, his breath visible in the cold air. By the time he was a few words into the song, the whole North Bank seemed to have joined in. The noise was frightening yet electrifying too. Excitement was at fever pitch and the game hadn't even started yet. I felt like the only one not singing, partly because I wasn't sure of the words and partly because I would have felt self-conscious.

*Hello hello we are the Arsenal Boys*
*Hello hello we are the Arsenal Boys*
*And if you are a Tottenham fan*
*Surrender or you die*
*'Cos we all follow the Arsenal*

I knew that somewhere in the vast bank of people behind me were the skinheads and hooligans that I'd read about in the *Sun* and heard about at school. Dave and I were pressed against the fence, just behind the goal, which was reassuring. If there was any trouble, I would just climb over it and escape.

By kick-off, the North Bank was full, in contrast to the Clock End, where small pockets of Burnley fans stood huddled together.

The game was everything a Bromley game wasn't – fast, skilful and full of action. I'd seen both teams on *Match of the Day* in recent weeks, but nothing could have prepared me for seeing them so close up. The players were all familiar – I even had Typhoo tea cards of Ian Ure and Terry Neill, which I had a habit of cutting from the side of the box before my mum had finished it and subsequently got into trouble.

When Arsenal scored, the whole of the North Bank surged forward like a tidal wave. And when the whistle went for full-time, I could feel the relief of the thousands behind me as Arsenal held out a late fightback from Burnley to win 3–2.

By the time we got back to Bromley, we were both still on a high and walked back to my house singing:

> *Hello hello we are the Arsenal Boys*
> *Hello hello we are the Arsenal Boys*
> *And if you are a Tottenham fan*
> *Surrender or you die*
> *'Cos we all follow the Arsenal*

●●●

The next day at school, Dave took me aside and showed me a drawing of what looked like white space-age football boots, with dozens of tiny star-shaped studs designed, he told me, to give the wearer added traction when turning.

Eyes gleaming with excitement, he claimed that these boots would fit the foot like a sleek glove with nothing protruding above the leather. Their big selling point was the buckle that fastened onto the sole, thus allowing the 'foot to football interface' to remain uncluttered.

The boot was shown from every conceivable angle – above, below, from the left, from the right, from the inside. There were arrows leading from each innovative feature to his longhand explanation. He'd obviously spent a lot of time drawing them. The detail was amazing.

He explained that he'd designed the boots especially for John Radford, the Arsenal centre-forward. I had already realised this – there was a big caption above the drawing saying 'THE SENSATIONAL JOHN RADFORD FOOTBALL BOOT'. They were Dave's answer to the George Best boots that were currently being advertised in all the football magazines. George's boots were different simply for the sake of being different. They were purple, with a white stripe from top to toe, and had laces on the sides. They looked more like bowling shoes than football boots. I wanted a pair desperately.

Dave's idea was for John Radford to bring out and wear his own boots, which would be designed by himself. His only slight concern was that the white colour might make Radford seem less masculine, but eventually decided he was worrying over nothing. He didn't want any money, just for people to appreciate John's genius.

Dave was determined that John would enjoy playing in these, so had made comfort, in the form of internal cushioning, a big part of the design. He certainly didn't want a repeat of the 'Denis Law fiasco' where the Manchester United inside-left could be seen in the pages of *Shoot!*

Magazine advertising Mitre boots. But he refused to play in them. Mitre finally agreed that he could play in Adidas boots, as long as he disguised them as Mitre boots.

Dave was confident that John Radford would not only enjoy playing in his boots, but also score more goals as a direct result.

He'd sent weekly work-in-progress designs to John at Highbury Stadium and had rushed to the front door every morning when he heard the mail drop, confidently expecting to hear from John or his representative.

They hadn't yet got back to him.

I had to admit the boots looked good and I made him promise to make sure they were stocked in Eric Fright's sports shop in Bromley High Street. My loyalty to this particular establishment was due to Eric Fright being the Bromley captain when they won the Amateur Cup in 1949.

My own boots, which I wore every Sunday in a proper men's league, had three white stripes down the sides to make them look like Adidas. But that was a deception. They weren't Adidas at all. The big giveaway was the word 'WINFIELD' stamped on, thus identifying it to everyone as a cheap, Woolworths' own brand of boot. They were also a size too big, but my mum had assured me that I'd grow into them.

What I really craved was a pair of boots with a swivel base, cleverly designed to avoid injury when turning. I was convinced they would help me score more goals and I'd already approached my parents with the idea of getting some for Christmas and they had agreed. But recently, I'd had a growing desire for something else.

A sheepskin coat.

My Highbury trip had convinced me that I was really missing out by not having one. I would never forget looking behind me and seeing a sea of sheepskin. If I was going to really belong in the first division of football supporters, I had to get myself one.

It didn't even have to be real one. I'd seen a really good copy of one in the window of C&As in Bromley High Street and hinted to my dad that he might want to have a look at it.

Dad told me that I had to decide whether I wanted the coat or the boots. It was up to me. It was a question of what I wanted more.

•••

After Dave had put away his drawing, he asked if I wanted to play Killball. I'd never heard of it – Sevenoaks certainly didn't play it – but eager to join in, I agreed.

Killball was played in the cloakroom, usually when it was too wet to play conventional football outside.

A game was in progress as we arrived, so I was able to get a good look.

The idea seemed to be for one player to dribble a crudely made paper-and-sellotape ball through a human corridor of vicious, giggling schoolboys, whose aim was to kick the dribbler anywhere they could – shins, ankles, thighs.

Whatever it took to prevent him from reaching the other end and kicking the ball against the wall.

It was a game designed to bring out the idiot in any boy. While the sensible thing to do would be to concede defeat before any real damage was done, most seemed prepared to get a goal regardless of bumps and bruises received.

In order for you to join the corridor of kickers, you had to take your turn dribbling the ball. That's what they told me, anyway. So I steeled myself and, with the ball at my feet, headed towards the wall.

They seemed to be taking extra delight in kicking me. I

don't know if this was because I was a new boy or they just didn't like me, but I was being kicked from all directions. I even went down a couple of times, my ankles weakened by the constant assault and unable to support my weight. The strange thing was that I was loving it. Every yard I managed to get the ball nearer the wall felt like a triumph. And when I finally scored it felt almost as good as my goal for Hayesford Park Reserves.

The only difference being that then I didn't have a mass of cuts and bruises covering my lower leg.

I became addicted to Killball. It didn't matter whether I was kicking or being kicked, I found it exciting and started hanging around the cloakroom during breaks, hoping there would be enough people for a game.

# CHAPTER SIXTEEN

Most people, when given the choice, would rather watch a First Division team on a winning streak than an Isthmian League one that had lost 21 of their last 22 games.

I could understand that. But despite the sheer excitement of my Arsenal adventure, I felt I should take the second chance I'd been given to see Bromley take on Oxford City in the FA Amateur Cup.

Apparently, Oxford's flu epidemic was now under control and the game would definitely go ahead. Because the game was being played a week late, the winners' second-round opponents were already known.

Wealdstone away. A tough, but not impossible, task.

Bromley had prepared for today's clash by increasing their midweek training regime to two sessions instead of one. Alan Basham felt this would help towards the end of the game, a time where Bromley traditionally collapsed.

Les Brockman was the only new injury. He'd managed to break his jaw while playing in goal for his Sunday league team.

Ginger Warman was ineligible, having already played for Horsham in the Amateur Cup before he rejoined Bromley. He was replaced by David Wise, who had been ineligible for the last game against Wembley in the London Senior Cup. A game that Ginger Warman had been allowed to play in.

I joined The Grubby behind the goal. He had three cups of tea beside him and handed one to me. I took a sip and it tasted as though it had about eight sugars in it. Satisfied, I carried on drinking.

There was worry etched all over The Grubby's face. Oxford

hadn't lost to Bromley in nearly four years and had already done the double over us this season.

More impressively, they'd almost caused a massive FA Cup upset a few weeks previously, by taking the lead against Fourth Division Swansea Town in the second round proper, before doing a Bromley and going on to lose 5–1.

Still, any team capable of going that far in the FA Cup would have to be in with a real chance of lifting the FA Amateur Cup.

●●●

I was getting desperate for a win. Any win would do, for either Bromley or Hayesford Park Reserves. Both teams seemed to be taking it in turns to outdo each other in levels of humiliation. Hayesford Park Reserves had recently finished the first half of the season with an 8–1 defeat to Albermarle, giving us a record of one draw and nine defeats in the last ten games. This was an identical record to Bromley's.

Charlie King was clearly not yet in the holiday mood. His programme notes reflected my frustration at all the recent injustices. He was still upset about Oxford pulling out last weekend because some of them had flu. He also referred back to that game a month or so ago, when Oxford won 1–0. It was, he said, 'a game we should surely have won 2–1 if justice had been done, only miraculous goalkeeping by the Oxford keeper saved them'.

His final salvo was aimed at the supporters, reminding them to 'give our boys the vocal support so badly needed'.

Sadly, the few hundred fans that turned up ignored Mr King's pleas and stayed silent. Perhaps that was because they were unable to believe what they were witnessing.

There was a sense of *déjà vu* about the first incident of the game that occurred after just a couple of minutes. The

Bromley goalie was injured and had to be carried off. It had happened to Ian McGuire against Clapton and Walthamstow and now it was Alan Soper's turn. He got a kick on the knee and Jeff Bridge was forced to take over as goalie.

As if being totally rubbish wasn't enough, we now had to play with our right-back in goal. Luckily, Soper soon returned, swathed in bandages, ready to face the onslaught.

The visitors were slowly getting on top.

But then, a mere six hours after their last goal, Bromley scored through a Bobby Lennox cross which the Oxford goalie fumbled and then contrived to drop into the net. An eerie silence fell over the ground as though no-one could quite believe what they had just seen.

Slowly, the applause started. It kept building and building, until just about every one of the 263 (officially 400) spectators was standing and clapping.

The second goal for Lennox was greeted with similar levels of enthusiasm and by the time Nottage had added a third to give us a 3–0 half-time lead, the ground felt as though it had slowly come alive again after a long period of hibernation.

It took an hour for Oxford to finally find a way past Soper as Oram bundled the ball into the net. But before my head had had the chance to hit my hands, I saw the referee, Mr T.G.O.P. Bune of Camberley glance over at his linesman, Mr B.A.W. Brackpool of Oxted, who had his red flag raised. The goal was disallowed. The feeling of relief was enormous. Being a Bromley supporter, you really needed at least a three-goal cushion before you could start believing that a win was possible.

The Grubby and I were taking it in turns to nervously circumnavigate the ground, cup of tea and saucer in hand, barely able to watch. The tension really was unbearable. Suddenly, this useless team of ours was poised for a glorious, unexpected win. Against our bogey team in a competition that really, really mattered.

As I was walking past the Supporters' Club hut, with time up on my watch and Bromley 3–0 ahead, the unthinkable happened. Oxford were given a penalty for what looked like a double offence – a Jeff Bridge foul and a Pat Brown handball.

Morton rammed home the spot-kick.

3–1 to Bromley.

From the kick-off, Oxford got the ball back and with a simple exchange of passes, Ramsden scored.

3–2 to Bromley.

I hadn't even walked a circuit of the ground and Oxford had scored twice. Bromley looked in tatters. Why hadn't Mr Bune blown for full-time? This had to be at least the third minute of injury time.

I felt a familiar burning hatred for Alan Basham. It was obvious to me that the extra training that week had been too much. The players looked exhausted. They were out on their feet. This wasn't right. Bromley were meant to be fitter than ever, while Oxford were supposed to be getting over the flu.

And now, Oxford were mounting another attack. Just three minutes ago, I'd been fantasising about a trip to Wembley, as my team had been 3–0 up. Now, a 3–3 draw seemed the most likely result.

A cross came over from the right but it was plucked from the air by Alan Soper. Before he had time to kick the ball out, the referee finally blew his whistle. The Bromley players celebrated wildly, The Grubby was grinning from ear to ear and I was trying hard to stop myself from crying. It had reminded me why I loved football so much. Suddenly all the passion I'd been forced to suppress was threatening to pour out.

When you support a team that consistently loses, a win

means so much more than it does to a successful team whose supporters seemed to take it for granted. It's almost as though you have to go through all the misery to truly appreciate the feeling of victory.

Bromley's worst ever run had come to an end. It wasn't against a rubbish team like Corinthian Casuals, either. But one of the better amateur sides. The nightmare was finally over.

We had Wealdstone in the next round of the Amateur Cup to look forward to – a team lower in the Isthmian League table than the team we'd just beaten, Oxford City.

It was a shame such a small crowd had turned up to witness such a historic event, but I was sure there'd be a big increase in numbers for the Maidstone game on Boxing Day.

Every season has a turning point. This looked like being ours. The early exits from the FA Cup, Kent Floodlit Cup and Kent Senior Cup, as well as having no chance of winning the league, had actually worked in our favour.

Bromley were now free to concentrate on winning the Amateur Cup. For the fourth time in their history. On the three previous occasions, they had won 1–0 with the goal being scored by the player in the number eight shirt.

So far this season, eight different players had worn it, the latest being Dave Wise. I saw this as a sign. A highly obscure one, but a sign nonetheless.

●●●

I was really looking forward to Christmas Day. But I was looking forward to Boxing Day even more, because it was always one of my favourite days in the football calendar. Boxing Day was traditionally a time where local derbies took place, since long-distance travel was particularly difficult.

Bromley were playing Maidstone at home. The fixture had

added significance – the majority of the Maidstone team were former Bromley players.

But that was tomorrow. Today was the day we all opened our presents. I still hadn't got out of the habit of waking early on Christmas Day, even though I hadn't put out a stocking in two years.

I crept through to the lounge and had a peek under the tree. There were four packages with my name on them – one, I knew, would be a box of Maltesers from my sister. We always got each other a box of Maltesers.

When the rest of the family appeared we all wished each other a merry Christmas and then got on with the business of opening presents.

I immediately tore the carefully wrapped paper from what looked like my main present and felt a surge of joy when I saw what it was.

It was a sheepskin coat. Not a real one, but the one I'd seen at C&A. They'd called it a 'driving coat' and it was made from a harsh synthetic material that felt a bit like foam rubber. It was a light beige colour, which, from a distant, looked like sheepskin. The lining was a white, fluffy wool substitute that smelled of chemicals and the collar was made from the same material. The pockets were deep, woolly and warm.

I put it on and went to look in the mirror. It looked fantastic – a perfect fit.

My next present was just as exciting. I had been under the impression that I'd be getting either a sheepskin or a pair of football boots with a swivel base. Incredibly, I had been given both.

I tried the boots on, savouring the smell of leather coming from the box, enjoying the feel of brand new black laces which threaded easily into the eyes of the boots. I then went out into the garden and practised swivelling on the rotating studs, which were arranged in a circle on the front part of the sole. It felt amazing – whichever way I turned, the boots turned. I couldn't wait for the next Hayesford Park Reserves game, even though it was still over a week away. We would be playing Cudham Reserves, a team so appalling that we considered we were in with a chance of beating them.

I packed my boots away, put my sheepskin back on and went for a walk, eager to be seen in my new coat. I went past 'Judo' Al Hayes's house, hoping he'd be out in the drive but he wasn't. I could see the red, green and yellow lights of his Christmas tree through a gap in the curtain and hear the excited screaming of children. He was spending the day with his family. Not even 'Judo' Al Hayes washed his car on Christmas Day.

Next, I went to the park, but it was closed. There was no-one around to admire my coat or to kick a ball around with in my new boots. I then went to the shops, but they too were closed. I got home just in time for Christmas dinner and sat at the table, unwilling to take my new coat off.

What a great Christmas it had been. A sheepskin coat, some new boots, a *Morecambe and Wise Christmas Special*, loads of sweets, a brilliant *Top of the Pops* with the Beatles, Clodagh Rogers and Blue Mink, a whole bottle of Cydrax fizzy apple juice to myself, record tokens from both aunts, Twiglets and *Carry on Christmas*.

And just when I thought it couldn't get any better, I unwrapped my final present – one I'd been saving up. It was the latest *All Stars Football Book* edited by Jimmy Armfield, the England left-back.

I was soon lost in its pages, savouring every picture and carefully reading every story. I couldn't believe how Armfield had managed to find time to fit in book editing alongside playing for Blackpool as well as his country. He'd done a really good job.

The day finished in the traditional way with the third annual Super Christmas Floodlit Cup, a Subbuteo extravaganza utilising the floodlights I'd got three Christmases ago.

As I only had three teams, participating clubs were selected because they played in either blue shirts with white shorts (Everton, Birmingham, etc.) or red shirts with white shorts (Manchester United, Charlton Athletic, etc.).

The all-white strip, which had been modified with blue trim, was Bromley only. They always won. This time, by 9–0 over Portsmouth, who, in the real world, were struggling in the Second Division.

After packing the teams away, I finally went to bed. Tomorrow was also looking like a big day, with the newly on-form Bromley taking on lowly Maidstone United.

I'd be there to see it. In my sheepskin coat. I felt almost as excited at the prospect of Boxing Day as I had on the night before Christmas.

•••

I wanted everyone in the ground to admire my new sheepskin coat, so I wandered around slowly, stopping frequently and posing in the hope that someone would notice. Despite these efforts, Derek was the only person who mentioned it. He disappointingly complimented me on my new driving coat instead of my sheepskin.

I bought my programme from Charlie King, who had recently added Programme Seller to his other duties as Ground Announcer and Chairman.

I then bought three cups of tea from Peter in the tea hut. After exchanging 'Merry Christmas', he asked if I could join him after the game. Intrigued, I agreed.

I then went to sit next to The Grubby and handed him his

teas. We sat in silence, studying our programmes.

The team news was undramatic. Jeff Bridge was spending Christmas in France, staying at a hotel owned by a former Bromley teammate, Colin England. Bobby Lennox was going back up north. John Sullivan wasn't publicly revealing his festive plans, but they didn't include playing for Bromley. He had made himself unavailable.

Not that he would've been picked.

The crowd was a good one – certainly bigger than for the last couple of games combined. I wondered if it was the result of the great win against Oxford, the lure of Maidstone United or simply a case of people desperate to get out of the house.

Both teams got an unusually good reception. It was odd seeing so many ex-Bromley players in the gold shirts and black shorts of Maidstone. It felt as though they'd wandered into the visitors' changing room by mistake and put the wrong shirts on.

Bromley looked full of enthusiasm and confidence, with one exception. A very grumpy looking Ginger Warman, who had the air of a child who hadn't got what he'd wanted for Christmas. My thoughts immediately turned to his recent disciplinary record which wasn't pretty. He'd only just finished a three-week suspension for being sent off in a Post Office match. The details of his offence had never been made public, which led to all sorts of speculation until Peter revealed that a bad foul was responsible.

His behaviour in Bromley colours hadn't been much better, with two bookings in the past month. I just hoped he'd last the full 90 minutes today, but wasn't overly optimistic.

The game quickly settled into a clash between two ultra-defensive sides both seemingly looking for a draw. Attacks were few and far between from either side until a flowing move, cruelly involving four ex-Bromley players, led to

Maidstone taking the lead just after half-time.

This seemed to incense Ginger Warman even more. He appeared to take it as a personal affront and launched himself into a series of bloodcurdling tackles.

When his former team-mate Bobby Evans returned the compliment with a tough-but-fair challenge, Ginger didn't take it well. He retaliated so violently that Evans had to go off for treatment.

The Warman sending-off that followed the incident was inevitable, as it had been from the moment he took the field. Bromley were now a man and a goal down.

But finally Alan Basham's fitness training paid dividends. In the last minute, usually the time for opposition teams to score, Bromley got an equaliser. Pat Brown made up for the dismissal of his fellow postman by putting Eddie Green through to finish with a fierce drive.

It had come too late for me to write about in my programme. I had already packed both of them away and was heading to the tea hut for my meeting with Peter.

I jumped in the air with excitement at seeing such a great goal just when I'd given up any hope of Bromley avoiding defeat. It was turning into an unforgettable Christmas.

And when Peter told me I'd got the tea-making job in the tea hut and that I'd even get paid, it felt like the best Christmas ever.

# CHAPTER SEVENTEEN

The holiday was spent mainly down at the park. I wasn't the only one with new boots. There seemed to have been an outbreak of seasonal boot buying and just about every boy was sporting a new pair. The George Best-autographed Stylo boots were definitely the most popular, and there were also a few pairs of Puma Hat Tricks.

There didn't seem to be any discernible difference in the standard of football, although we were all convinced otherwise, putting every good shot or accurate pass down to the new boots.

I was taking every opportunity to turn sharply, so I could swivel on the rotational studs. This meant I went on aimless meandering runs, filled with as many turns as humanly possible, even when there was no-one anywhere near me. I think I just loved the feeling of swivelling around.

The only downside was that new boots can get quite uncomfortable, especially if you don't ease them in. Which was why, one by one, boys were wandering home, complaining of sore feet and blisters.

But however much pain they were in, I knew they would all be back tomorrow for more.

●●●

The bad news that had filtered through from South London was that Corinthian Casuals had beaten their landlords, Tooting and Mitcham, and had trebled their total points for the season. Although it was technically an away game, I felt slightly better knowing that it had also been a home game, which made their winning slightly more understandable.

I was glad to see Bromley were taking the threat seriously. The headline on the back page of the *Bromley and Kentish Times* read 'BROMLEY PLAN TO END POOR RUN'.

It was what I wanted to see. After 22 league games without a win, it was good to see the club were taking steps to turn things around.

I eagerly read the article and, by the end, was feeling a little bewildered. The plan seemed alarmingly vague. From what I could make out, the big idea was to beat Corinthian Casuals and Walthamstow Avenue at home, as well as Maidstone and Dulwich away, thus avoiding finishing in the bottom two and having their worst-ever season.

That was it. That was the much-trumpeted plan.

Part one of this would be taking place at Hayes Lane the next day, with the home fixture against Corinthian Casuals. Dave would be coming with me and I was desperate for Bromley to do well in front of him.

It was also important for them to play well because it was the last game before the massive Amateur Cup second-round tie at Wealdstone's Station Road ground a week later.

I felt sorry for Charlie King. He might well be going on a round the world cruise to places like Australia and Africa, but I was sure he'd rather be going to Wealdstone.

I knew I would.

•••

I had severely over-committed myself. Not only had I arranged to start work at the tea hut but I'd also promised to take Dave along to the game, which was one of the most important of the season.

It was the first of Bromley's 'must win' games in their

plan to avoid finishing last. My lack of organisation meant that Dave was forced to watch the entire match on his own, while I made tea for the thirsty supporters. This was a serious blow as I had intended to give him background on all the players and a running commentary, in the hopes of persuading him to come and watch all the games with me.

Although Corinthian Casuals had won against Tooting, I was confident they wouldn't be able to follow it with a win at Hayes Lane. My theory was that they only beat Tooting because they were able to watch them practise – and therefore get a look at their tactics – due to sharing a ground.

Bromley would be a different matter, especially since we were now unbeaten for two matches.

I got to the ground at 2.30pm and reported to the tea hut. Peter was already there and the giant water boiler in the corner was emitting a mixture of gurgling sounds and a shrill whistle. This, I was told, indicated that it was boiling.

Part of my training was to measure out the tea leaves from

## Fight is on to avoid finishing next to bottom

NEXT-TO-BOTTOM Bromley hope to gain their first Isthmian League win since September 13 when they entertain bottom club Corinthian Casuals at Hayes Lane this Saturday (k.o. 3). Bromley must beat Casuals and take points from fellow strugglers Walthamstow, who they have still to meet at home, Dulwich (away) and Maidstone (away) if they are to finish any higher this season (writes Tony Flood).

Unless Bromley continue the improvement shown in their last two games, they are certain to finish 19th of the 20 Isthmian League clubs, making this their worst-ever season.

They have never finished lower than 17th since they rejoined the Isthmian League in 1952-3 after an absence of nearly 50 years. In the 1952-3 season Bromley came third, and in 1953-4 they won the Isthmian League championship. Since then Bromley have finished 3rd, 2nd, 3rd, 4th, 9th, 6th, 1st, 14th, 7th, 15th, 9th, 16th, 14th, 13th and, last season, 17th.

So they will be all out to regain some pride by beating Casuals.

Bonney, C Brown, Lewis, P Brown, Pettet, Warman, Wise, Nottage, Green, Lennox.

This means that John Sullivan is left out. Jeff Bridge will return from holiday in time to play against Wealdstone on Saturday week in the away F.A. Amateur Cup second round tie.

Providing there is a definite result in the Wealdstone match, Bromley travel to play Erith and Belvedere on Saturday, January 17 in the Kent Senior Cup, the winners being away to either Tonbridge or Deal Town in the next round.

NOT FIT

a massive box and put them into a huge metallic teapot. I was impressed to learn that it could hold enough tea to fill over 50 cups.

Although this wasn't my first job I was still nervous. I'd been sacked from my last job at the chemist's for being too demanding and before that the only work experience I had was a paper round for a year and various bob-a-job week tasks for the Boy Scouts – the highlight of which was washing 'Judo' Al Hayes's car for a shilling.

My job at the tea hut was less glamourous, but no less exciting. I was responsible for taking orders and pouring the tea. Peter then took the money, which was often accompanied by grumbling as the price had recently gone up to 6d.

When the first customer appeared at the hatch, Peter showed me how it was done. 'Yes, mate?' he asked and the man who was standing there said 'White with two, please'. This, I learnt, was tea speak for a cup of tea with milk and two sugars.

The next customer wandered up. I was thrust into action, thankful that my first customer was known to me. It was The Grubby.

'Yes mate?' I asked. He wanted three teas, all with milk and four sugars. Only after he had put in his order did it seem to register that I was the one serving him and therefore wouldn't need my usual cup of tea. He changed his order to two teas with milk and four sugars.

After a slightly confused Grubby had returned to his place behind the goal, I served a steady stream of customers without mishap.

It felt great to be part of the inner circle at Bromley FC. Especially as the tea hut was a stepping stone to the big one – working in the Supporters' Club hut on the other side of the ground. I wore my enamel badge on my sheepskin coat with even more pride than usual.

Just before the game kicked off, I saw Dave enter the ground. He reluctantly walked over to the main stand and sat down, looking round. He finally saw my frantic waves and grudgingly waved back. I don't think he was too pleased about having to watch on his own.

Still, I'd get to see him afterwards, by which time I was convinced he would already be a loyal Bromley fan. I hadn't warned him how useless the opposition were – I wanted him to get the impression that Bromley were really good – not that Casuals were really bad.

I got back to work, stopping occasionally to take a sip of tea or have a bite to eat.

I spent much of what I earned at the tea hut on Club Biscuits. It made a change paying for them, as until recently, I had been getting them free, in common with a significant percentage of boys at school.

It had started when one of them had written to Jacobs, the manufacturer, after noticing that the photos on the wrapper showed more raisins than were actually in the biscuit. They wrote back apologetically and sent him a box packed with their products.

Word soon spread and before long literally hundreds of boys were writing to Jacobs with similar complaints. Jacobs obligingly sent boxes by return of post until they cottoned on to the fact that just about the entire population of Beckenham was feeling hard done by when they looked at the wrapper of a Club biscuit. After that, people got nothing but a polite apology.

Unfortunately, after I'd got through my box of free samples, I was left with a taste for their product which made the tea hut an expensive place for me to work.

•••

The view from the hut wasn't quite as impressive as I'd hoped. The good thing was that we had a slightly elevated position. The bad thing was that the position was rubbish, overlooking a corner flag. It was the wrong end, too. Bromley were attacking the other goal, which meant I wasn't likely to see much action.

How wrong I was.

Something had changed with Corinthian Casuals. They still didn't look like proper footballers, with their chocolate and pink shirts, but they were playing with a confidence I hadn't seen from them before.

The action was all taking place in front of me, prompted by our nemesis from earlier in the season, Chris Joy. It was he who set up the opening goal, with a blistering shot that Soper could only parry into the path of their right-winger and we were in the unthinkable position of being 1–0 down to Corinthian Casuals.

Their second goal followed a few minutes before half-time, just as the water was reaching boiling point and I was preparing to pour it into the pot. The centre-forward beat the offside trap and we were suddenly two down to the worst team in the league.

Even Peter was at a loss for words. We poured the half-time refreshments in stunned silence.

As luck would have it, much of the activity in the second half also took place at our end. Eric Nottage hit the bar with a great header and then Alan Bonney punched the ball into the Casuals net, while trying to make it look like he'd headed it. I didn't know what he was thinking – not only was it cheating, but it was something nobody would ever be able to get away with.

The scorer of the visitors' second goal added a third just before the end, leaving just enough time for Postman Pat Brown to get a consolation for Bromley seconds from the final whistle, when he headed home from an Eddie Green corner.

As the players trooped off, I went around the terraces with my Double Diamond tray, picking up the used cups and saucers.

Watching the small crowd file out of the ground, I thought back to September, when I had left the Corinthian Casuals away fixture thinking that I was glad there was one team I could look down on.

I was willing to bet that the handful of Casuals supporters who had witnessed today's game were now thinking exactly the same thing.

Dave and I walked back to my house, eager to arrive in plenty of time to see the new *Dr Who*. Even though it was obvious that Patrick Troughton was irreplaceable, I was interested to see what Jon Pertwee would be like. According to the *Radio Times*, Brigadier Lethbridge-Stewart from the previous series would be appearing in the first episode, so there would at least be one familiar face.

I didn't want to broach the subject of the afternoon's

**The threat of coming last now faces Bromley**

BROMLEY 1, CORINTHIAN CASUALS 3

ALAN BONNEY

football just yet. It was going to be hard to come up with a convincing defence for Bromley's ineptitude and I needed time to come up with something plausible.

One theory was that Dave's presence was responsible. It made sense – we had gone two games unbeaten, he goes to watch the next one and we lose to the bottom team. On the way home, he had accused me of jinxing Arsenal, after seeing their result on a colour TV in the window of Radio Rentals on the High Street. They'd been held at home by Blackpool and had now gone four games without a win since I'd been to Highbury. Dave thought that Bromley's uselessness had some-how rubbed off on the Gunners thanks to me.

There was a definite air of tension between us. We later agreed never to watch each other's teams again.

However, the tension resurfaced later that night, as we fell out for the only time that season.

It wasn't about football, but about women.

What had started out as a discussion on the relative merits of Una Stubbs and Diana Rigg soon turned heated. He insisted Diana was better looking, but it was obvious to me that Una was much prettier.

Neither Dave nor I was prepared to give ground. As the anger took hold of me, my voice got higher and I started to screech in defence of Una Stubbs. He was just as loud in his claims of Diana Rigg being more fanciable and the vein on his forehead stuck out as he, too, was overcome by fury.

I wanted to punch him and I could see that he wanted to punch me. I was shaking with anger – how could he not see Una's obvious beauty?

We spent the rest of the evening gazing intently at the TV, jaws set in a determined manner, studiously ignoring each other.

•••

By the time we went into WH Smith to spend my record tokens the next day, we were back on speaking terms. I loved going upstairs to the record department with the equivalent of money in my pocket. It almost made up for the hundreds of times I'd been in there unable to afford anything.

Under normal circumstances, I would have been tempted by *Abbey Road*, the Beatles' latest, and *Ssssh* by Ten Years After, which The Grubby insisted was the greatest album ever made.

Then there was the matter of 'Two Little Boys' by Rolf Harris. Although I'd never have admitted it to anyone, this was a single I really loved. The trouble was, I hated listening to it when other people were around, because I found the 'leave you dying' lines incredibly emotional and had difficulty disguising its effect on me. Not only was it a great single, but it was also the last Number One of the sixties and I was convinced it would soon become a collectors' item.

The other single I badly wanted was 'In the Year 2535' by Zager and Evans, even though Dave had cruelly joked that the song was about the year Bromley would next win a game.

There were plenty of records I wanted to spend my tokens on. But this was not the time for buying something I wanted. It was time to buy something that would make me look cool at school, despite Dave's protestations.

I picked *Tighten Up Volume 2* from the rack. It was a reggae collection and I knew a few songs from it – 'Liquidator', 'Longshot Kick De Bucket' and 'Elizabethan Reggae'. I didn't particularly like them, but that wasn't the point. Next, I found a copy of *Motown Chartbusters 3*, which had few things I actually liked on it. There was just enough left over to treat myself to the 'Ruby Don't Take Your Love To Town' single by Kenny Rogers, which I was determined no-one at school would find out about.

As for the LPs, I was equally determined that everyone at school was going to find out about them.

# ISTHMIAN LEAGUE HOW THEY STAND

## 9TH JANUARY 1970

|                  | P   | W  | D  | L  | F  | A  | Pts |
|------------------|-----|----|----|----|----|----|-----|
| Wycombe W        | 24  | 16 | 6  | 2  | 52 | 16 | 38  |
| Enfield          | 22  | 15 | 6  | 1  | 50 | 12 | 36  |
| Sutton Utd       | 25  | 14 | 7  | 4  | 50 | 26 | 35  |
| St. Albans City  | 28  | 13 | 8  | 7  | 42 | 34 | 34  |
| Barking          | 24  | 14 | 5  | 5  | 58 | 24 | 33  |
| Hitchin Town     | 24  | 10 | 8  | 6  | 39 | 27 | 28  |
| Wealdstone       | 24  | 12 | 3  | 9  | 36 | 30 | 27  |
| Hendon           | 21  | 9  | 7  | 5  | 39 | 28 | 25  |
| Oxford City      | 24  | 10 | 5  | 9  | 38 | 39 | 25  |
| Kingstonian      | 24  | 9  | 6  | 9  | 35 | 33 | 24  |
| Clapton          | 25  | 9  | 6  | 10 | 39 | 44 | 24  |
| Tooting & Mit    | 18  | 9  | 4  | 5  | 39 | 25 | 22  |
| Leytonstone      | 23  | 9  | 4  | 10 | 33 | 25 | 25  |
| Dulwich Hamlet   | 26  | 6  | 9  | 11 | 31 | 43 | 21  |
| Woking           | 25  | 8  | 5  | 12 | 35 | 36 | 21  |
| Ilford           | 25  | 5  | 10 | 10 | 27 | 47 | 20  |
| Maidstone Utd    | 24  | 6  | 4  | 14 | 31 | 49 | 16  |
| Walthamstow A    | 24  | 5  | 4  | 15 | 28 | 52 | 14  |
| **BROMLEY**      | **25** | **3** | **3** | **19** | **18** | **74** | **9** |
| Corinthian Cs    | 26  | 3  | 2  | 21 | 23 | 67 | 8   |

# CHAPTER EIGHTEEN

Going back to school after the holidays was marred by only one thing – The Grubby had decided not to go back to school.

He'd got a job at Debenhams on Bromley High Street, working in the carpet department. They'd evidently been impressed with him when he'd gone for an interview for a part-time job a few months earlier and had rung him offering him full-time work. I wouldn't see him until Bromley's next home game. Bizarrely, they didn't have any scheduled for over a month.

It was a novelty for me to enjoy going to school. I made sure my reggae and Motown LPs were tucked prominently under the arm of my sheepskin jacket as I walked through the wooden doors on the first morning back.

My hair had also been cut shorter. I hadn't been brave enough to get the full crop, but it was short enough for me to feel the cold chill of winter on my neck and ears.

To complete the look, I had a pair of monkey boots, which were a bit like Doc Martens but without the steel toecaps.

I was making a statement. I just wasn't sure what it was.

•••

On my first day back, all the talk was of three of the skinheads who had achieved celebrity status by featuring in a tabloid expose of football hooligans.

Being highly impressionable, this was enough to set off a fresh bout of hero worshipping which stopped just short of asking them to autograph the photo in the paper.

More than anything, I wanted to be like them.

So when one of them started talking to me about the *Tighten Up Volume 2* LP I was carrying round, I was only too eager to offer to lend it to him.

He seemed pleased about this and then we talked football for a few minutes. I felt flattered that he was even talking to me. What's more, other boys were seeing it.

I handed over the LP, like a worshipper making an offering to a god.

I never saw *Tighten Up Volume 2* again.

•••

Bromley's judgment of a good footballer was far from flawless. Amongst their more forgettable moments was getting rid of Ginger Warman's brother Phil when he couldn't make the Bromley first team. Warman Junior went on to play 364 games for Charlton Athletic.

There was also the case of Peter Cadman, a man who had gone from Bromley Reserves to Carshalton's first team and become their top scorer. He was now being talked about as a potential amateur international.

The latest example of Bromley's unique inability to recognise talent when it was right under their noses came in the form of John Faulkner.

He'd been a reserve-team fixture, but was kept out of the first team by a succession of unconvincing centre-halves.

Faulkner then decided on a move to Sutton United, where he quickly became one of their stars and played a big part in an FA Cup run which had culminated in a stunning upset win over Bromley's conquerors Hillingdon Borough.

This had earned Sutton a home tie against the Football League champions, Leeds United. Although they lost 6–0,

Faulkner made such a good impression that Leeds offered him a contract.

When I read about him lining up against Burnley in his debut, alongside greats like Giles, Bremner and Lorimer, I wondered how Bromley had once again managed to get it so wrong.

Bromley had the worst defensive record in the Isthmian league and were about to come up against Wealdstone in the second round of the Amateur Cup. And we were going into the game with Phil Amato at centre-half, instead of someone who was good enough for the best team in the country.

●●●

The first thing I did when I got to Wealdstone was check out their tea huts. Although I'd never taken much notice of them before, I now started taking a professional interest. What water-boiling equipment did they have? Did they use tea leaves or the recent innovation, tea bags? What snacks did they sell?

The Wealdstone huts both seemed to be short-staffed. The queues were too big and the service far slower than we provided at Hayes Lane.

I wasn't surprised to learn from the programme that the club were looking for more volunteers to work in them.

I took my tea, which was good although possibly a bit over-stewed, to the terraces by the halfway line. This was where we always stood, waiting for the toss of the coin which would decide which goal Bromley would be attacking. We then went and stood behind it.

There was a sizeable Bromley contingent, which didn't surprise me. This was our last chance for glory in a major competition.

The other main aim for the season would be finishing above Corinthian Casuals, a less lofty ambition than winning the FA Amateur Cup.

There was a good atmosphere at Wealdstone. The home side were having a good season and relied on a physical approach, much like Leeds United, although Wealdstone obviously weren't quite as good.

The pitch was wet and slippery, but the home supporters were saying that it had been that way for weeks. This was one of the good things about non-league football – supporters of both teams mixed freely.

Bromley had brought a strong team, the same 11 that started against Oxford in the previous round, and they looked full of purpose when they ran out onto the field. It was as if they realised this was their last chance to salvage something out of a season that had gone badly wrong.

The early signs weren't good, in that Wealdstone scored twice within the first 15 minutes. The first one was due to the mud. The ball got stuck in it and Bernie Bremer, the hometown favourite, forced the ball home. A few minutes later, he struck again with a lucky shot from the edge of the area.

The talk immediately turned to Barking. We were swept by a wave of fear that a repeat of the 8–0 loss to them earlier in the season was a real possibility.

Bremer seemed determined to get his hat-trick and this is probably what saved Bromley from total annihilation. He was on a single-minded mission and refused to pass or even communicate in any way with his teammates, instead preferring to ignore everyone else and shoot every time he got the ball.

At the other end, our end, Bromley were finally starting to threaten. Phil Amato's cross was met by Eric Nottage for about the millionth goal of his career. For once, it didn't feel like a consolation goal, but one that had got us back in the game.

Bremer then hit the bar as a reminder that his personal crusade wasn't yet over, but it was Bromley who scored next. A great cross by David Wise was met on the volley by Eddie Green and the scores were level at 2–2.

This was cup football at its most exciting. The game couldn't have been closer with Bromley and Bernie Bremer taking it in turns to attack.

Just before half-time, the travelling supporters' hearts sank as someone who wasn't Bremer put Wealdstone back in the lead from a corner.

As the players trooped off for their oranges, we weren't too dispirited. Only 3–2 down and still in with a chance of a win or even a replay at Hayes Lane. The pitch had, by now, turned into a quagmire which nullified the more skilful Wealdstone midfield.

The second half was undoubtedly Bromley's best 45 minutes of the season. Despite playing uphill, they mounted attack after attack.

Wise and Pettet had shots blocked on the line. Eddie Green's drive missed the target by a matter of inches.

Meanwhile, Alan Soper was in inspired form. The Wealdstone fans barely believed me when I told them he'd been in bed with flu the day before. But it was true. Peter had told me on the way to the ground.

Somehow, the score hadn't change since half-time. Then, in the last minute, Eddie Green scurried down the touchline and put in a curling cross towards Eric Nottage, the master converter of such chances and easily our top scorer. Nottage rose at the far post, just needing the slightest touch to level the scores.

But the ball somehow evaded his forehead. It went out for a Wealdstone throw and Mr RF Wood (Brighton) blew his whistle for full-time.

We had lost . . . but in the most glorious fashion possible. For the first time in a long time, we had been every bit as good as our opponents. This, of course, was no comfort whatsoever. If anything, it made it worse.

I looked over at Roy. His thick lens magnified his eyes and the beginnings of a tear were clearly visible.

I think we all knew how he felt.

•••

I was seriously wondering just how much bad news it was possible for me to take. The Wealdstone result really hurt. We could easily have won. We should have won.

The next day, I was looking through the other results when I saw the news I had feared. Corinthian Casuals had won their league match against Maidstone 4–2, giving them a three-game winning streak. This meant that Bromley were now just one point clear and in serious danger of finishing last for the first time in their history.

What were they going to do to make sure this didn't happen?

In Charlie King's absence (he had just left for his round the world cruise) the committee had sprung into action, perhaps sensing an opportunity to make some changes.

Acting Chairman Bill Woodward announced that for the foreseeable future, committee meetings and training nights would be held on Tuesdays, so that more up-to-date news on injuries and availability could be obtained.

Bromley had also signed a new centre-half, John Miles from Maidstone United. The fact that he had been playing for the team with the third-worst defensive record in the league didn't fill me with confidence, but at least he was really tall, which had been Gasmask's main asset.

The bad football news continued the next day, when

Hayesford Park Reserves lost 6–0 at home to Farnborough Youth – a team that had only won twice all season.

The result, and my performance in particular, had a galvanising effect on me. I had noticed that I tended to fade spectacularly after about half an hour, spending the rest of matches as more of a spectator than a player. I decided to take my lead from Alan Basham and increase my fitness. This would include walking more and cycling to Bromley games instead of getting the bus. The only reason I hadn't done this before was because I'd had nowhere to keep my bike safe; but now I'd be able to bring it into the tea hut.

But before I could start getting fit, there was the trip to Erith and our last chance to salvage something from the season.

●●●

The coach to Erith and Belvedere for the Kent Senior Cup tie was full.

It was while I was talking to Roy about Bromley's chances that everything slowly came together in my mind – the Arsenal trip, the school celebrity skinheads, Charlie King's exhortations for supporters to get behind the team.

Suddenly, I knew what I had to do.

The huge losses to Oxford City and Hillingdon Borough had been notable for the sheer volume of noise produced by the home supporters. They created an intimidating atmosphere for the visitors and I suddenly realised that I would be able to influence the outcome of this afternoon's match. On my previous trip to Erith and Belvedere for the Kent Floodlit Cup fixture, the home support had been virtually non-existent – polite clapping had greeted the goals. All of them.

It would be easy to make Bromley feel as though they were playing at home.

All it needed was a leader for the Bromley supporters – one who could lead the chants and show the team that they had plenty of support. It was a role I felt I was destined to fill.

Once inside the ground, we stood in small cliques on the terraces behind the goal Bromley would be attacking in the first half.

I stared fiercely at the opposition fans who were scattered behind the goal at the other end. From a distance, I felt confident that my fake sheepskin would look like the real thing. They would think I was a genuine skinhead. Now was the time to show them that Bromley were a force to be reckoned with.

I raised an imaginary black and white scarf over my head and screamed 'Gimme a B' to my fellow Bromley supporters.

There was an embarrassed silence.

I looked around desperately at the 43 people who had come down on the coach with me. Some stared back with bemusement. Others avoided looking at me.

I wished I'd never started, but now felt compelled to carry on as it felt slightly less humiliating than asking for a B and then leaving it at that.

'Gimme an R,' I roared.

No-one gave me an R. Not Derek, not Roy and not Peter. Neither did John Self, the Supporters' Club Honorary Secretary. I thought I'd be able to count on him, but no.

I felt my face flush with embarrassment. It was too late to pull out now. My voice was faltering and had taken on a pleading, rather than demanding tone.

'Gimme an O.'

At last, someone responded. The shout of 'O' came from an unexpected source – behind the Erith and Belvedere goal at the opposite end. One of the home fans had clearly taken pity on me.

Satisfied that I'd saved face and proven myself as the

leader of the Bromley end at the tender age of 14, I sat down on the cold concrete to enjoy my cup of well-made tea.

Erith and Belvedere ran out onto the field looking supremely confident. They had every right, having beaten us twice already in the space of a few months.

Postman Pat was controversially relegated to the bench and the number five shirt had been given to new signing John Miles. Eddie Green was 'going away on business', which puzzled me a bit as I'd thought he was another postman.

Apart from that, the team was essentially the same side that had won just one game out of their last 26.

The pitch was a mudbath. Only the odd blade of grass was visible and we later learnt that the referee had only passed it fit for play minutes before the kick-off.

Bromley's plan was soon obvious. At the slightest hint of danger, such as a corner, the entire team apart from Bobby Lennox took up defensive positions.

Then Lennox, who had almost caused me to go to Ravenswood School instead of Langley Park when I found out he was a teacher there, came close to putting Bromley into the lead with a great shot from the edge of the penalty area. But apart from that lone effort, it was all Erith and Belvedere.

Bromley's ten-man defence was holding. At half-time, it was still goalless and we switched ends so we could still stand behind the goal Bromley were attacking. As we passed the Erith fans, who were also switching ends, I ruined my skinhead image by wishing them good luck for the second half.

The next 45 minutes was similar to the first 45 minutes – plenty of Erith attacking and plenty of Bromley defending. Alan Basham's plan had clearly been to play for a replay and his team seemed to be on track.

Then, in the last minute, things took a turn for the worse.

Not in the usual form, which was conceding a goal, but in the sending off of Roy Pettet.

He'd been fouled by Brendan Greatorex, the Erith and Belvedere skipper, and retaliated by pushing him. The referee, Mr FR Pestell (Rochester) pointed sternly towards the changing rooms. Bromley had lost their inspirational captain.

Overcome with emotion, I decided to try once more to inspire my fellow supporters into seeing our team through those difficult dying minutes.

I raised my hands above my head, like I'd seen that North Bank fan do a few months back before the Arsenal v Burnley game. At the time, I'd been impressed by how rapidly everyone else joined in. I decided to adapt his chant, even though the name of today's opponents made it all a little unwieldy.

'Hello hello we are the Bromley Boys,' I sang clearly, confident that this time I wouldn't be a lone voice.

'Hello hello we are the Bromley Boys,' I continued, as Derek and the others groaned. Not at me, but at a Warman header that had gone just wide. That was when I realised I was being ignored.

Once again, I was left to continue the chant on my own. As I was doing it, I became painfully aware of just how ridiculous the words coming out of my mouth were.

What had sounded so powerful and inspiring coming from thousands of voices at Highbury just sounded pathetic coming from one squeaky voice at the Park View Ground in Erith.

Especially the words:

> *'And if you are an Erith and Belvedere fan*
> *Surrender or you die*
> *'Cos we all follow the Bromley'*

I finished on a near whisper, just as Mr Pestell's whistle signified the end of the game, which had ended in a 0–0 stalemate.

There would be a replay at Hayes Lane the following Saturday.

I hoped that not many Erith and Belvedere fans would make the trip. I also hoped they'd stay well clear of the tea hut.

I really didn't want to be recognised.

●●●

There was a new comic called *Scorcher*, which had come out the previous week. Tempted by the free 'great soccer wallchart', I had bought my copy on the day it came out, but hadn't got around to reading it until now.

The story that stood out for me was Billy's Boots.

Billy Dane was a boy around my age who had found a pair of boots belonging to Dead Shot Keen, a 1920s England centre-forward, in his Gran's attic.

When Billy put the boots on, he was instantly transformed from being a rubbish footballer into one who couldn't stop scoring brilliant goals.

My new boots with the rotating studs had failed to have the same kind of effect.

I still hadn't added to my goal in the first game of the season and today's game, the 13th of the season, was against Farnborough Youth, who had beaten us on the previous Sunday. By a strange coincidence, both Hayesford Park Reserves and Bromley were playing the same team two weeks running.

Roy had been switched to midfield in a bid to stem the leaking of goals, while another dustman had taken his place at right back.

No-one had mentioned my antics at Erith, much to my relief. But because I'd been ignored, I felt I had to prove myself all over again to Derek, Roy and Peter.

My plan was to try harder than ever to help Hayesford

Park Reserves finally get a win. Even when we were 3–0 down, I was running back to help defend, making tackles and hoofing the ball clear.

And when we got our first corner of the match – in fact, our first corner for several weeks – the ball found me a yard from the line and I instinctively headed past the Farnborough Youth goalie before he had time to react.

Instead of celebrating, I picked the ball out of the net and ran back to the halfway line with it, looking grim and purposeful, like I'd seen an Oxford player do in the Amateur Cup match when he'd scored to bring the score back to 3–2.

I ran out of steam not long after, as did the rest of the team, and we eventually went down 7–1. But I'd had my best game in a Hayesford Park Reserves shirt and had never been happier with a six-goal defeat.

●●●

The Grubby hadn't changed at all, even though it seemed like ages since I'd last seen him. He had taken up his usual position behind the goal with plenty of time to spare before the Bromley and Erith and Belvedere players ran out for their Kent Senior Cup first-round replay.

While I was waiting for the giant urn to boil, I wandered over to talk to him. The first thing I noticed was that he was smoking Benson and Hedges instead of his usual Embassy. He explained that now he was working he could afford a better lifestyle.

I was surprised at his switch of brands. I knew he was quite close to being able to get a Goblin Teasmade with the Embassy coupons he'd been collecting. The Goblin Teasmade was pretty much his ultimate dream – a gadget that woke you up with a steaming cup of tea every morning.

I arranged to watch the last quarter of the game with him.

That was our least busy time and I was allowed to leave the hut until after the final whistle, when it was my job to collect all the empty cups.

I was particularly excited by today's game, as it represented a realistic chance of winning as opposed to an irrational hope.

In theory, Bromley had done all the hard work the previous Saturday. Successful cup teams are happy to draw their away games and win the replay at home. Manchester City, the current FA Cup holders, had done just that by drawing at Newcastle in the fourth round and winning the replay 2–0.

Even the most pessimistic Bromley supporter (which would have been Roy) was confident of going through to the next round, where they would face either Tonbridge or Deal away, both of whom were beatable. Even by Bromley.

To load the dice even further in our favour, Pat Brown was back in the starting line-up.

An unfamiliar feeling come over me. Hope.

So it was even more crushing than usual when Bromley made the kind of start we'd seen all season. Alan Soper inexplicably strayed out of his goal to try and deal with a speculative lob. It went over his head and into the net. If he'd stayed on his line, he would have caught it comfortably.

1–0 to Erith and Belvedere became 2–0 to Erith and Belvedere when a far-post header easily beat Soper, whose defenders seemed to have deserted him.

The best save of the match came just after half-time, when Jeff Bridge leapt to his right to palm the ball over the bar. As he was a right-back and not a goalkeeper, a penalty was awarded and it became 3–0.

Bromley were out of the Kent Senior Cup, just like they were out of every other cup.

I was sick at the sight of Erith and Belvedere. They had now beaten us three times in the space of a few months and I never wanted to see them or their stupid all-blue kit again.

The depths to which Bromley had sunk was perfectly illustrated by a photo that took pride of place on the back page of the *Bromley and Kentish Times* following the match.

It showed David Wise, Colin Brown and Alan Bonney posing together, grinning happily. The caption pointed out that the three of them had all nearly scored for Bromley against Erith and Belvedere.

Back in the Stonebridge era, you had to score at least one goal to get your picture in the paper.

Now, apparently you just needed to come close to scoring.

•••

The next morning, Hayesford Park Reserves had a hastily arranged friendly with a Cudham XI. To be more accurate, it was a Cudham x as only ten of them turned up.

This prompted Peter to make a tactical decision of such brilliance, I felt he should immediately apply for Alan Basham's job.

He offered them one of our players, as we had 12. They naively accepted, and welcomed Roy into their team.

Hayesford Park Reserves had never have a better chance of winning a game for the first time in their history.

I had been demoted from my striking role, despite my goal last week, and another dustman had been brought in. He promptly scored the opening goal.

If there had been any spectators at Whitehill Rec that day, they would have seen Hayesford Park Reserves playing better than at any time in our history. It was as though the pressure had been lifted now that we weren't playing in a game where points were at stake.

Even Derek, freed from his role of watching balls flash past him and into the net, got in on the action. He scored a great goal, which was followed by a third and then a fourth. A team that was averaging less than a goal a game suddenly couldn't stop scoring.

By half time, we were 4–1 up and I felt wonderful, even though my contribution had been minimal. I had never been in a team that was winning – I don't think many of us had.

Predictably, we fell to pieces in the second half, which, coincidentally, was when their missing player turned up and replaced Roy.

Panic seemed to spread through the Hayesford Park Reserves team as the enormity of what was happening sunk in. We were actually in the lead and had a chance of winning a game. Like many of my teammates, I was suddenly paralysed by fear.

The Cudham xi pulled it back to 4–3, thanks to a goal from their centre-forward and an own goal from Sean, our right-back.

We managed to hold on, and the final whistle was the cue for wild celebrations. The Cudham players looked a little puzzled.

It was as though they didn't understand why a win in an irrelevant friendly was so important to Hayesford Park Reserves.

●●●

Alan Basham appeared to have devised a new method of giving false hope to Bromley supporters.

He would regularly announce what seemed to be impressive new signings to make up for players who had left the club, not bothered getting in touch, missed training, got injured or gone on holiday.

For the away game at Dulwich, the latest additions to the Bromley team would be unveiled. Defender Michael Miles was following in his brother John's footstep's by coming over from Maidstone. Tony Day, a left winger, had also joined. He seemed to be overqualified to play for Bromley, having represented both the London FA and the Surrey FA while with his previous club Croydon Amateurs.

Miles and Day would be taking the places of Postman Pat Brown and David Wise, both of whom missed training. Under Alan Basham, missing training was pretty much the worst offence possible and it automatically meant not being selected for the next game.

I think this was meant to be an incentive to attend training.

Within a few minutes, the Dulwich game had taken on a depressingly familiar shape. Even though it had been identified as the second of the 'must win' games in Charlie King's masterplan to avoid finishing bottom, Bromley were playing as though they were merely trying to minimise the margin of defeat.

Their packed and overworked defence weren't helped by Alan Bonney's apparent determination to add to his season's tally of two own goals. Twice he came close, twice Alan Soper was forced into making the save.

Our lone forward, Eric Nottage, was playing with a heavy cold. This was obvious by the fact he kept taking a handkerchief from his sleeve and blowing his nose. The chilly, wet conditions can't have helped and he was eventually substituted, much to the visible relief of an elderly woman who was sitting in the stand and might well have been his mum.

Dulwich were a team on form and they played like it. The first goal came right at the end of the first half and their second came ten minutes from the end.

Bromley had now no points at all from their must-win games. For the first time, I was having to acknowledge the possibility of us finishing bottom of the Isthmian League. This was something I had avoided thinking about until now. I'd always assumed that things would improve. But the tight feeling in my stomach as I studied the league tables trying to find a way out of the mess told me, for the first time, that Bromley might conceivably be as bad as they appeared to the outside world.

It really hurt.

•••

Bromley were going through a terrible time, with no points to show for the year to date. Hayesford Park Reserves had a similar record.

John Miles star of over-worked Bromley defence

But at least I was enjoying school.

Dave had invited me to his house after the weekend and he was proving an invaluable social asset. Even though he didn't belong to any particular clique, he was on the fringes of several.

By aligning myself with him, I was finding it much easier to make friends than it was at Sevenoaks. He even occasionally hung around with the skinheads, due mainly to a shared love of Arsenal.

He still hadn't forgiven me for allegedly jinxing his team. They had now gone eight games without a win since I went to Highbury and his anger with me was matched by my anger with him – Bromley hadn't won in five games since he had been to Hayes Lane.

There was also still some unresolved hostility over the Una Stubbs v Diana Rigg debate. But apart from those minor things, we were getting on well. It was just a shame my luck hadn't spread to Hayes Lane.

●●●

Alan Basham had seemingly decided that the best chance of beating Leytonstone would be to drop all our best players. So out went Ginger Warman, ostensibly because of his disciplinary record, while Pat Brown and David Wise missed out because they once again hadn't gone to training on the Tuesday night.

I couldn't believe it.

If I'd had a season ticket, I would have torn it up in protest, but as one would have cost me almost £2, it was never even a possibility.

The whole obsession with fitness was incredible. Even I could see there was much more to the team's problems than that. And now the players were coming out and saying as much.

Roy Pettet went public with his belief that a lot of his teammates weren't up to Isthmian League standard. Alan Bonney, who was possibly one of those Pettet was referring to, agreed.

He added that the defence, of which he was a part, were not to blame. It was everybody else.

There was a feeling amongst supporters visiting the tea hut for a pre-game cup of tea that if Bromley lost this game, everything could fall apart.

Mutiny at Hayes Lane was a serious possibility.

•••

Leytonstone couldn't have had an easier win all season. Or at least since they last played Bromley. This time, they won 4–1 against a very fit and very useless home side.

We were now cast firmly adrift with Corinthian Casuals at the bottom of the table. And the men in chocolate and pink shirts were just one win away from overtaking us.

As I cycled home, I was in a rage, working out my frustrations by peddling as fast as I could. I was now sure that Bromley wouldn't win another game all season. I wondered if they'd ever win a game again.

As I approached the junction at Shortlands, still seething, I realised that I was heading for a group of five or six sheepskin-wearing Palace skinheads, on their way home from their cup game against Chelsea. They'd seen me and were standing in the road, waiting.

It was too late to turn around so I carried on cycling, hoping that the perceived threat didn't really exist outside of my mind. It was when one of them shouted 'get him' that I realised it did.

I tried ringing my bell, but that had no effect other than to make things worse. I then panicked and headed straight for them. I couldn't think. Fear had overtaken me completely.

At the last second, instinct took over and I swerved to avoid them, before turning right onto Shortlands Road and quickly putting a few hundred yards between me and my pursuers.

But even then I wasn't in the clear. Cruelly, the lights at Shortlands Station were red so I obediently stopped. I could hear the dull thud of Doc Marten boots hitting concrete getting louder and louder as the skinheads closed in on me.

If I'd been thinking straight, I might have got off the bike and wheeled it to safety or just gone through the red light, but I wasn't thinking straight.

I was in a state of high panic. But despite this, I remembered to use the basic skills which had earned me my cycling proficiency badge. My right arm, which was shaking, was stuck out at a 90-degree angle to indicate my intentions.

Just as I was bracing myself for a beating, the lights changed to green and I raced off and kept on at full speed until I got home.

Once inside, I hung up my sheepskin, locked my bedroom door, closed the curtains and lay curled up on my bed, feeling terrified.

It seems I just wasn't cut out to be a skinhead.

# CHAPTER NINETEEN

I stayed on my bed until it was time for *Match of the Day*, which made it easy to avoid the football scores. This meant I had no idea what I was about to witness.

An hour later, I was sitting on the couch in a stunned state. George Best had almost single-handedly beaten Northampton Town in an incredible FA Cup fifth-round tie.

He'd scored six of United's eight goals, equalling the record. But it was the style he'd taken his chances with that was so impressive, frequently walking the ball into the net after he'd run out of defenders to beat.

I felt inspired.

In the morning, Hayesford Park Reserves were taking on Forresters, the league leaders. I was determined to put in a George Best-like performance and I drifted off to sleep that night fantasising about rounding the Forresters goalie with almost embarrassing ease and tapping the ball home to complete my double hat-trick.

•••

The only good thing about the 21–0 defeat that morning then was that it happened to Hayesford Park Reserves and not Bromley. In a season of lows, this was the lowest.

One incident will be lodged in my memory forever. Roy's attempted back pass from 30 yards out scorching past a bewildered Derek and smashing against the crossbar. If it wasn't for that piece of luck, we would have conceded 22.

Another memorable aspect to the loss was the fact we were playing against ten men.

By the end of the game, the Hayesford Park Reserves players had been reduced to watching in horrified admiration as their Forresters counterparts took it in turns to score.

It was a measure of their total domination that Derek was voted as our player of the day. To add to the humiliation, I had recklessly told several boys from school to watch out for our results. It was my way of telling them that our games were so important, the results were printed in the paper.

This had now backfired horribly. It wasn't something I'd be able to keep secret. But I was going to try my best. I wasn't going to tell anyone what the score was – not even Dave. This was going to be particularly difficult, especially as I would be going to his house for the first time after school on Monday.

•••

By the time I'd told Dave about the weekend's post-Bromley-game incident, the amount of skinheads involved had grown to about a dozen, while the amount of goals Hayesford Park Reserves had conceded had shrunk to a much more respectable ten.

Dave lived on the RAF base at Biggin Hill and when we arrived, I was pleased to see a set of 5-a-side goals on a large play area. A slightly older boy, thin and lanky with unfashionable glasses and unruly straw-coloured hair, was dribbling a brown plastic ball past imaginary defenders then kicking it into the unguarded net.

Dave explained that the boy's name was Keith and he was undoubtedly pretending he was Paul Aimson. Aimson was, apparently, the star centre-forward for Fourth Division York City, Keith's favourite team.

We wandered over to join him. I went in goal, Dave went out to the right wing and Keith stayed in the middle for Dave's crosses. Naturally, we each adopted the identity of our favourite player, so Eddie Kelly was crossing the ball for Paul Aimson, who tried to head the ball past Alan Soper.

We were all fairly convincing in our roles, in that Dave crossed the ball like a midfielder who couldn't get a regular game for the first team, Keith headed it like an obscure Fourth Division striker and I kept goal like someone who had conceded a club record amount of goals.

We carried on playing until the last bit of daylight had gone, before reluctantly parting company with Keith and heading to Dave's house for tea.

Once we got there, he made us both a cup of tea. He then introduced me to his sister, who I couldn't help but notice had a wall covered with pictures of Jon Sammels, the Arsenal central midfielder. I happened to know from my obsessive reading of football magazines that his full name was Jonathon Charles Sammels, but what he was doing on her wall was a mystery.

Dave admitted that he was responsible. A while ago, he'd decided that Arsenal should have a pin-up boy and managed to convince his sister that Jon Sammels was the best-looking player in the game, despite the existence of one George Best.

He also insisted that Sammels would one day play for England, and that would be when his matinee idol good looks would be universally recognised.

His faith had only been slightly shaken by constant references to 'that powder puff' from the other fans he stood alongside on the North Bank.

Few shared Dave's opinion about Sammels' claims to an international cap and no-one else was converted to worshipping him for his looks.

Touchingly, his sister had kept the posters up, long after it had become clear that she didn't find him particularly handsome.

Before I met her, I had felt complete indifferent towards Jon Sammels. Now I was extremely jealous of him.

His pictures were on the wall of the most beautiful girl who had ever spoken to me.

•••

The next day at school, I tentatively approached Dave about his sister. I admitted that I fancied her and asked him to use his influence with her to get some inside information. He promised he'd do some subtle digging.

I tried explaining that she reminded me of Linda Ronstadt, especially the picture on the cover of *Hand Sown, Home Grown*, but he seemed more interested in having a game of Killball.

This seriously tested my patience. I really needed to talk about his sister, to find out everything about her. She was the first real crush I had had, or at least the first one I had a chance of going out with. The only other woman I wanted to go out with was Una Stubbs from *Till Death Us Do Part*, but she had recently got married to another actor. This news had affected me almost as strongly as Alan Stonebridge's departure.

This left Dave's sister.

Only by buying him a Mars bar did I manage to find out a bit more about the girl I had been fantasising about since I met her. The fantasies usually consisted of sitting side by side in the Supporters' Club area watching Bromley together.

When Dave told me that he didn't think she had a boyfriend, my hopes soared. I vowed there and then that I would ask her out.

I gave myself a deadline of the end of the season, which was three months away, to pluck up enough courage to ring her.

●●●

While my love life was looking up, Bromley were still falling to pieces.

Ginger Warman, who was second top scorer, had got a 28 day suspension for his misdeeds against Maidstone. He was also fined £5, which seemed a bit unfair to me. I didn't know how much postmen got paid, but I thought he'd have to deliver quite a lot of letters to pay it.

Pat Brown and David Wise were also in trouble. Neither had turned up to training for the second week running, although manager Alan Basham had encouraging words for the former.

'Brown could be a fine player if he was fit,' he said, somehow missing the point that Postman Pat had consistently been a fine player for the past five seasons.

He then damned several more of his players with faint or no praise, saying that Roy Pettet 'has the ability to do well in midfield', Alan Bonney 'makes too many mistakes at the back', while Eric Nottage has 'never been a brilliant distributor of the ball'.

The committee met to discuss the declining morale and decided that carrying on with Alan Basham as trainer-coach was the best option.

His next task? An away game at Tooting and Mitcham, a club who had recently earned my affection by beating Corinthian Casuals 5–0. They had also earned my fear by beating Enfield in their next game.

●●●

I got up early on the day of the Tooting and Mitcham match, eagerly awaiting the post. I couldn't have been more excited if either Pat Brown or Johnny Warman had been delivering it personally.

It was Valentine's Day and I had somehow managed to convince myself that Dave's sister had been so impressed with the two minutes she'd spent in my company, even though I hadn't actually managed to speak, that she would be sending me a card.

As I looked outside, eagerly awaiting the postman's arrival, I noticed that the snow, which had started several days ago, was still falling heavily.

It had been so bad that only two Isthmian League games were possible. Both of them were crucial to Bromley's chances of avoiding bottom place. At the same time we would be playing Tooting and Mitcham, Corinthian Casuals would be taking on Dulwich Hamlet.

Being superstitious, I was feeling quite confident of wins for Bromley and Dulwich, plus a Valentine's card for me, as I reminded myself that good luck comes in threes.

What I hadn't considered was that bad luck also comes in threes.

It soon become apparent this wasn't going to be my day.

Disaster number one was the sheer crushing disappointment of the mail. No card from Dave's sister. No cards from anyone.

Disaster number two was the loss in what seemed to be sub-zero temperatures at Tooting. Despite taking the lead twice, Bromley had gone down 5–2. The highlight was a great full-length diving save by centre-half Alan Bonney from a Tooting long-range effort. Despite the impressive technique, the referee gave the home side a penalty and they were level. Three more goals in the last 20 minutes compounded the misery.

But the biggest disaster was saved until last. I heard later that Corinthian Casuals had beaten Dulwich to lift them off the foot of the table for the first time in living memory.

Bromley were now rock bottom.

It had been the kind of day to crush the spirit of any man, let alone a 14-year old boy. I went to bed at 8pm, just to make sure nothing else could go wrong.

As it turned out, this was the worst thing I could have done. I lay awake until 4.15am restlessly thinking about the day's disasters. The lack of Valentine card hurt most – although there was a slight possibility that something had gone wrong at the Post Office and there could still be one in Monday's post.

Being last in the Isthmian League was also an awful feeling. It hadn't happened in my lifetime and I found myself wishing I'd been born in a different era – the 1948/1949 season would have been a much better time to have been a Bromley supporter than now. They had won the Athenian League as well as the Kent Amateur Cup. Not to mention the big one – the FA Amateur Cup.

After that win, the team inched their way through Bromley High Street in an open-topped bus, as a crowd of around 20,000 cheered loud and long.

A famous picture from the time showed a young chairman, Charlie King, beaming amidst an unprecedented haul of trophies. He had a look of pride I hadn't seen on his face in all the years I'd been watching Bromley.

At least he'd tasted the good as well as the bad. The team we had now was the only one I'd ever known.

Last year, I had spent Valentine's Day in hospital with appendicitis. The pain I had experienced then was nothing compared to what I was going through now.

•••

I was always the last one to catch onto new crazes, and the Esso World Cup coins were no exception.

They had been out for a few weeks and most boys were already swapping ones they had doubles of. I didn't get my first one until the journey home from Tooting.

Derek had stopped for petrol and I noticed a sign advertising the coins. Curious to find out more, I went inside and came out a short while later with a blue presentation folder which had cost me 2/6, and a small blue and white foil packet, containing my first World Cup coin.

It was Brian Labone of Everton.

I was ready to start collecting. My aim was to get the whole set in time for the World Cup.

As you got a coin every time you bought four gallons of petrol, and two coins for eight gallons, I began pressuring the driver of whatever car I was in to fill up at Esso. It meant I was accompanying my dad pretty much every time he went out, in the hopes of persuading him to fill his tank. I also kept a close eye on the petrol gauge in Derek's car, letting him know every time it dipped below half full.

There were thirty coins in all and when I looked through the names of Esso's version of the England squad, there was one player I was delighted to see missing.

My arch enemy, Jon Sammels.

# ISTHMIAN LEAGUE HOW THEY STAND

## 14TH FEBRUARY 1970

|  | P | W | D | L | F | A | Pts |
|---|---|---|---|---|---|---|---|
| Wycombe W . . . . | 25 | 17 | 6 | 2 | 55 | 16 | 40 |
| St. Albans City | 31 | 16 | 8 | 7 | 53 | 36 | 40 |
| Enfield. . . . . | 23 | 15 | 6 | 2 | 50 | 14 | 36 |
| Barking . . . . | 27 | 15 | 6 | 6 | 65 | 27 | 36 |
| Sutton Utd . . . | 25 | 14 | 7 | 4 | 50 | 26 | 35 |
| Hitchin Town . . | 27 | 12 | 9 | 6 | 46 | 30 | 33 |
| Tooting & Mit . | 22 | 13 | 4 | 5 | 52 | 27 | 30 |
| Wealdstone . . . | 27 | 13 | 4 | 10 | 40 | 32 | 30 |
| Oxford City. . . | 28 | 12 | 6 | 10 | 44 | 49 | 30 |
| Leytonstone . . | 26 | 11 | 5 | 10 | 38 | 26 | 27 |
| Kingstonian . . | 28 | 10 | 6 | 12 | 41 | 42 | 26 |
| Woking . . . . . | 27 | 10 | 6 | 13 | 40 | 45 | 26 |
| Hendon. . . . . | 22 | 9 | 7 | 6 | 41 | 31 | 25 |
| Clapton . . . . | 29 | 9 | 6 | 16 | 41 | 61 | 24 |
| Dulwich Hamlet. | 29 | 7 | 10 | 13 | 36 | 49 | 24 |
| Ilford . . . . . | 28 | 5 | 14 | 12 | 30 | 60 | 24 |
| Maidstone Utd . | 28 | 7 | 5 | 17 | 36 | 59 | 19 |
| Walthamstow A . | 27 | 7 | 5 | 17 | 34 | 59 | 19 |
| Corinthian Cs . | 28 | 5 | 2 | 23 | 28 | 75 | 12 |
| **BROMLEY . . . . .** | **28** | **3** | **3** | **24** | **22** | **88** | **9** |

# CHAPTER TWENTY

On the journey to Kingston for our league fixture with Kingstonian, I added to my Esso World Cup coin collection with a Henry Newton and an Alan Oakes. I was a bit disappointed. The big names seemed to be evading me, although Dave had promised to give me one of his three Norman Hunters.

We were in Derek's car. As usual, there hadn't been enough supporter interest for a coach.

Also as usual, Bromley had given debuts to a couple of newcomers. These newcomers usually sounded great on paper and invariably disappointed in the flesh.

Anthony Allshorne seemed the most promising – a former Chelsea youth player. Michael Lloyd was the other debutant. His career had had a less glittering start than Allshorne's, having spent his early days at Croydon Amateurs.

Although Bromley were now at the bottom of the table, we felt quietly confident of a win which would take us back above Corinthian Casuals. We'd won 4–2 at Kingstonian last season and it had been one of the easier wins.

This confidence stayed with us for most of the game, even though Bromley only managed one shot on goal in the entire 90 minutes, which, in itself, was an improvement on some of their recent efforts.

The shot was from David Wise and came after just over an hour of total Kingstonian domination. It was so one-sided that we moved behind Alan Soper's goal in order to see some action.

And we saw plenty. There were missed open goals, great

saves, ten-man defence and a lot of shouting from Alan Soper. The home team looked great, though. They were wearing brand-new shirts, which had been donated by their supporters' club. I wondered if we could do something similar for our team. I made a mental note to bring the subject up in the car on the way home.

As for the Bromley newcomers, it was generally felt that Michael Lloyd would have made a big impression on Alan Basham. He was the kind of player the manager/coach seem to favour – very fit and with limited skill. I could see him having a long career under Basham.

In the end, all Kingstonian had to show for 90 minutes of attack was a solitary goal. But it was enough to give them the points and keep Bromley at the foot of the table.

The only good news was that Corinthian Casuals had also lost.

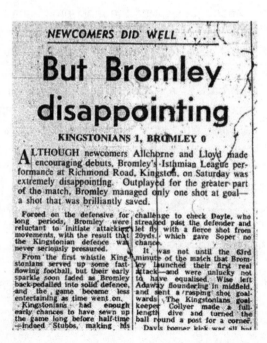

**NEWCOMERS DID WELL**

# But Bromley disappointing

### KINGSTONIANS 1, BROMLEY 0

ALTHOUGH newcomers Allchorne and Lloyd made encouraging debuts, Bromley's Isthmian League performance at Richmond Road, Kingston, on Saturday was extremely disappointing. Outplayed for the greater part of the match, Bromley managed only one shot at goal— a shot that was brilliantly saved.

Forced on the defensive for long periods, Bromley were reluctant to initiate attacking movements, with the result that the Kingstonian defence was never seriously pressured.

From the first whistle Kingstonians served up some fast-flowing football, but their early sparkle soon faded as Bromley back-pedalled into solid defence, and the game became less entertaining as time went on. Kingstonians had enough early chances to have sewn up the game long before half-time —indeed Stubbs, making his

challenge to check Doyle, who streaked past the defender and let fly with a fierce shot from 20yds. which gave Soper no chance.

It was not until the 63rd minute of the match that Bromley launched their first real attack—and were unlucky not to have equalised. Wise left Adaway floundering in midfield, and sent a rasping shot goalwards. The Kingstonian goalkeeper Collyer made a full-length dive and turned the ball round a post for a corner. Davis' corner kick was all but

I'd told Dave to tell his sister that my favourite player was Jon Sammels in the hopes that it would convince her we were meant to be together and that I liked Tom Jones, whose poster I had also seen on her wall.

One morning at school, just before Killball, he told me that he'd talked to her about me. He said that he hadn't mentioned my liking for Jon or Tom for my own good. She didn't really like Jon Sammels. And she didn't like Tom Jones, either – their mother had persuaded her to get the poster against her better judgment.

He hadn't asked her what she thought of me, claiming that it would be best if he could build up my case for me before revealing his hand.

I had mixed feelings about this – at least she wouldn't be able to reject me if she didn't know I was interested in her. But if she did like me, we could be going out by now.

She was starting to take up more and more of my thoughts. The song that was on in her bedroom when I met her, 'A Whiter Shade of Pale' by Procol Harum, had become enormously meaningful for me. Every time I heard it, I thought of her. And I heard it up to ten times a day, since I owned the single and had taken to playing it with increasing frequency.

•••

It didn't take me long to discover the downside of Killball.

Having survived almost an entire corridor of feral boys kicking me, I was about to kick the ball into the wall when I felt a sharp pain in my ankle and went down in a screaming heap.

My first thought was that it was broken. I looked up, expecting concerned faces filled with sympathy, but I should have known better. Most of them were laughing hysterically at the sight of my rapidly swelling and yellowing ankle.

Would they have been laughing so much if they'd known that the injury could rob Hayesford Park Reserves of its centre-forward for the key clash with Barnet Reserves in 11 days time?

Yes, they probably would.

•••

There were several mysteries going into the must-win Maidstone away game.

Mike Mile's mystery illness, for one. It had been variously diagnosed as German measles and a skin infection. Whatever it was, it had been enough to potentially rule him out for the rest of the season.

His brother John was embroiled in another mystery. A rumour had swept the club concerning a possible move back to Maidstone, the club he'd recently left. Someone wanting to leave Bromley wasn't unusual, but wanting to do it after just three weeks smacked of indecent haste. When Peter asked him about it, the elder Miles brother denied there was any truth to the story.

But I was not convinced. Something would happen in the last few minutes of today's game which would persuade me that he had already secretly signed for Maidstone.

Just about everything that led up to that incident was pointing towards Bromley's first league point of the year and maybe even our first win in six months.

David Wise had put us ahead with a glancing header and Bromley were outplaying the home side so comprehensively that if it had been a wrestling match, Maidstone would have submitted.

But then John Miles stepped in to change the course of the match.

First, he missed a cross and Mickey Angel, formerly of Bromley and now of Maidstone, headed past Soper.

Then, with time just about up, came the incident which had several Maidstone supporters sitting near us literally crying with laughter. There can be no greater humiliation than that.

It started when Alan Soper came too far out of his goal following a corner and the ball was lobbed over his head towards the Bromley goal. Miles, who was scrambling back, had the simple task of heading it clear.

Instead, he somehow managed to head it against the bar and then tripped over his own feet and fell back into the net, ripping a huge hole in it.

He then sat there with a helpless expression and watched, along with the rest of us, as the follow-up shot went into the goal and through the hole that he had just made.

I leaned over the fence, picked the ball up and rolled it back through the hole to a dazed-looking Alan Soper.

Once again, Bromley had found a novel way to turn a comfortable draw into an embarrassing defeat.

No-one knew if Miles was going back to Maidstone or not. But I think we were all hoping that he was.

At least another mystery was cleared up. I had been wondering why an obscure Metropolitan Sunday League team called Southborough were suddenly getting rave match reports in the paper – often in a prominent position on the back page. Even when they'd lost, they were reported as having been unlucky or outplayed their opponents. And their goals were invariably described as being 'brilliant'.

It suddenly made sense when I read the latest match report and saw that one of the Southborough scorers was Tony Flood – the same Tony Flood whose day job was football writer for the *Bromley and Kentish Times*.

•••

We went to the Viva Maria Restaurant for my 15th birthday. It more than lived up to its billing on the front of the Bromley programme as a 'first class restaurant'.

I had thought long and hard about inviting Dave's sister. I'd picked the phone up on several occasions, only for my courage to desert me at the last second. In the end I decided that if I didn't ask her, she wouldn't be able to turn me down.

For my present from my parents, I'd requested record tokens and that was what I got.

Even though walking was still really painful, Dave and I went to WH Smith to spend them after school the next day. He was pressuring me to buy some Bob Dylan, particularly *Blonde on Blonde*, which he insisted was a masterpiece.

I listened to a couple of tracks (each of which seemed to last about 20 minutes) in the listening booth and they sounded good, so I bought the LP. I then looked at what else I could get.

Now that my skinhead ambitions were on the back burner, the new *Tighten Up – Volume 3* LP held no interest, although I was briefly excited to see a track by the Kingstonians on it.

Unlike at Christmas, I decided to buy records I actually liked. This meant singles. There was 'Wanderin' Star' by Lee Marvin, 'Temma Harbour' by Mary Hopkin and 'Space Oddity' by David Bowie, which I only bought because he was from Bromley.

With the remaining money, I reserved a copy of England's World Cup song, 'Back Home', which was coming out at the end of the season. I asked them if they could ring me the moment it arrived. I badly wanted to be the first person at school to own it.

Afterwards, we went to Debenhams to see The Grubby. He was sitting on a rolled-up carpet, smoking and drinking tea, which, come to think of it, he was doing every time I saw him.

I arranged to meet him at our usual place behind the goal on Saturday. Despite Bromley's poor run, our enthusiasm hadn't diminished.

We were both excited about the team's chances, despite us both knowing better.

●●●

A South Thames Cup game against Kingstonian at Hayes Lane was not an occasion I would have expected to see one of Bromley's most notorious skinheads angrily striding towards where The Grubby and I were sitting.

I'd seen him around, but didn't know him by name. I glanced at The Grubby, whose face had suddenly taken on an alarmed expression. This made me even more nervous. The Grubby was not someone who scared easily.

The skinhead sat right down beside us. I was getting ready to run. What did he want? If it was money, I would gladly have given him some. But before I had the chance to make him the offer, The Grubby started apologising. Bizarrely, he seemed to be saying he was sorry about a key, which he was handing over to the skinhead.

Then it got really strange. The skinhead smiled, patted The Grubby on the arm and wandered off in the direction of the exit.

The Grubby explained that the skinhead was his brother and he'd forgotten to give him their front-door key, which meant he'd been locked out. He knew he'd find The Grubby at Hayes Lane, so had come to get the key.

The shock of discovering that my hippie friend had a

high-profile skinhead brother was immense. It made about as much sense as Alan Basham's team selections.

I decided to concentrate on the game, or rather what was left of it.

The South Thames Cup was probably the least prestigious trophy in football. This was a competition that had started last season, but had carried over to this season as only a handful of first-round games had been completed. The South Thames Cup had been known to stretch over three seasons, which seemed to be down to the indifference of the participants. Just how lowly it was perceived was shown by the fact that Bromley had made the previous final, where they lost 2–1 to Sutton nearly two years ago.

Now that both Bromley and Kingstonian had run out of excuses not to play, the fixture was finally going ahead. This, I suspected, was only because Mr Arthur Coward, the chairman of the South Thames Cup, had announced that if games weren't completed by the end of the month, he alone would be deciding who went through to the semi-finals.

I would like to think being forced to play for such an irrelevant trophy was responsible for Bromley's disastrous start to the game, but deep down I knew that it was because they were rubbish.

After two minutes, Alan Soper dropped the ball at the feet of the Kingstonian number ten, who stabbed it home. A few minutes later, it was the number nine's turn when he took advantage of confusion between Postman Pat and John Miles.

We were basically out of the South Thames Cup before the game had reached the five-minute mark.

The visiting number seven added another goal on the hour, but it was completely unnecessary. The damage had already been done.

The tie was meant to have been played over two legs, but

after having to postpone the second leg because of a waterlogged pitch, the clubs apparently agreed that Bromley had no chance whatsoever of overcoming a three-goal deficit and that it would be best if Kingstonian went straight through to the next round.

Mr Coward gave the decision his official blessing and Bromley's last hopes of winning something had gone for the season, just like that.

•••

Even though my ankle was still bruised and sore, I decided that if Alan Stonebridge could play with boils on his leg, I could play with a bruised ankle.

I made a great show in the changing room of wincing when I pulled my sock over the injured ankle. This was intended to show how brave I was being as well as setting the scene for my excuse if I didn't have a good game.

The disadvantages of my new boots soon became apparent. Every time I tried to swivel, it put a strain on the ankle causing me agonising pain. Kicking the ball had the same effect. As did running.

I was substituted after ten minutes and watched from the sidelines as Hayesford Park Reserves put in their best performance of the season, going down 2–1 to Barnet Reserves after a late, late winner.

I didn't like to think about the fact that my contribution was limited to limping up and down the touchline, acting as linesman.

The following Saturday, I was so nervous cycling down Bromley High Street on the way to Hayes Lane that I barely noticed the pain in my ankle, the howling wind blowing into my face or the cold rain dripping down my back.

The nerves were because of what could potentially happen to Bromley that afternoon.

We were playing Barking who had won 8–0 the last time the two teams had met. Back then, Barking were a fairly decent middle-of-the-table side. Now they were in great form. Second in the league, having scored loads more goals than anyone else. Last week, they'd put six past Tooting and Mitcham, who were considered a good team. I shuddered to think what they'd do this week.

It was a measure of how bad the season had been that I felt enormous relief when I arrived at the ground and saw the word 'POSTPONED' pasted over the poster advertising the Bromley v Barking fixture.

Under normal circumstances, I would have been angry and frustrated. I also would have climbed over the fence, and made my own pitch inspection just to make sure it really was unplayable.

Instead, I just turned around and cycled home.

It didn't really feel like a postponement, though. More like a stay of execution.

## ISTHMIAN LEAGUE HOW THEY STAND

### 13TH MARCH 1970

| | P | W | D | L | F | A | Pts |
|---|---|---|---|---|---|---|---|
| Wycombe W . . . . | 25 | 17 | 6 | 2 | 56 | 16 | 40 |
| Barking . . . . . | 29 | 17 | 6 | 6 | 73 | 29 | 40 |
| St. Albans City . | 31 | 16 | 8 | 7 | 53 | 36 | 40 |
| Sutton Utd . . . . | 27 | 16 | 7 | 4 | 54 | 26 | 39 |
| Enfield. . . . . . | 24 | 15 | 7 | 2 | 51 | 15 | 37 |
| Hitchin Town . . . | 27 | 12 | 9 | 6 | 46 | 30 | 33 |
| Leytonstone . . . | 29 | 13 | 6 | 10 | 45 | 29 | 32 |
| Tooting & Mit . . | 27 | 14 | 4 | 9 | 59 | 40 | 32 |
| Wealdstone . . . . | 28 | 14 | 4 | 10 | 44 | 35 | 32 |
| Oxford City . . . | 29 | 12 | 7 | 10 | 44 | 49 | 31 |
| Kingstonian . . . | 30 | 11 | 6 | 13 | 43 | 44 | 28 |
| Hendon . . . . . . | 23 | 10 | 7 | 6 | 42 | 31 | 27 |
| Woking . . . . . . | 29 | 10 | 6 | 13 | 40 | 45 | 26 |
| Dulwich Hamlet . . | 30 | 7 | 10 | 13 | 36 | 49 | 24 |
| Clapton . . . . . | 31 | 9 | 6 | 16 | 41 | 61 | 24 |
| Ilford . . . . . . | 31 | 5 | 14 | 12 | 30 | 60 | 24 |
| Maidstone Utd . . | 29 | 7 | 5 | 17 | 36 | 59 | 19 |
| Walthamstow A . . | 29 | 7 | 5 | 17 | 34 | 59 | 19 |
| Corinthian Cs . . | 30 | 5 | 2 | 23 | 28 | 75 | 12 |
| **BROMLEY . . . . .** | **30** | **3** | **3** | **24** | **22** | **88** | **9** |

# CHAPTER
# TWENTY-ONE

The following Saturday was Alan Basham's lucky day.

It was announced over the tannoy that he had won £5 in the Bromley Football Club 200 Club lottery, which wouldn't have made me overly suspicious if it hadn't been for Bromley winger Tony Day winning the previous draw a fortnight earlier.

Apart from being £5 richer, Basham also had a full squad to choose from for the first time in ages.

Ginger Warman was back for the rearranged game against Barking, having served his time. So was Roy Pettet, our best midfielder, and Alan Bonney, our best defender. Bonney had announced himself ready to return now that his cracked fibula had healed (my mum, a nurse, told me that it was another word for the calf bone).

For once, Bromley were at full strength.

Basham's luck continued for the whole of the first half, with Barking failing to take advantage of a strong wind behind them, thanks to a combination of poor finishing and Soper brilliance.

The first half hadn't produced any goals, which was a major shock. I'd almost let the tea get cold because I was concentrating so hard on the match. Keeping the league's top scorers scoreless was an incredible achievement.

Alan Basham's luck finally ran out two minutes after the restart, when Barking went one up. When they went two up a few minutes later, I was transported back to the terraces at Barking's Vicarage Field ground earlier in the season where a second-half blitz had left their supporters so dazed that they had lost track of the score. Something similar was a distinct possibility today.

But just when they needed it most, Bromley got a huge slice of good fortune. Mick Lloyd took a speculative shot from 35 yards out which went high in the air, landed in front of the Barking goalie who had wandered to the edge of his six-yard box and bounced over him into the net. With that kind of luck, I felt sure he'd win £5 in the next Bromley Football Club 200 Club lottery.

The visitors were so stunned they only scored once more after that, the traditional last-minute goal that Bromley were so fond of conceding at Hayes Lane.

Not many teams were so bad that their supporters would get a warm glow from a 3–1 defeat, but to Roy and I it felt like yet another potential late turning point in the season.

The improvement wasn't just on the scoreboard – the defending had actually bordered on competent at times and the attack looked a lot more threatening than it had in recent months.

This definitely felt like a shift. Like Crystal Palace, who were improving to the extent that they had a chance to avoid relegation, Bromley were playing as though they didn't want the embarrassment of finishing last.

It was then that I realised the problem with Bromley had nothing to do with fitness. The players, like the supporters, had been so crushed by the experience of loss after loss that they no longer believed winning was possible.

•••

The only thing that stopped me getting teased about being a Bromley supporter at school had been how badly Arsenal and Crystal Palace were doing.

But now, both teams were threatening to turn their seasons around. Palace had started to string a few good results together and Arsenal had just had their first win in 13 games.

It suddenly seemed that I was the only boy supporting a team doing badly.

More than ever I needed Bromley to win a game. The person who worked out the Isthmian League fixtures seemed determined to prevent this from happening.

The next match would take me back to the scene of the season's biggest disappointment – Lower Mead, Station Road, Wealdstone, Harrow, Middlesex.

•••

It was traumatic walking into the Wealdstone ground, which was tucked just behind the ABC cinema.

I was tempted to go there instead – watching *Carry On Up the Jungle* seemed a far less painful way to spend a Saturday afternoon.

But I soon felt the familiar excitement and anticipation, when we went through the turnstiles and into the ground.

This was enhanced when I learnt that Phil Amato had been rested. My theory was that this was a nice way of saying he'd been dropped, because Alan Basham was scared of Amato's fiery temper.

Like the rest of the success-starved Bromley faithful, I was also glowing in the praise of the Barking players following the last game. They'd apparently said how impressed they'd been with our defence. As this was a defence that had conceded nearly 100 goals in 30-odd games, it was a rare compliment.

It was as if it was now official that Bromley were an in-form side, even if that hadn't quite translated into points just yet.

Roy, Peter and Derek all seemed to sense we had a real chance. There was a good feeling amongst our small group. Even the Wealdstone tea tasted good.

Our confidence was partly down to the team's performance against Barking, partly because of what happened the last time we came to Wealdstone, but mostly the blind optimism that keeps football supporters coming back to watch their team week after week.

From the moment Ginger Warman kicked off, Bromley played with an urgency and skill we hadn't witnessed since the winning streak had come to an inglorious end all those months ago. Eric Nottage and Pat Brown both came close to scoring in the first few minutes.

We were outplaying Wealdstone at Lower Mead – a ground where we had lost every game we'd played in the entire history of the Isthmian League.

Just before the break, Bromley forced three corners in a row. From the third, Ginger's cross was glanced past the Wealdstone goalie by Postman Pat to give us a well-deserved lead.

A lead we held on to without much trouble as full-time approached.

The defence had been outstanding. I had no doubt that Wealdstone would agree with Barking's assessment. The Miles brothers were making a big difference and Soper was having another great game.

I looked at my watch. It was nearly 4.40pm.

Surely this was it. The first win all year. Our habit of conceding last-minute goals had been dealt with by Basham's fitness regime. The team were now capable of playing for the full 90 minutes and time was just about up.

The excitement amongst the travelling fans was immense. We were all whistling in vague approximation of the whistle of Mr CI Boswell (Gillingham), urging him to blow for full-time. He kept looking at his watch. Maybe it had stopped. I hoped not.

Wealdstone launched a last, desperate attack. Gary Hand, the left-back, scurried down the wing, put in a cross and Dave Swain, their top scorer, broke our hearts with a late, late equaliser.

A gasp of despair and disbelief came from the small group of faithful Bromley fans. But the disappointment of not winning was soon replaced by the joy of getting a draw. It was our first point of the year and a huge relief to those of us who had feared going a full 12 months without getting a single point.

I couldn't help myself – overcome with emotion, I clambered over the fence and ran onto the pitch, making a beeline for Alan Soper. When I reached him, I was suddenly tongue-tied, but managed to pat him on the back and say 'Well played, Sopes' (a nickname I had spontaneously given him).

He forced a smile, even though I could tell he was shattered after coming so close to experiencing winning a league match for the first time in six months.

I walked with him to the tunnel, which was slightly awkward as I couldn't think of anything else to say, but didn't want to leave his presence.

Eventually I was faced with the choice of either wordlessly following him into the changing room or turning round and going back to the coach.

I chose the latter.

•••

On the way home, I was so happy with the result and the way the team had played that I didn't even mind all the Esso stations we passed without stopping to fill up.

The coach dropped me off at the end of my road, where Dave was waiting for me. After filling him in on the Wealdstone game we got home, made ourselves a cup of tea and sat in front of the TV, in nervous anticipation.

The Eurovision Song Contest was about to start. Like today's Wealdstone/Bromley game, last year's contest had ended in a draw, even though Lulu deserved to win. This year, Mary Hopkin was representing the United Kingdom and she was amongst the favourites.

I wanted Luxemburg to win. The singer was called David Alexander Winter, which meant he and I almost had the same name – mine being David Alexander Roberts. His song was called 'I Fell From Heaven' and, although it wasn't very good, I felt it could easily win. It was the kind of song that usually did well. Dave was a fan of the Irish entry, 'All Kinds of Everything' by Dana, which I didn't think stood much of a chance.

As soon as the voting started, I knew I was in trouble. Everyone seemed to be voting for Dana, who eventually won easily, much to Dave's delight.

David Alexander Winter of Luxembourg finished rock bottom, making history in the process by scoring no points whatsoever.

Luxembourg had inadvertently become the Bromley of the Eurovision Song Contest.

•••

Afterwards, we got to talking about his sister.

I'd asked him to ask her what she'd say if I asked her out.

The thinking behind this strategy was that if she said she would say no, I could claim I was only joking.

So he asked her.

And then asked me if I wanted to know what she'd said. I said that I did and steeled myself for rejection.

The good news was, she liked me. The bad news was it was only as a friend. This was the one thing no teenage boy liked to hear. I felt crushed and suddenly didn't feel like talking any more. It was even worse than I felt after we'd lost to Wealdstone in that Amateur Cup tie. Worse than when I heard Una Stubbs had got married.

At least it explained the lack of Valentine's card.

I vowed to try and forget about women and just concentrate on football.

# ISTHMIAN LEAGUE HOW THEY STAND

## 26TH MARCH 1970

|                  | P   | W  | D  | L  | F  | A  | Pts |
|------------------|-----|----|----|----|----|----|-----|
| Barking . . . . . | .32 | 19 | 7  | 6  | 81 | 32 | 45  |
| Wycombe W . . . . | .27 | 18 | 7  | 2  | 58 | 18 | 43  |
| Sutton Utd . . . . | .30 | 18 | 7  | 5  | 60 | 28 | 43  |
| St Albans City . . | .31 | 16 | 8  | 7  | 53 | 36 | 40  |
| Enfield . . . . . | .25 | 16 | 7  | 2  | 52 | 15 | 39  |
| Hitchin Town . . . | .30 | 15 | 9  | 6  | 57 | 31 | 39  |
| Leytonstone . . . | .31 | 13 | 7  | 11 | 47 | 32 | 33  |
| Wealdstone . . . . | .30 | 14 | 5  | 11 | 45 | 39 | 33  |
| Tooting & Mit . . | .29 | 14 | 4  | 11 | 62 | 47 | 32  |
| Hendon . . . . . . | .26 | 11 | 9  | 6  | 46 | 33 | 31  |
| Oxford City . . . | .30 | 12 | 7  | 11 | 45 | 53 | 31  |
| Kingstonian . . . | .31 | 12 | 6  | 13 | 47 | 45 | 30  |
| Ilford . . . . . . | .34 | 7  | 14 | 13 | 38 | 66 | 28  |
| Woking . . . . . . | .31 | 10 | 7  | 14 | 43 | 50 | 27  |
| Dulwich . . . . . | .32 | 8  | 10 | 14 | 40 | 53 | 26  |
| Clapton . . . . . | .33 | 9  | 7  | 17 | 42 | 65 | 25  |
| Maidstone Utd . . | .31 | 7  | 5  | 19 | 36 | 62 | 19  |
| Walthamstow A . . | .31 | 7  | 5  | 19 | 35 | 68 | 19  |
| Corinthian Cs . . | .32 | 6  | 3  | 23 | 30 | 76 | 15  |
| **BROMLEY** . . . . . | **.32** | **3**  | **4**  | **25** | **24** | **92** | **10**  |

# CHAPTER TWENTY-TWO

The next morning I learnt that anything Bromley could do, Corinthian Casuals could do better.

When Bromley had lost last week, the Casuals had drawn. And just when we'd finally drawn a game, they'd won. This meant they were now three points clear of Bromley, a gap which looked like a gaping chasm, considering we'd only got one point all year.

The news for Hayesford Park Reserves was even worse. Anything we could do, every other team in our division could do much, much better.

Our form had completely deserted us, as evidenced by the latest game against Chelsfield Colts.

For once, I blamed Derek for the defeat. He hadn't been able to make it so a replacement goalie was needed. There was only one volunteer who was idiotic enough to believe that playing for 90 minutes behind a non-existent defence was going to end in any way other than disaster.

Me.

I still clung to the belief that I was a more than adequate replacement and certainly looked the part in the warm-up, confidently catching the ball and tipping a couple over the bar with unnecessarily flamboyant dives.

The problem came when the game started. My first save almost bent my hand backwards and I yelped in pain. I had never had to face such a hard shot. The ultimate ignominy followed seconds later when Roy of all people had to come to my rescue by clearing the ball off the line.

From then on, it was a procession of goals, eight in the first half and a further six in the second. It was only after the game when I realised that while it was really embarrassing when your team lost 14–1, it was doubly so if you were the goalkeeper.

I had also ruined my dad's driving gloves, which I'd used on the basis that any gloves were better than no gloves. Even if they were made from really expensive leather.

Afterwards, we went to the pub and sat outside, talking about the game. This was about the only time I was conscious of being a boy playing in a men's team. While they all drank shandy, I always had a couple of pints of blackcurrant and lemonade.

It was still one of the most enjoyable things about playing for Hayesford Park Reserves.

Sometimes, it was the only enjoyable thing.

•••

When Charlie King had left for his round the world trip, Bromley had only won four times. Now, three months and 30,000 miles later, he was back and Bromley had still only won four times.

What's more, when he left we were about to play Wealdstone away and when he returned we were also about to play Wealdstone away. He must have felt as though time had stood still.

He had missed the 1–1 draw at Wealdstone last weekend as he'd only just got back, but he was soon back in action at his beloved Hayes Lane.

He was selling programmes outside the ground before the Hendon fixture, as I turned up in plenty of time before my shift at the tea hut. He looked tanned but worried. The fact that he'd had results telegraphed to him on board ship had probably meant he'd been unable to completely relax.

I'd read in the paper that the first thing he'd done on his return was give a vote of confidence to the underachieving Alan Basham, which was more disappointing than surprising.

It didn't make any sense to me. Since Basham had taken over from the committee, Bromley hadn't won a single league game. And that was about five months ago. I wanted to know what hold he had on the club and Mr King in particular.

Peter hadn't yet arrived, so the tea hut was still locked. I leaned against it and read the programme.

The team news wasn't good. Jeff Bridge, who had spent Christmas at former teammate Colin England's hotel in the French alps was going back there for Easter. This meant that Phil Amato was being recalled after his 'resting'.

Then Roy ran over looking flustered, which was pretty much his normal state. He'd heard that Peter wouldn't be able to make it and wanted to know if I'd be OK running the tea hut on my own.

Pride and panic collided in my brain.

I had been well trained and knew all the jobs off by heart. Boiling the urn was the first job, before preparing the pot. I got the Cadbury Fingers and Jacob's Club Biscuit packets out of the cupboard and put them out on display. Next, I got the cups and saucers out and lined them up. Roy had brought the milk over. After making sure the sugar bowls were full, I was ready to open the shutters for business.

The good thing about me being out in sole charge now was that the crowd wasn't expected to be very big. Hendon were a good side, one of the big two in the Isthmian League. Traditionally, them and Enfield were the two teams you could count on losing to. This season, that list had expanded to include pretty much everyone else as well.

They were only about halfway in the table, but had loads of games in hand due to several successful cup runs. They had several internationals and always seemed to treat Bromley games like light-hearted training runs.

By this stage, Charlie King had taken up one of his other duties as ground announcer. This included revealing the name of the latest winner of £5 in the Bromley Supporters' Club '200' club. It was a certain Mr E Nottage, c/o Bromley Football Club.

He then ran through the changes that anyone who read the *Bromley and Kentish Times* already knew about and left us with the usual sounds of marching music.

●●●

The busiest times in the tea business are in the ten minutes before a game and at half-time.

The secret is to anticipate the number of customers and to prepare accordingly. I decided that I would probably be serving around 70 customers, most of whom would just require one cup. The exception to this was The Grubby, who would want two.

As I glanced up at the teams running onto the field, it was clear that I was a lot more nervous about the afternoon ahead than they were.

The first and only sign that an upset was on the cards came just as the first wave of tea drinkers had been served. Right in front of me, Mick Lloyd put in a perfect cross which '200' club winner Eric Nottage nodded past the England amateur goalie, John Swannell.

Bromley had taken the lead. I wanted to run out of the hut

to where The Grubby was sitting and share the excitement with him. But that would have been unprofessional.

Alan Soper then made one of the mistakes that so frustrated Bromley fans. He could be brilliant at times – every bit as good as Swannell. But he could also do some really embarrassing things. I suppose that was why he was playing for Bromley instead of someone good.

On this occasion, he made a great save from John Baker's header then undid the good work by dropping the ball and watching it roll into the net.

What made this worse was that Bromley were playing so well and would have deserved to go in at half-time leading.

If Hendon's first goal was the result of Soper's generosity, their second was down to pure good fortune. A hopeful shot from 20 yards out hit John Miles and bounced to another England amateur international, Rod Haider, who tucked home the winner.

It had been another excellent Bromley performance, but I was so fed up with Hendon's luck that I never wanted to see them again.

Unfortunately, we were playing them away later that week.

●●●

All Bromley had to do was beat a below-strength Sutton side at home and they would have a mathematical chance of avoiding finishing last. According to my calculations, anyway.

Sutton's idea of a weakened team was only having two England internationals instead of their usual three. Ken Grose, the history-making substitute from the game earlier in the season, had made the starting line-up. I was distressed to see that the man who had effortlessly scored a 20-minute hat-trick against us was a defender who had only revealed his goal-scoring prowess in the one game that season.

Charlie King's programme notes once again steered clear of reality by pointing out that Alan Basham was now well advanced in his plan to build a team 'capable of restoring our club's prestige.'

To contradict that, the next sentence announced that in tonight's line up, Phil Amato would be at left-back.

From my limited view from the tea hut, I spent the first half-hour of the game watching Sutton goalkeeper Bone jump up and down, trying to keep warm. All the action was at the other end. He had only one save to make, from David Wise, who managed to injure himself in the process of shooting and had to be carried off.

The inevitable Sutton goals both came at the start of the second half. One of their remaining England internationals, Larry Pritchard, dribbled past Amato to put the visitors into the lead, and then defender Ken Grose got his fourth of the season against Bromley to take Sutton to the top of the table and ensure Bromley finished bottom.

Alan Basham and Charlie King felt we needed strengthening in just three positions to make Bromley a 'very different proposition' for next season.

I don't know what positions they were talking about, but as far as I was concerned, only Soper, Nottage, Bridge, John Miles, Pat Brown and Ginger Warman were good enough to wear the famous white shirt.

●●●

It was the school holiday, so I had arranged to go and stay with Dave until the weekend, when we would be going our separate ways – he was off to Highbury and I was going to Hendon.

## BROMLEY'S BARREN SPELL CONTINUES

A BARREN Easter for Bromley, with no points and only one goal to show for 180 minutes of football—admittedly against two of the strongest non-league sides in the country. But there were signs that the team is improving and greater fire power in attack could have brought in a couple of points.

So Bromley's run of reverses now means they have won three points out of 46 and have gone 23 league games without a win, facts which speak for themselves and show why Bromley are currently propping up the Isthmian League.

Secretary, Charles King said this week, that there was the nucleus of a reasonable side at Hayes Lane—a not unreasonable statement in view of recent encouraging displays.

"I think we only need strengthening in another three positions—and we have things already in hand to achieve this for next season—will make us a very different proposition," he said.

The most interesting news from Hayes Lane for the remainder of the season, however, will not come from the pitch but probably from a full scale committee meeting which is planned in about a fortnight's time. Big long-term decisions could well be taken at this meeting.

The team which faced Sutton United, has been given a vote of confidence for this Friday's clash at Hendon.

The kick-off is at 7.30 p.m. and the match has been brought forward to keep in with the authorities' request to keep the F.A. Amateur Cup Final, day free of major non-league matches.

On Saturday, Hayes Lane stage the final of the London Youth Cup between Crystal Palace and Millwall, kick-off 11 a.m.

Bromley's remaining league fixtures for the season have been finalised. They are: Tooting and Mitcham, home, on Tuesday, April 14, Walthamstow at home on the 18th and Enfield away on April 30.

### BROMLEY 1, HENDON 2

BROMLEY can count themselves unlucky last Saturday, going down by the odd goal in three to powerful Hendon, at Hayes Lane, although their famous visitors were well below par.

It was all the more frustrating for their sparse band of loyal supporters, particularly in view of their recent revival.

They saw their team grab a shock lead after 17 minutes, when Eric NOTTAGE rose well to head home Lloyd's cross, and then saw their hopes dashed as Hendon grabbed goals close to both sides of the interval.

Super can be faulted for the first, after 20 minutes, although he did make a good save from Baker's header only to drop the ball and see it roll into the net.

This marred an otherwise excellent display, culminating in some brave saves in the closing stages, as Hendon turned on the pressure.

The winner was a piece of bad luck for Bromley, Jameson's hopeful shot cannoned off John Miles, putting England man, Rod HAIDER, through to score easily.

BROMLEY. — Super; M. Miles, Amato; P. Brown, J. Miles, Baxter; Lloyd, Marman, Nottage, Wise, Day. Sub.: Hall.

### BROMLEY 0, SUTTON UNITED 2.

Theoretically Bromley still have a chance, admittedly a slim one, of evading bottom spot in the Isthmian League, but after Tuesday night's defeat by a below form Sutton, the possibility of them accomplishing this looks very remote indeed.

Sutton goalkeeper, Bone, had one shot to save in the first 30 minutes of this match, which demonstrates clearly just how ineffective Bromley's striking force is. That came from Dave Wise in the 14th minute and he injured himself in the process.

Looking on the bright side, however, Bromley's defence must be given credit for keeping Sutton out for more than an hour.

Particularly outstanding was full-back Mick Miles, who turned in an uncompromising display of quick tackling and untrammelled use of the ball.

Soner, too, distinguished himself in the home goal making several good saves from the lively Sutton forwards, who found plenty of space to work in.

The second half opened with a spell of Bromley pressure, but Sutton broke away without too much difficulty and Pritchard dribbled through on the left to net easily with an acute angled drive.

The second goal duly followed 10 minutes later when Bonner was admitted to have handled Gradi's low drive with Bonner out of position and stretched Ken Grow converted the spot-kick.

This virtually ended the game as a contest and all that Bromley fans were left to cheer about, was some brave running from Johnny Warman and probing attacking by Pat Brown.

BROMLEY. — Super; M. Miles, Amato; P. Brown, J. Miles, Baxter; Lloyd, Marman, Nottage, Wise, Day. Sub.: Brown.

---

As we were sitting in his room, listening to *Blonde on Blonde*, I spotted something on his desk that made me realise instantly that we would be friends for life.

It was a large scrapbook, with the word ARSENAL painted in big red letters and a detailed sketch of the cannon from the team's badge, which must have taken him hours to draw.

I felt my heart rate increase with the excitement of this discovery. I had thought I was the only one who kept such a detailed record of my team – and now, thumbing through his book, I realised I wasn't alone.

I got even more excited when he explained that there were several other volumes in the cupboard, but this was one from a couple of years ago that he'd been reading last night.

It had page after page of yellowing match reports,

rumours of new signings (which had almost never come to fruition) and articles about players.

This was the kind of thing a true friendship was built upon, I realised. A shared love of something. In our case, football. His scrapbook seemed to contain every mention Arsenal had ever had in every newspaper.

Most impressive of all was the comprehensive record of Arsenal's participation in the *Quiz Ball* TV programme, in which various football teams had to decide whether to take the easy route to goal and answer one-point questions, or do it the hard but direct way, with four-point questions.

There were also two- and three-point questions, but successful teams rarely bothered with those.

Ian Ure had captained an Arsenal team which included Terry Neill and Bertie Mee as well as their guest supporter, the Radio Two disc jockey Jimmy Young.

In his neatest handwriting, Dave had faithfully recorded every answer given by the team and had devoted a whole spread to their triumphant run a couple of seasons ago.

This was when they had overcome a strong Leicester City line-up (including the in-form Lady Isobel Barnett) in the semi-final thanks to Ian Ure getting all four goals, before beating Dumbarton 7–3 (Neill 2, Ure 2, Young 3) in the final.

As it was the only trophy the team had won in the 1960s, Dave had given this modest achievement a disproportionate amount of space and prominence.

The scrapbook also featured a photo of Frank McLintock, with his arm around someone who looked a lot like Dave's dad. It turned out to be his uncle, who was holidaying in Costa Brava and found himself at the same hotel as the Arsenal captain. I wondered if he'd said 'It's not for me, it's for my nephew' when he asked if they could have their photo taken.

Dave's Arsenal scrapbook was like a less obsessive version of my Bromley scrapbook.

Once he had taken me through every single page, Dave announced it was time to go. He was going to Highbury to see his heroes take on West Ham, who would presumably be fielding their strongest side – something I still hadn't forgiven them for failing to do at Bromley.

While he would be watching Hurst and Moore (Peters had just moved to Spurs for a record fee of £200,000), I would be at Hendon for a meaningless Isthmian League fixture.

With a wistful glance at his sister's closed door, I left Dave's house and cycled off to meet the coach at Hayes Lane, which would take me to yet another game we had no chance of winning.

●●●

Hendon basically carried on where they had left off six days earlier. Bromley went into the game having conceded 96 goals and came out of it having brought up the 100 for the season. There was even time for number 101.

Alan Soper, so often the hero, was at fault with goals number 97, 98, 99, 100 and 101.

His mistakes were, in order:

1. Giving away a free-kick by taking too many steps, which resulted in a goal.
2. Letting a corner-kick float over his head and into the net.
3. Dropping a shot at the feet of a Hendon forward, who gratefully accepted the gift.
4. Giving a penalty away by pulling down a Hendon midfielder.
5. Getting himself stranded and watching helplessly as a header found the empty net.

**The ton up, as Bromley get another hiding**

I felt sorry for him. He'd had a great season, but his confidence must have been shot to pieces.

After the final whistle, I once again climbed over the fence and ran onto the pitch, keen to re-establish contact with Alan Soper and reassure him that he was still brilliant, despite today's lapses.

But it wasn't to be. The thought of a warm bath on a bitterly cold afternoon was clearly uppermost on his mind, because as soon as he saw me coming towards him, he broke into a light jog and reached the tunnel without looking back.

It hadn't been a productive day, to say the least. I hadn't managed to talk to Dave's sister (I still harboured hopes of changing her mind about me) or Alan Soper, the coach hadn't stopped off at an Esso petrol station and Bromley had never looked like winning.

At least I had another game to watch the next day. One that was even bigger than Hendon v Bromley.

•••

One man who was missing from the Leeds line-up to face Chelsea in the FA Cup Final was former Bromley reserve John Faulkner. His career since moving to Leeds hadn't gone as well as he would have hoped.

He'd played twice for the first team. In the first game, against Burnley, he scored an own goal. In the second, against Manchester City, he broke his leg.

But this tenuous Bromley connection was enough for me to support Leeds as Dave and I watched the game on TV at his house. He wanted Chelsea to win, mainly because I didn't.

The rivalry became so heated that we had a bet. If my team won, he would have to go to school with a T-shirt that had 'Bromley are better than Arsenal' painted on it. And if his team won, I would have to go to school wearing a T-shirt saying that Arsenal were better than Bromley.

It was a bet neither of us wanted to lose and definitely added to the excitement of the match.

First Leeds took the lead and then Chelsea equalised. Leeds took the lead again and Chelsea equalised again. Dave and I seemed to be swapping emotions every 20 minutes or so – the seesaw nature of the game meant hopes were raised then dashed before being raised then dashed all over again.

Being a Bromley supporter, this was something I was used to.

The match ended in a draw, the first one ever in a Wembley Cup Final and we were both spared any further humiliation.

●●●

I had never been to a game where I wasn't convinced that the referee was biased against my team.

But the most blatantly biased refereeing I have ever seen cost Bromley two points against Tooting and Mitcham, and ensured that we would finish the season bottom of the table.

We had three perfectly good goals disallowed, while Tooting and Mitcham were given two goals that clearly weren't.

The first hit the woodwork and bounced on the goal line before John Miles scrambled it clear. Unbelievably, Mr Clark pointed to the centre-spot.

It was just like Geoff Hurst's goal in the World Cup Final, the only difference being that while everyone in England knew that Hurst's effort did cross the line, the one from Hutchins of Tooting and Mitcham clearly didn't. I had a perfect view from the tea hut.

But Mr Clark hadn't finished yet. He then failed to give Ken Jelly, Tooting and Mitcham's superstar striker, offside even when it couldn't have been more obvious that he was. Everyone except the man in black could see that Jelly was at least three yards ahead of the last defender. The grateful centre-forward ran through to beat Soper from close range. He'd already scored 52 goals in the season. It wasn't as though he needed to be given any more.

'How much are they paying you, mate?' shouted an incredulous voice from the Main Stand, putting into words what everyone must have been thinking.

Next, it was Eric Nottage's turn to feel hard done by, when a brilliant header flashed past the Tooting and Mitcham goalie. The celebrations were cut short by Mr Clark's decision to disallow the goal for no apparent reason.

The official then continued with his vendetta against Bromley in general and Nottage in particular by disallowing another perfectly good goal, this time for offside when he clearly wasn't.

Things had got so bad that I actually felt incredible rage when Mr Clark disallowed yet another goal – this time from Bobby Lennox – even though the Bromley striker clearly punched the ball into the net. By this time I could no longer differentiate between right and wrong. If the referee disallowed a goal, I now automatically felt a great injustice had been done.

The final scoreline was Bromley 2 Tooting and Mitcham 4, but if it was adjusted to take into account all the unfair decisions, it would have been Bromley 5 Tooting and Mitcham 2.

I was so angry that I went home and wrote a letter to the president of the Isthmian League, complaining about the totally biased performance of the referee and gave detailed descriptions (with diagrams) of the Bromley goals he had disallowed, as well as the Tooting and Mitcham ones he had given.

I finished by saying that, in my opinion, he should never be allowed to referee again. And if they didn't believe me, they could ask anyone who was at the game.

A week later, I got a reply. It thanked me for my letter and said that my comments had been noted.

Reading between the lines, I took this to mean that Mr Clark had blown his whistle for the last time.

I was glad the league had acted so decisively.

●●●

The Hayesford Park Reserves season ended without a win. The last game was against Albermarle Reserves, who were outclassing us to such an extent they were up 6–0 after half-an hour.

They seemed to have men to spare. Every time we got the ball, there were several markers. And every time they attacked, they seemed to outnumber us. It felt as though we were playing 12 men. I counted them. We were.

After pointing this out discreetly to the referee (I didn't want to be seen as someone who told tales), the extra player was sent to the sidelines.

It didn't make any difference. Albemarle Reserves were

# BROMLEY HAVE THREE GOALS DISALLOWED AND LOSE AGAIN

### BROMLEY 2, TOOTING AND MITCHAM 4

SLIPSHOD defending from both sides and some ludicrous decisions by referee Mr. F. Clark combined to make this a game almost bordering on high farce. Add to this three disallowed goals for Bromley and it all made for an interesting, if not classic, Isthmian League clash at Hayes Lane on Tuesday night.

Bromley are now definitely bottom, a position they have looked unlikely to avoid since the beginning of the year.

They threw this game away in the first two minutes, when they gave Tooting's leading scorer, Ken Jelly, a man with more than 50 goals this season, the softest of chances, and thereafter spent the remainder of the match striving desperately to haul themselves back on terms.

They nearly succeeded, too, in an inspired period of attacking just after the interval.

They hit back with a Nottage goal and then the same player had a brilliant header disallowed," which would have brought the scores level.

Again, with the score at 3—2 in the visitors' favour, Tony Day was just off target with a bullet header from Mick Miles' accurate cross.

The small crowd had hardly time to settle down when Tooting took the lead.

A long ball was punted out of defence and caught the whole Bromley defence napping.

Jelly streaked through to slide the ball home.

Soper found himself pretty busy in the next 20 minutes, as he kept out shots from Webb and Tooting's tricky left-winger, Kelly.

had another "goal" disallowed for offside.

Six minutes later, Tooting restored their two-goal advantage. Jelly, from a suspiciously

Bob Lennox gets up to head this cross in the early stages of the game against Tooting, last Tuesday night.

**MANOR LOSE LEAD AND THE MATCH**

still much better than us, even with the same amount of players and they ran out 9–2 winners.

We had finished the season anchored to the bottom of the table, with just one point to show for seven months of freezing weather, hard bumpy pitches, niggling injuries and wasted effort.

Our record made painful reading. We'd played 18 games and lost 17 of them, drawing one. We'd scored 16 goals and conceded a dismal 128.

As we were in the lowest division of the Orpington and Bromley District Sunday League, we couldn't be relegated. We'd already reached rock bottom.

Instead, we were invited to 'apply for re-election'.

If Bromley finished bottom, they would also avoid relegation for the same reason. They couldn't go any lower.

Together with Corinthian Casuals, we had completely lost touch with the other 18 teams in the Isthmian League.

And I had finally discovered why this had happened.

Shamateurism.

**ORPINGTON AND BROMLEY DISTRICT SUNDAY LEAGUE**

|  | P | W | D | L | F | A | Pts |
|---|---|---|---|---|---|---|---|
| Forresters . . . . . .18 | 18 | 16 | 1 | 1 | 125 | 17 | 33 |
| Albemarle Res . . . .8 | 8 | 14 | 1 | 3 | 1 | 28 | 29 |
| Chelsfield Colts . .18 | 18 | 12 | 2 | 4 | 95 | 46 | 26 |
| Eton Park . . . . .18 | 18 | 9 | 3 | 6 | 71 | 41 | 21 |
| Barnet Res . . . . .18 | 18 | 9 | 1 | 8 | 41 | 50 | 19 |
| Glenwood Res . . . .18 | 18 | 7 | 4 | 7 | 46 | 47 | 18 |
| Farnborough Youth . .18 | 18 | 7 | 2 | 9 | 49 | 49 | 16 |
| Cudham Res . . . . .18 | 18 | 4 | 1 | 13 | 33 | 107 | 9 |
| Chelsfield Villa . .18 | 18 | 3 | 2 | 13 | 43 | 87 | 8 |
| **Hayesford Park Res** . .18 | 18 | 0 | 1 | 17 | 16 | 128 | 1 |

It was a word I'd heard many times, but never understood what it meant, until I plucked up the courage to ask Peter.

He explained that Isthmian League rules meant you had to be strictly amateur, but most teams got around this by paying expenses or giving other perks.

Among the very few strictly amateur teams left were Bromley and Corinthian Casuals.

Most of the rest found ways of rewarding players for their efforts, especially the glamour teams who attracted much bigger crowds than Bromley. I'd even heard that Sutton's manager earned £1,500 a year while Alan Basham earned nothing. I think I was meant to be outraged by this, but it seemed an accurate reflection of their respective abilities.

No Bromley player or official was getting anything – not even their bus fares to the ground. At least several of them seemed to have better luck picking up £5 in the weekly Bromley Supporters' Club '200' club.

The more I thought about the shamateurism issue, the more convinced I became that it explained our lowly league position.

The FA had announced an inquiry. I couldn't wait to hear the results of it, especially if it meant that everyone apart from us and Corinthian Casuals would get points deducted.

If all went well, the Isthmian League table could have a completely different look by the time the season ended.

This was the kind of straw I was now clutching at, as I prepared for Bromley's last home game of the season.

●●●

April 18, 1970 was one of the quietest match days I'd experienced at Hayes Lane. The visitors, Walthamstow Avenue, were fourth from bottom of the table but well clear of the danger zone. They didn't seem to have brought any supporters with them and there were very few Bromley fans, even though it was the last chance to see Bromley play at home for several months.

The terraces were completely empty and the main stand held less than a dozen spectators. A cold wind blew across the ground.

The air of desolation was enhanced by a flat-sounding Charlie King, clearly less than rejuvenated after his recent cruise, announcing on the tannoy that although this had been the worst season in living memory, the support had been tremendous and next season was going to be a lot better.

There was no real conviction behind his words.

As I made my way towards the tea hut, Peter met me half way. The news he had sent a wave of excitement through me – so much so, that I had to get him to repeat it.

I hadn't been mistaken. Peter had asked me if I wanted to work in the Supporters' Club hut today. This was what I had been working towards all season. A place in the inner sanctum of Bromley supporters.

I slowly walked over to the hut, relishing every step. Like the tea hut, it wasn't busy. A story that was the same all over the ground. The turnstile operators were just as under-employed and the programme sellers were stuck with large stacks of unsold programmes.

As I unlatched the white gate to go into Supporters' Club area, my heart was almost bursting with pride. And then it got even better. I was told that I might as well sit on the little bench in front of the hut until they got a bit busier.

I felt like a king and the bench felt like a throne. Behind the goal at the far end, a lone figure with long ginger hair had taken his usual place. I hoped he'd seen me.

I treasured every moment of the match, apart from the

four Walthamstow Avenue goals which were scored right in front of me, during a second-half blitz that took the scoreline from a respectable 0–0 to an embarrassing 4–0.

The view was incredible. I had never been so near to the action. At one stage, I was close enough to hear Phil Amato say 'Leave it, Bridgey' as Jeff Bridge had tried to take a quick throw directly in front of me.

It got even better when Roy and Derek joined me and we sat together in the fading Spring sunshine, in the shadow of the floodlight pylon doing what we loved to do best. Watching Bromley.

The fact that we were losing 4–0 didn't seem to matter. It was as though all hope had already been beaten out of us and we had even accepted that we weren't going to catch Corinthian Casuals.

Just talking amongst ourselves and intermittently shouting encouragement to a wildly discouraged bunch of players made me realise that what made a football club wasn't just the teams, it was also the fans. They were as much a part of the club as the players.

We talked about finishing bottom of the league and discovered that we'd all dealt with it in different ways. Derek, the practical one, was already looking forward to next season, where Bromley would be able to start afresh. Roy, the emotional one, had fallen into a deep depression, while Peter, the mysterious one, was typically giving nothing away about how he felt.

As for me, I had been able to think of little else. Bromley Football Club was the most important thing in my life and the season's succession of failures had taken its toll. Over the last few months, I had become morose and uncommunicative; something that had been put down to teenage hormones, but that wasn't the real reason. It was really down to Bromley. All

## BROMLEY'S WORST IN 25 YEARS

### LOCAL TEAMS SOON OUT

BROMLEY were defeated but not disgraced in the London Inter-Borough U-19 Basketball Rally Championships at Crystal Palace last Saturday, when they failed to reach the final stages.

Drawn in a strong pool that included Newham, who went on to reach the final, Bromley was three and lost three matches.

Successes were against Hillingdon, Redbridge, and Houslow, while reverses came at the hands of Newham, Ealing and Bexley.

Bromley were handicapped by having played together for only six weeks and their lack of experience told in the fiercely contested matches.

Mr. Paul Longborn and Mr. Neil Brown, organiser and coach respectively, of the team, are planning a closer link with local schools in order to tap all the available talent.

Last year, a schools' league was started for the first time in Bromley and following its success, Mr. Longborn is hoping to start a summer tournament.

"I think we could have a real chance of winning next year, especially in six of our team will be available," he said.

The two girls' teams A and B also failed to reach the finals, but they, too, were under the handicap of having been formed only weeks before the competition.

Mrs. Sonia Batten, leader of the All Saints Youth Club, Orpington, said she hoped the two girls' teams would form the nucleus of a new borough netball club.

### Avenue's blitz is sad end to home games

**BROMLEY 0, WALTHAMSTOW 4**

HARDLY unexpectedly, the season finished on a flat note at Hayes Lane last Saturday, where the home team were clinically destroyed by four second-half goals.

There was the by now familiar entry in the programme that "all concerned are busy making arrangements, which it is hoped will bring better results next season," a few words of commiseration over the public address system for the loyal band of supporters, thanking them for their unswerving support, and then the curtain came down at home on Bromley's worst playing season since the war.

Bromley did have one more game in the league, against Amateur Cup holders Enfield, away next Monday evening but the mud boggles at the intriguing question which could be thrown up.

To return to Saturday's game, however, there was very little on the credit side.

There was some method and solid build-ups and the defence played hard to hold out with half-time.

Several players, notably Dave Wise and Ken Lyneza, produced some work-rate moves without achieving anything positive.

Eric Nottage, who still looks a useful player after all these years, was given to support up front and constantly found himself on his own, facing three or more opposition players.

The Bromley goal had some narrow escapes in the first half, only being kept intact by some pot ditch clearances and poor shooting from the visitors.

Lyneza was a live wire early on for Bromley and a cross from the right almost caught out Parsons, in the Walthamstow goal.

Minutes later, the same player found space for himself well on

Brooke headed in a left-wing corner.

They followed this with some near misses before rattling home two more goals in the final ten minutes through Gillett and Terry.

Bromley: Isard; Brown; Bridge; Miles; H. Moss; J. Gage; Wise; Lyneza (Wooten); Nottage; Gilbey.

#### TOUGH CLASH WITH THE CUP HOLDERS

Bromley round up what has been for them a disastrous season, with a tough away match at Enfield, the current Amateur Cup holders, on Monday, kick-off 7.30 p.m.

The team will not be revealed until after the Thursday's training session, but it will most likely be drawn from 12 last Saturday's team plus Colin and Pat Brown.

Enfield have a sparkling chance of doing the "double" and adding the Isthmian League title to their cup.

ERIC NOTTAGE

### JOHN HIT BY LEEDS JINX

THE Leeds United jinx struck down John Faulkner in only his second league appearance last Saturday when he fractured a kneecap in the match against Manchester City at Elland Road.

Faulkner, of St. Mary Cray, joins a long list of Leeds casualties who include the man he was replacing at centre-half, Jack Charlton, the England pivot.

John was carried off at Elland Road during the match against Manchester City. Watching the game from the stand was another injured Leeds player, Paul Reaney, who has a broken leg.

It has been a harsh and dramatic baptism to professional soccer for 22-year-old John, who was signed from Isthmian League side Sutton last month.

In his league debut against

### FIXTURES AND RESULTS

**ORPINGTON AND BROMLEY SUNDAY LEAGUE**

**BROMLEY LEAGUE**

**BECKENHAM AMATEUR LEAGUE**

---

I wanted was to see a performance that would give me hope for the future, but once again, I'd seen the opposite.

There was only one game to go after this — the nightmare fixture away to Enfield. Strangely, there was sufficient supporter interest for a coach to be completely booked out.

After the game, while all the other Bromley fans trudged out of the ground for the last time that season, I was still sitting on the bench, reluctant to ever leave it.

•••

There were a lot of nervous football fans at school. The Arsenal contingent were as surprised as anyone else that their team had reached the Inter-Cities Fairs Cup Final, where they would face Anderlecht – my favourite Belgian team. The fate of the Palace fans was in the hands of Sunderland and Sheffield Wednesday. If either team won their final match of the season, Palace would go down to the Second Division.

The sole Bromley supporter had less at stake, but a good performance at Enfield could possibly stop me being the only football fan in the entire school whose season would end in an unmitigated disaster.

# CHAPTER
# TWENTY-THREE

Enfield pretty much won everything they wanted to win. They were the current Amateur Cup holders and Isthmian League champions, a title they were about to retain.

They were so good that their right winger, Adams, had scored more goals during the season than the entire Bromley team put together.

And he wasn't even their leading scorer.

That was John Connell, one of the most famous non-league players in the world. He seemed to be a regular fixture in the pages of *The Amateur Footballer,* which I dutifully bought every month from the Supporters' Club hut even though it was really boring.

I didn't envy Alan Soper. I doubted he'd got much sleep the previous night worrying about Enfield's star-studded attack. I know I hadn't.

It wasn't just Enfield and Bromley supporters who were at Enfield Stadium that Monday night. There were fans with Sutton United scarves as well as a small Wycombe Wanderers contingent. I presumed they had all come to see just how many goals Enfield could rack up against one of the worst defences in English football.

It felt a bit strange talking about our chances of a keeping the scoreline in single figures, but that was the best we could realistically hope for.

Only three of the Bromley team had played when the

teams had last met at the beginning of the season, while the Enfield line-up was almost identical to tonight's.

As soon as the referee took the field, I knew we were doomed. It was Mr KG Salmon, who I held personally responsible for our loss in the first league game of the season at Wycombe. He was now in charge of the last league game, too.

The first ten minutes only enhanced the feeling of a season going full circle. It was like the opening fixture against West Ham all over again. I was checking my watch every few minutes, becoming increasingly hopeful of a result that would shock the football world.

Enfield just couldn't find a way through a superbly well-organised Bromley defence, with Alan Bonney in particular standing out.

This sudden ability to play far better than usual was contagious – the Miles brothers were so effective that Enfield were reduced to taking shots from 30 yards out.

Unfortunately, this was something they were very good at and John Connell hit the bar with one such effort after 20 minutes. This seemed to give the home side confidence and a few minutes later John Connell (obviously) gave them the lead.

But, just like in the earlier meeting between the teams, the expected floodgates didn't open. And just as in the earlier meeting, Bromley unexpectedly drew level. It was through Eric Nottage, a man who had been called an 'old warhorse' in just about everything I'd ever read about him throughout the season. He calmly beat Ian Wolstenholme in the Enfield goal and it was 1–1. Against Enfield. Away.

I looked at my watch. The defence just had to hold out for an hour or so, for a result that would shake the very foundations of amateur football.

From then on, it was one-way traffic.

It was the first time in a long time that I'd seen the team

in white dominate a game so extensively. The reason for this was that Bromley were playing in red, to avoid clashing with Enfield's white shirts and blue shorts.

It was hard to see how anyone could have possibly mistaken Bromley for Enfield, even if they'd been wearing identical kits.

The game was agony to watch – wave after wave of attacks were being repelled by the great Alan Soper, whose form was every bit as impressive as it had been in 'The Soper Match' earlier in the season, when he had almost single-handedly kept Woking scoreless.

Anticipation of a shock result was growing – not just amongst the Bromley fans, but also amongst the Wycombe and Sutton United fans, who I learnt were there to support Bromley. Both of their teams were still in with a chance of winning the title, as long as Enfield lost tonight.

Then halfway through the second half, something happened that caused three sets of supporters to simultaneously groan in frustration and one set to celebrate wildly. Enfield took the lead. The goal was a good one – it had to be to beat Soper.

Bromley didn't crumble as I expected them to. They fought back and came close through Mick Lloyd, but Enfield held out for the narrowest of wins.

As the final whistle blew on our worst ever season, the Bromley supporters spontaneously stood and burst into heartfelt applause, having experienced the rare feeling of pride in the team's performance. If they'd played that well over the previous six months, things would have turned out differently.

We all shook hands with each other, laughing in disbelief at how close Bromley had just come to beating the best amateur side in the country. As we made our way back to the coach for the last time that season, the atmosphere was like the end of term at school, where everyone was just relieved the torture was over – until it all started up again.

I was in a happy daze, barely able to register the impressive nature of Bromley's performance. The only slight doubt in my mind was that maybe Enfield hadn't quite been at their best, considering this had been their eighth league game in 17 days.

●●●

As I stared back at Enfield's ground from the coach, I decided to forgo the card game so I could work out my annual end-of-season awards. I planned to get Dave to design them, as he was really good at drawing. I was then going to present the certificates to the players after the first of next season's pre-season friendlies.

The Best Player award was a tough one, because they'd all been pretty useless. I toyed with the controversial idea of not awarding it to anyone, but instead went with someone who, I felt, hadn't had a bad game in the Bromley shirt. Alan Stonebridge. He was the club's second top scorer for the season, despite leaving half way through it.

Although I wouldn't be able to present his certificate in person, I would send it to him care of Carshalton Athletic.

Best Goal had to take into account several factors, as Brian Moore had once explained on ITV's *The Big Match*. It wasn't just the brilliance of the goal, but also the importance of the game, the conditions and the strength of the opposition. Once again, the path led straight to Alan Stonebridge. His penalty against Enfield at Hayes Lane was one I felt I would never forget. The pressure on Stonebridge must have been enormous and he took his chance coolly. I knew having a penalty as best goal would also be controversial, but I was comfortable with my decision.

Not many teams would merit a Goalie of the Season award, but not many teams would have had as many goalies over the course of a season as Bromley. This was another straightforward one. Despite letting in 30 goals he should have easily saved, Alan Soper was my pick. I only hoped he wouldn't run away when I approached him to present him with his certificate.

Winners of the less prestigious awards were:

> John Miles – Best Defender
> Roy Pettet – Best Passer
> Johnny Warman – Best Dribbler
> Phil Amato – Worst Player

The latter was one award I wouldn't be presenting. Amato was highly temperamental and might react badly. The Morrie head butt hadn't been totally erased from my mind.

As I put my pen back in the pocket of my sheepskin, I reflected on how good the season had been apart from what had happened on the pitch.

It had started off with me watching games on my own, from high up in the stand. Since then, I'd made friends with some fellow supporters like The Grubby, Derek, Roy and Peter and become a real part of Bromley Football Club, by helping run the tea hut as well as playing regularly for their Sunday league team. And just when I'd thought it couldn't get any better, it had. Being able to watch a game from the Supporters' Club hut was something I would never have imagined was possible all those months before. But sitting on that truncated bench felt like one of the greatest achievements of my life. I felt as though I had finally been accepted.

This was echoed in my feelings about life at school.

The season had, again, started badly. But if becoming a boarder was the low point, being expelled from Sevenoaks was the high point and the start of my change in fortune. After a false start at Langley Park, when I tried to get in with the skinhead crowd, I had made some good friends, including Dave. Despite our differences over football and women, he and I genuinely seemed to enjoy other's company and we spent a lot of time together outside school.

I definitely felt I'd grown up since the start of the season. If adult life was going to prove to be a series of crushing disappointments mixed in with the occasional glimpse of joy, which I suspected would be the case, then supporting Bromley had prepared me well for the future.

I'd also learnt that supporting a club meant sticking with them when times got tough. The reward came when they did have a win – it meant so much more than being one of tens of thousands of spectators who turned up week after week to watch their expensively assembled team thrash yet another hapless opponent. When Bromley actually won a game, it meant I could take a real sense of achievement out of the result and I'd be walking around with a smile on my face for the whole of the following week. Or until they next lost.

It was in this mood of feeling really quite pleased how things had worked out that I decided to re-assess the criteria for judging what sort of season it had been for Bromley.

In the post-match euphoria which these days came from a close defeat, it suddenly became obvious that the true measure of a team's success was not where they finished in the league, but how they did in their home and away games against the team who ended up winning the title.

The fact that Bromley had held Enfield to a 1–1 draw back in August and now come agonisingly close to a similar result in their final game meant my team were as good as anyone in the Isthmian League, despite the apparently overwhelming evidence to the contrary.

There were other factors that proved Bromley were an improved side from the previous season, where they had finished much higher in the table. The biggest loss had then been 9–0 to Sutton. This season the 8–0 defeat at Barking had been the worst.

Then there were the games against Hillingdon Borough. Last season, we'd lost 7–0 to them in the FA Cup. This season it was a much closer 4–1.

By the time I got home from Bromley's 28th game in a row without a win, I had managed to convince myself that it had been a magnificent season, marred only by finishing a distant last in the table with just ten points from 38 games, having scored a pathetic 31 goals and conceding 111.

I don't think the *Bromley and Kentish Times* agreed with this assessment. I eagerly turned to the back page of the edition that came out a few days after the game and was shocked to see that it was the first time football hadn't made the lead story all season.

The big news was that the Beckenham Ladies Swimming Club were facing an increase in charges for hiring the local pool.

●●●

Back in August, I had been looking forward to seeing Moore, Hurst and Peters at Hayes Lane. Now, almost a year later, I couldn't wait to see them play in the World Cup in Mexico on our new colour telly. Dave and I had decided to watch all 32 games, starting with the hosts against Russia.

We were even more in love with football than ever –

everyone at school was. Our teams had all redeemed themselves in their final games of the season. I was ecstatic with Bromley's result at Enfield, the Arsenal fans were overjoyed because their team had won the Inter-Cities Fairs Cup thanks to goals from my love rival Jon Sammels, Dave's hero Eddie Kelly and John Radford, who managed the feat without wearing his Sensational John Radford Football Boots. The Palace fans were just as happy, as they celebrated somehow avoiding relegation.

As I looked through my almost-complete collection of Esso World Cup coins and listened to the England squad's single 'Back Home', I felt proud and optimistic. There were plenty of signs pointing towards an England victory.

Bromley's future seemed equally assured. The performance against Enfield a few weeks ago showed that even without Alan Stonebridge, we had managed to assemble a team capable of winning the Isthmian League when it kicked off again in just a few months time.

The 1969/70 season was already a distant memory.

# ISTHMIAN LEAGUE HOW THEY STAND

## END OF SEASON

|                   | P   | W  | D  | L  | F  | A   | Pts |
|-------------------|-----|----|----|----|----|-----|-----|
| Enfield. . . . . .  | .38 | 27 | 8  | 3  | 91 | 26  | 62  |
| Wycombe W . . . .   | .38 | 25 | 11 | 2  | 85 | 24  | 61  |
| Sutton Utd . . . .  | .38 | 24 | 9  | 5  | 75 | 35  | 57  |
| Barking . . . . .   | .38 | 21 | 9  | 8  | 93 | 47  | 51  |
| Hendon . . . . . .  | .38 | 19 | 12 | 7  | 77 | 44  | 50  |
| St Albans City . .  | .38 | 21 | 8  | 9  | 69 | 40  | 50  |
| Hitchin Town. . .   | .38 | 19 | 10 | 9  | 71 | 40  | 48  |
| Tooting & Mit . .   | .38 | 19 | 5  | 14 | 88 | 62  | 43  |
| Leytonstone . . .   | .38 | 17 | 7  | 14 | 57 | 41  | 41  |
| Wealdstone. . . .   | .38 | 15 | 10 | 13 | 53 | 48  | 40  |
| Oxford City . . .   | .38 | 15 | 7  | 16 | 61 | 78  | 37  |
| Kingstonian. . . .  | .38 | 13 | 9  | 16 | 55 | 57  | 35  |
| Ilford . . . . . .  | .38 | 8  | 15 | 15 | 42 | 73  | 31  |
| Dulwich Hamlet . .  | .38 | 8  | 12 | 18 | 46 | 66  | 28  |
| Woking . . . . . .  | .38 | 10 | 7  | 21 | 46 | 69  | 27  |
| Walthamstow A. . .  | .38 | 11 | 5  | 22 | 52 | 81  | 27  |
| Clapton . . . . .   | .38 | 9  | 7  | 22 | 45 | 87  | 25  |
| Maidstone Utd . .   | .38 | 7  | 8  | 23 | 48 | 84  | 22  |
| Corinthian Cs . .   | .38 | 6  | 3  | 29 | 30 | 99  | 15  |
| **BROMLEY** . . . . . | **.38** | **3** | **4** | **31** | **28** | **111** | **10** |

# Epilogue

What happened next?

Well, England didn't win the 1970 World Cup. Or the one after that. Or the one after that. Or the one after that. Or the one after that. Or the one after that. Or the one after that. Or the one after that. Or the one after that. Or the one after that.

Bromley had to wait until August 22nd to get their first win of 1970. It was against Corinthian Casuals and the scorer of the only goal was Jim Roberts. By that time, everyone had forgotten my claims that he was my uncle. The team managed to finish the season a far more respectable fifth-from-bottom.

I left Bromley in the mid-seventies and have only watched the team play twice since then. The first time was at Hayes Lane, where 21 players were involved in a mass brawl after Junior Crooks (an Extrudor Operator) headbutted the opposing goalie. The second time was at Swindon in the FA Cup a year later, when Bromley lost 7–0 and got a standing ovation from the home fans.

•••

Dave and I are still friends. He became a reporter and moved to the US where he is now a sub-editor in Florida, which means the only way he can watch Arsenal is on American TV. He met some of the skinheads at a school reunion on his last visit home and described them as being 'pleasant, middle-aged family men'.

The Grubby never left Bromley. He had awful luck with his

health, but never complained about it. He is now working as a caretaker at his local church hall.

Derek continued to watch Bromley until family commitments meant he no longer had the time. He still has his tax-consultancy business and is a referee in the Orpington and Bromley District Sunday League. At 60, he has recently become a father for the third time.

Peter continues to be a mystery. The last I heard, he had moved down to Bath and was working for a government organisation.

Alan Stonebridge took early retirement from teaching in 1997, but has recently returned to it part time. He still coaches football in schools and local clubs, with a particular interest in encouraging girls to take up the game. His son, Ian, played for England at Under-18 level, alongside Joe Cole, Gareth Barry and Michael Carrick.

Eric Nottage, who owned his own electrical firm, retired recently. He still lives in the Bromley area and one of his regular jobs was maintaining the Hayes Lane floodlights.

After finishing his football career (and subsequent pizza making career), Jeff Bridge moved to South Australia, where he taught until retiring in June 2008. His wife sent me a recent photo and he looks in great shape.

Alan Basham reaped the benefits of staying fit by continuing to run his own building company well into his sixties.

Graham Gaston left the printing business and became a paramedic in Sevenoaks. Like so many of his team mates, he has recently retired.

After many years as a salesman, Phil Amato now runs his father's shoe business.

'Judo' Al Hayes changed his name to Lord Alfred Hayes and found fame on the American TV wrestling programme,

*Tuesday Night Titans*. He went on to become an announcer on *Prime Time Wrestling*, a career that was interrupted when he was taken hostage live on air by Sergeant Slaughter and his Iraqi allies.

Jon Sammels became a driving instructor in Leicester. Ian Ure was a social worker at Lower Mass Prison in Scotland.

Dave's sister never married.

As for Roy, I completely lost touch with him.

●●●

In 2007, Bromley won promotion into the Blue Square Southern Conference, which is only a couple of divisions away from the Football League. It was arguably the biggest achievement in their history.

Even though I was now living in New Zealand, I was able to watch the highlights of the play-off final against Billericay Town on Bromley's website. It finished 1–1 and went to penalties, where Bromley won 4–2.

The crowd was enormous – far bigger than I had ever seen at Hayes Lane. The new stand looked far more impressive than the old Main Stand, which had burned down in 1992. There were now lifts, a café, five-a-side pitches and a brand-new club shop.

The ground had been renamed The Courage Stadium and there was no room for the tea hut, which had been torn down, or the old Supporters' Club hut which seemed to have undergone a similar fate.

After the match highlights, there was an interview with Mark Goldberg, the Bromley manager. Standing just behind him, soaking up every word, was a grinning spectator in his early sixties. The wild, curly hair was unmistakable, even though it was now mainly grey. The glasses were bigger and thicker than he'd needed nearly 40 years beforehand and the face plumper and more lined. But Roy's beaming smile was the same one I'd seen way back when our team had beaten Oxford City just before Christmas in 1969, or when we had almost held Enfield in the last game of that season.

I felt incredibly happy that Bromley had finally made it into the big time. And I was even happier that one of the Bromley Boys had been there to witness it.

# Acknowledgements

Thanks to Derek Dobson for the memories and memorabilia, Tom Bromley for his enthusiasm, Bob Dunning for his knowledge of 1960s football boots, David Hayes for the advice and anecdotes, Birrell and Kevin Cummins for their suggestions and ideas, Mike Brunel for his support, and Mum and Dad for deciding to move to Bromley back in 1961.

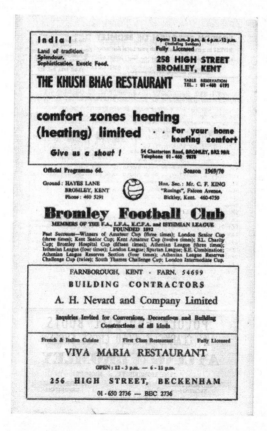